NOT TODAY
HOW I CHOSE LIFE

I could not have written this book without the
help and support of these wonderful people:
Ian Jones & Bournemouth University,
Roisin Wood & Kick It Out,
Katherine Conway & Aon,
Theresa & Katie Farrenson,
Kerry Chotty and Jo Lake.

Thank you to everyone that contributed
to the crowdfunder for the book, especially
Miki Downing Beavis, Angela Field, Jade Harker,
Heidi McCormack, Anwen Muston, Sandra Redhead,
Alan Spink, Florentina Taylor, Philippa Thompson
and everyone that pre-ordered their copy.

Without your faith in the project
this book would have never happened.

To Sallie

Always stay strong

Always stay true to yourself

NOT TODAY

HOW I CHOSE LIFE

MY BATTLE AGAINST
THE DEMON WITHIN
(A LOVE STORY)

SOPHIE COOK

loads of love

Sophie Cook xx

WARNING

This book contains graphic references to mental health, self harm and suicide that some people may find disturbing.

If you are affected by any of the issues discussed please contact a mental health professional or support service.

Speak up, ask for help and stay safe.
Sophie x

Printed in the United Kingdom
1st Edition, 2018
2nd Edition, 2019
3rd Edition, 2021
ISBN 9798518906983
Sophie Cook Talks
www.sophiecook.me.uk

CONTENTS

1st half: Lost

2nd half: Found

Extra time

For Vicki, Noel and Sadie
That you might understand x

"It's only after we've lost everything
that we're free to do anything."

Chuck Palahniuk, Fight Club

1ST HALF
LOST

"Monsters are real, and ghosts are real too.
They live inside us, and sometimes, they win."

Stephen King

PROLOGUE

It starts with a murmur.

Just a few cheers that soon became a roar as 4000 raised voices become one.

Occupying around a third of Charlton Athletic's ground, the Valley, the AFC Bournemouth fans are in good cheer as the club had already achieved the impossible earlier in the week, sealing promotion to the Premier League with a 3-0 victory over Bolton at Dean Court. This was to be our day, Watford were on course to be champions but, what the hell, we were already up, this is going to be a party, win, lose or draw.

On the touchline I look up to the stands realising that the news has just come in that Watford have blown the title race and that everything has changed.

As the club photographer for the Cherries I'd captured four momentous seasons with my home town club. From shooting half a season without pay in League 1 after the previous photographer was made redundant, a promotion to the Championship and finally to this astonishing moment. The club that my Dad had taken me to see in the 1970s, standing on the rundown terraces, cheering on a fourth division side were not only going to the Premier League, we were being promoted as Football League Champions.

For a club that had previously only achieved one season in the second flight under our legendary former manager Harry Redknapp this was a truly historic moment. People talk of the Premier League as being THE dream, well for AFC Bournemouth fans it wasn't even the stuff of fantasy. Our dream was to still have a club next season, to stay in the football league and to beat our local rivals Southampton.

The final whistle blows and I run straight onto the pitch, capturing the emotions of the players, recording this moment for posterity. Flags appear proclaiming us as Champions and are draped around players shoulders. Champagne arrives and, despite the quality, is, for the most part, sprayed rather than drunk.

While I join the players in the changing room a podium is erected on the pitch in front of the away end and the Football League Championship trophy is unveiled to the fans.

Heading back out onto the pitch the players are introduced to the crowd one by one and presented with their medals. Players wave to families and friends, pose for selfies and embrace each other. Last onto the podium is our captain, Tommy Elphick, he's presented with his medal and then, accompanied by fireworks and a massive cheer, he hoists the Championship trophy aloft.

This is the day that changes everything, the financial future of the club is secure, we will be welcoming Manchester United and Chelsea to Dean Court instead of Tranmere and Stevenage. We will be on the world stage and nothing will ever be the same again.

And yet, standing on the pitch, being sprayed with champagne by our triumphant players, which, for the record is nowhere near as much fun as it sounds, in reality it's sticky and buggers up your camera gear, emotion washes over me.

Elation to be right at the centre of the action as my childhood club reaches the promised land of the Premier League, and fear.

This is the greatest day in the 116 year history of my club and yet I am terrified.

I'm scared that I won't be there to see the great teams visit my club, I'm scared that this will be my last ever match photographing my beloved Cherries.

I'm scared that the lifelong secret I'm about to reveal will mean the end of my career in football just at the very moment of our greatest triumph.

1
WHEN I WAS A BOY

The whine of the turbojet engine rose in intensity as the throttle was pushed forward, increasing the flow of fuel to the combustion chamber, more air was sucked into the intake and the engine roared as it built rapidly up to its maximum 3500 lbs of thrust.

Slowly at first but soon gathering speed the hydroplane made its way across the dark, icy surface of Coniston Water. The aluminium hulled vessel looking and sounding more like a jet fighter, almost flying as it traversed the lake at 300mph. Its distinctive blue livery almost blending with the cold azure of the water, a comet tail of spray flying up behind the craft.

"Full house, full house, power off now!"

The pilot shut the throttle and applied the water brake, slowing the boat as the turbojet engine sputtered and flamed out. Impatient to complete the return run he initiated an engine relight as the vessel turned in a wide arc at the southern end of the lake.

Less than two minutes after completing the first run, at 8.48am the pilot gave a last nod to Mr Whoppit, his teddy bear mascot and announced that he was starting his return run.

As the boat passed the marker buoy she was travelling at 320 mph, faster than she'd ever been before, but within seconds her starboard sponson started to bounce in the choppy water.

"Pitching a bit down here... Probably from my own wash... Straightening up, now on track... Full power... Tramping like hell here... I can't see much... and the water's very bad indeed... I can't get over the top... I can't see anything... I'm going!"

In its final seconds the craft lifted from the surface of the lake, the angle of attack increasing all the time until the blue hull somersaulted into the air before crashing back nose first into the cold water breaking the vessel in two just behind the cockpit.

As the broken remains of Bluebird descended through the dark waters to the bed of Coniston Water carrying with it Donald Campbell, eight time world speed record breaker on land and water, a lone voice came across the radio:

"Complete accident, I'm afraid. Stand by!"

300 miles to the south a woman went into labour.

· · · · ·

I was born in the Royal Victoria Hospital in Bournemouth on January 4, 1967, to Deric Robert Cook, aged 19 of Bournemouth and his wife, my mother, Judith Cook, nee Moody formerly of London, England, also 19 years of age.

England were the World Cup Holders, The Beatles had just released Revolver, America had yet to reach the moon although it knew where Vietnam was, Kennedy had been dead for 4 years, and Harold Wilson was the Prime Minister.

There was nothing much of note during my first three years, my first words and steps but all in all I can't convince myself that my contribution to the sixties was as important as that of John, Paul, George, Ringo, JFK, Martin Luther King, Janis Joplin or even Dr. Timothy Leary.

At 20 months old I was joined by my brother, David. We're not exactly alike, we two, I'm fair he's dark, I've got straight hair he's got curly hair. There was always a joke in the family that he was the milkman's, but since the milkman at the time was in his sixties and my brother looks like a clone of our Dad I wouldn't be too sure.

When I was three my Dad decided that the best way to support us all was by joining the Royal Air Force and learning a trade. Senior Aircraftman Cook, Aircraft Mechanic Airframes was posted to RAF Bruggen in West Germany where my Dad serviced the airframes of the Phantom jet fighters. We lived in a Dutch farmhouse, just a few miles from Roermond and the air base, which featured vacant pigsties, a large, dark barn and a much loved, old grey horse.

Unfortunately my Dad had to leave the air force after only four years due to a perforated eardrum, the result of too much time working next to the screaming howl of the Phantoms twin Spey jet engines without adequate hearing protection. And so it was that we all moved back home to Bournemouth.

The house on Castlemain Avenue, Southbourne that was my childhood home seemed huge to me at the time, housing as it did, four generations of my family. My brother, parents, and I were joined by my maternal grandparents Bill and Mary and my great-grandmother Bertha.

With my parents busily trying to bring the money in, a lot of the childcare responsibilities fell upon my grandparents and great-grandmother. Bill had seen service with the RAF in Burma during the Second World War and was a carpenter by trade, always creating some item of furniture or shelving to improve the house and my grandmother worked in the accounts department of various local firms.

Bertha, my great-grandmother, born in the closing years of the previous century, seemed to be a link to a world that I would never know. Her body stooped slightly by age and carrying a couple of extra pounds she was known by the affectionate nickname of Fatgran, a name which nearly five decades later seems hideously unkind but which was in fact, I believe, a term of endearment.

My grandmother Doris, being a statuesque 5'10" was Biggran. I have no idea of the exact origins of these nicknames, maybe it was having to differentiate between the two Nans in the household, maybe it was just the childish language of a pair of toddlers trying to communicate their love.

I remember very little of my early years, the first thing that I do remember is, not so much a memory as a parental anecdote, that when I was a toddler I ate a slug that I'd found under the gooseberry bush believing it to be a sausage. I'm not quite sure what that says about me but I'll try to make a point not to mention it to any psychiatrists I might ever visit.

David and I shared a single bed in our parents bedroom, one of us sleeping at each end and, as is the way with kids, we would get up and creep around upstairs when we were supposed to be asleep. I never knew how, perhaps it was miniaturised surveillance cameras or psychokinetic powers, but as soon as we moved my Dad would shout up at us from below to get back into bed. I didn't know about Dad's connections within the CIA and British Intelligence for sure, but he must have acquired the surveillance gear from somewhere.

Of course now that I'm a parent I realise only too well that no matter how quiet kids think they're being the reality is that they sound like a troop of bad thespians clog dancing, all theatrical stage whispers and heavy feet.

. . . . .

"Are you excited?" Mum asked from the front passenger seat of my Dad's Ford Anglia, the light blue car famous from the Harry Potter movies. The car was real but unfortunately its ability to fly was not and the long tortuous journey along country roads from Bournemouth to South Wales seemed to be taking an eternity, certainly long enough to dull enthusiasm in anyone but the most excitable of 7 year olds.

"I'm going to be playing football every day", chipped in my brother, already obsessed with the sport at age 5 and focused on the idea of being a professional player one day. He did go on to be signed by QPR as a teenager back in the days when clubs would gather hundreds of youngsters as part of a numbers game in the hope that you had enough raw materials that at least some of them would make the grade, unfortunately the lack of opportunities and the commute from the south coast to London meant that his dream would never be fulfilled.

"And what are you going to do Steven?" my mother asked me.

· · · · ·

Arriving at Butlins, Barry Island during the summer of 1974 the holiday park resembled a wartime army base, all H-blocks, painted curbstones and manicured lawns, except that instead of having short, aggressive Sergeant Majors shouting at squaddies they had falsely chirpy and ever happy Redcoats trying to control hundreds of precocious urchins, high on junk food and E numbers, resplendent in flares and tank tops.

This being the 1970s the height of good parenting consisted of a bottle of Coke and a packet of crisps whilst your parents went off to the bar, indeed one of my main chores as a child was the regular trip to the cornershop to purchase cigarettes for my parents. 20 St Moritz menthols for my Mum and Rothmans or Guards for my Dad, if I was lucky I was allowed to spend the few pennies change on sweets, the quarter penny chews were good value, I liked the Fruit Salads but was never much of a fan of the Blackjacks.

So with my parents happily enjoying adult time in the bar, and my brother off participating in constant kickabouts, I was free to spend the time as I wished.

· · · · ·

"Hi, I'm Debbie, this is Kim and my brother John," the girl in front of me was around my age, blonde and dressed in denim dungarees scuffed at the knees and a check shirt.

This was the moment of truth, this was the test, could I do it?

The tension rose up in me, the confusion and pain finding form and trying to choke my words.

"Cat got your tongue? Don't be shy, we won't bite."

Shy? Yeah that was it, that was why I was struck dumb and found it impossible to vocalise the words that I so wanted to say.

"Come on, let's go." Debbie turned to leave, taking her entourage with her.

It was now or never, this was my opportunity.

"Jenny!"

"It's Jenny" I blurted.

"Well nice to meet you Jenny, do you want to check out the amusements?"

And so, there I was, Jenny, hanging out with other kids my age, totally accepted for the person that I knew myself to be, here with these people that didn't know me and that I would never see again.

At seven years old, fresh faced and with long fine, blonde hair I could easily pass for a girl, albeit a slightly tomboyish one. But with the unisex childrens fashions of the day it was easy to blend in and make friends. The week that followed was one of unprecedented freedom and authenticity, playing with my new friends and being totally accepted as Jenny, the girl from Bournemouth.

I don't know at what age I first felt that something was wrong with the combination of my mind, body and soul but this is my earliest memory of acting on it.

I WAS JENNY.

I WAS A GIRL.

This felt so authentic and so liberating that I knew it was right and yet I knew that it was only a temporary respite from the mental anguish that I felt at my confused identity. In a weeks time I was heading back to reality and back to the life that the rest of the world had ordained for me.

At the end of the week as our respective parents packed and loaded luggage my new found friends gathered to bid farewell.

"Bye Jenny, have a great trip home."

"Thanks Debbie, it's been a great week, have fun," I said as I hugged them goodbye.

When I turned back to my parents I was met with raised eyebrows and questioning looks.

"What was that all about?"

"No idea Mum," I said with all of the quick thinking of a 7 year old caught with their hand in the cookie jar, "weirdos they've been doing that all week."

My Mum exchanged a glance with my Dad who shrugged and continued loading bags into the already overladen car.

As I watched them recede into the distance through the rear window of the car, sat wedged between a suitcase and a bag of dirty laundry, I said goodbye to Jenny myself.

She'd been a welcome release, but alas, it was one that I wouldn't know again for many years.

$$\cdots\cdots$$

In 1977 we all moved out of the house that we'd shared in Bournemouth. My Dad and Grandad were both working for a boatyard near Southampton, a small firm that specialised in making pleasure yachts, and it seemed like a good idea to move a bit closer. The chosen destination for this upheaval was a village of a couple of thousand inhabitants, nestled in the beautiful East Hampshire countryside called Liss. At the time the village had two modestly sized council estates, a Victorian Junior school which I was to attend, a gorgeous new 1970's glass and steel Infant school which David went to, about five pubs and two churches.

Liss may not have been the vast Metropolis that Bournemouth was, but it was still a pretty cool place to grow up. The village was small enough to be friendly, and surrounded by typical southern English countryside it gave us a beautiful rural childhood. One of my most precious memories of this or any other times were the hours that Grandad and I used to spend walking the dogs in the woods around the village. We would talk about everything and nothing, we are both great observers of life, we love knowledge and the process of thinking. There'd be badgers sets, which side of a tree moss grows on, fungi, birds, squirrels, aeronautics, radio theory, history, politics, we'd talk for hours, the world was our oyster and the woods our auditorium.

1977 was also the year of the Queen's Silver Jubilee, an occasion that I remember purely for two reasons: 1. The school gave us all free Silver Jubilee mugs, and 2. We went down to Portsmouth to watch the review of the fleet, I've never seen so much of the navy in one place, it was a good job the Russians didn't attack that day.

$$\cdots\cdots$$

I always loved science fiction movies and my childhood held some classics, from seeing the first Star Wars, not yet known as A New Hope, on its release at the age of 10 to Close Encounters, but there were two TV shows that particularly captured my attention. Whenever Mr Benn would walk through the second door of the changing room in the fancy dress shop that led to adventure I would wonder if it was possible for me to do the same and become a girl.

Of course transforming into someone else was a regular occurrence for Doctor Who but I would have to wait until their 13th regeneration in 2018 before the Doctor finally became a woman.

I'd never let go of Jenny, the girl inside me, although I had no idea how to communicate with her or allow her the freedom to be. I would dream about how I would one day wake up to be the woman that I knew myself to be and that the pain would be over. But every time I looked in the mirror there stood a boy where I should be and I would break down in tears of despair.

. . . . .

In 1979 I started at my secondary school, Bohunt in Liphook, East Hampshire. The school was brand new, we were the first intake of pupils and as such we never had bigger kids above us in the school. The school was so new that the buildings were not even finished and so we were educated in old portacabins and prefab barracks from the fifties which were converted into classrooms at the army base in Bordon. It was a curious experience, going to school on an army camp, fenced off from the soldiers in case our savage ways disturbed them.

It was during my first year at Bohunt School that one of my friends, Julian Cawkell or 'Cawky', did something that changed my life. He lived in one of the villages near the school in a nice semi-detached house, his Dad worked on a new fangled technology called computers back in the days when the only ones we ever saw on TV were the size of a house, used tape spools or were the green screen Commodore Pet PC's that had begun to make their way into our classrooms. By the time we left school five years later they lived in a big house in the country with a couple of acres of gardens and a double garage. Who knows, by now Cawky's Dad may well be the person that Bill Gates calls when he needs a sub, talk about being in at the ground floor.

One day Cawky excitedly told us about a record that he'd bought, not only was it great music but it had an entire culture and way of life attached to it. That night I took the record home and taped it on my parents stereo, listening for the very first time to the music that would become such a part of my life and dreaming of the provocative images on the cover. From that moment on we were all confirmed Mods, all it took was one listen to Quadrophenia.

· · · · ·

This was 1979, the time of the great Mod revival. The Jam were on the telly virtually every week, there were Mod bands everywhere, Secret Affair, The Purple Hearts, The Merton Parkas, The Lambrettas, The Chords. Then there was all the ska and 2-Tone, The Specials, Madness, The Selector, The Body Snatchers, The Beat. Life had never seemed as energetic and vital as it was in those glorious Moddy years between '79 and the early eighties when indifference spread it's cancer yet again through music as it had in the mid-seventies.

I'm sure now that music, like everything else in life, is cyclic. It sinks into wells of mediocrity and is devoid of inspiration, then it takes a violent explosion, a revolution, to kick it out of its slumber and we get a period of vitality. The excitement of the sixties gave way to the indulgence of 70s prog rock and then along came punk. After the late seventies music went back to sleep as surely as Bagpuss goes to sleep at the end of each thrilling episode of the children's TV show. New romantics and electronic bands gave way to formulaic pop. Then the nineties came along and all of a sudden these electronic bands started making chemical fuelled dance music, as exciting in its way as Motown must have been when it first hit these shores, although maybe a little more repetitive. Then along came grunge and Britpop to bring us back, full circle to punk and the sixties.

· · · · ·

Abbie Andrews was, to my mind, the most beautiful girl in school, I had a terrible crush on her for the entire five years that we were at Bohunt together. My love for her was unconditional, she had lustrous shoulder length auburn hair that I would dream of touching. My love was not even dented when she was singled out by the school's nit nurse and the long locks disappeared for a while. To me she was perfect. Unfortunately I was crushingly shy and there was no way that I could have told her my feelings.

My chance to impress Abbie came on a school trip to Calais. Nowadays schools go on trips to Kenya and the USA but back in the late 70s staying with a french family in a tower block in a French port barely a mile from the ferry terminal was considered cosmopolitan. Calais belonged to the post-war school of utilitarian architecture that believed that concrete boxes and factories are the ideal living environment and compared to the beautiful rolling hills of East Hampshire Calais felt like an industrial wasteland.

In order to gain the attention of the girl of my dreams I set out to impress her with my impeccable taste in music. Unfortunately for some inexplicable reason my copy of Abba's latest release obtained from the local Hypermarche didn't immediately convince her that I was 'going out with' material despite being limited edition red vinyl.

Eventually about five years later we went out with each other for a few weeks following leaving school, but I soon went into the air force and we never saw each other again. There is still a tree beside the pond in Newman Collard Playing Fields in Liss that bears the inscription 'SC 4 AA' and if you ever want to borrow a limited edition red vinyl copy of 'Voulez-Vous' it's still there in my record collection amongst The Jam albums and Who boxed sets.

. . . . .

I'd been a Mod for nearly a year now, and boy was I cool, or so I thought. I'd seen Quadrophenia for the first time in an English bar on holiday in the south of France, you know the sort, full English breakfast, Watney's Red Barrel, pie, mash and liquor, and I was going to be The Face.

Easter 1980, thirteen years old and ready to take on the world, I decided that now was the time to become a real Mod. Telling my Mum and Dad that I was off to see my friends, I walked out of the house in my parka, down to the railway station and bought a ticket to Brighton.

On the train I met a couple of Navy guys who were stationed at the nearby radar station, these were grown-up Mods, all of seventeen years old. We chatted about what was going to happen and they gave me the benefit of their experience. As the train got closer to Brighton I could feel the tension growing, we'd picked up a few more people when we changed trains at Portsmouth and there was now quite a crowd of us. Drawing into the Victorian splendour of Brighton railway station all we could see on the platform were coppers, police everywhere.

Back in the 60s and 70s the police had a special relationship with Mods in Brighton, they seemed to have extra powers, no doubt granted to them by an outraged local population still decades away from becoming the diverse, liberal city that I now call home. Years later whilst riding my scooter over the South Downs towards the Sussex town I ran into the only police roadblock that I'd ever encountered on mainland Britain.

The police were pulling over all of the scooters, giving them a good going over for such heinous crimes as illegally spaced letters on the number plate or noisy exhausts and taking everyone's details, just in case they caused trouble.

We were led out of the railway station and down towards the town, our numbers had grown to a couple of hundred by now and the atmosphere was buzzing. Chants of "We are the Mods" ringing out, it was the adrenaline rush of being in a crowd of people all wanting the same thing, to belong. There I was thirteen years old, walking through the streets of Brighton, I WAS a Mod, and for the first time the perpetual outsider felt like he belonged.

Then it happened.

As we walked down Queens Road from the station towards the sea ten leather clad rockers appeared in front of us. The crowd erupted, we were away, a couple of hundred Mods chasing ten rockers. I didn't know what was supposed to happen if we caught up with them, all I knew was that we were supposed to chase them. I'm sure that if we'd started gaining on them then we would have slowed down. It was the chase, the thrill of the hunt, playing out rituals that had been handed down to us from the generation before.

Seconds later the sirens started. We could hear them all around us, even over our screaming as we ran. The Navy lads that I was with split off to run down a side street into North Laine and I went with them, unfortunately so did the Police Land Rover. Suddenly there wasn't a couple of hundred of us anymore, there were four of us. We tried slowing to look as unobtrusive as possible, but the police weren't having any of it. The Land Rover, in full riot gear complete with wire mesh over the windows, mounted the curb in front of us and five coppers jumped out, grabbed us and threw us up against the railings of a rather pleasant Georgian terraced property.

"Where are you going? What are you doing? Who are you? How old are you? Where are you from? What do you do? Wouldn't your parents be ashamed of you? Do you want a police record?"

"Nowhere. Nothing. Steven Cook. Thirteen. Liss. At school. Dunno. No. Hmm that pavement's dead interesting."

We gave the police a good listening to I can tell you, in return they confiscated our shoelaces. People always look quizzical at that bit, but you see they take your laces off you so that you can't run, if you can't run, you can't chase rockers, if you can't chase rockers you can't riot and the whole thing becomes a bit of a waste of time.

The lads that I was there with had been through it all before, and even had spare laces in their pockets, I just made do with the drawstrings from the bottom of my parka. After that we hung around for a bit, and eventually I caught the train home alone. I'd only been there a few hours but I was hooked, the high had been so good that I knew I was always going to be a Mod. When I got home, my parents asked me how my day had been and I replied that it had been alright, y'know. To this day they still don't know about my day trip to Brighton.

· · · · ·

During my school years I was doubly unfortunate, in that I was both a Mod and suffered from an embarrassing case of acne. I was also a relatively quiet child who enjoyed books and was therefore open to all kinds of bullying. I was never the type of person to raise my voice to argue or fight, when confronted with a situation that I didn't like I was much more likely to bottle it up and dwell on the negative aspects.

Christopher Wilson was a gangly, greasy youth, a product of his environment, he lived on the roughest council estate in our village and he seemed to revel in chaos. He was in many ways the antithesis of myself, and for some reason he took great offence at my existence. It became his greatest ambition to make my life as miserable as possible, he would pick on me at school, on the way home from school and on any spare occasion that would crop up during the day.

I'm not sure how long this went on for, when you're in your early teens a few weeks can be a lifetime, especially when they're miserable ones. It all came to a head one afternoon on the way home from school, he'd been picking on me for ages and I just thought sod this. I turned round to him, squared up and pushed him into a convenient privet hedge, I then scarpered. The following day I caught an earlier train to school, and for the rest of that week in order to avoid his retribution, as I recall none ever came but I did keep an eye over my shoulder for a while.

My acne also left me wide open for a different form of childhood torture, the classroom name callers. What made it worse was that some of the worst people for this were people that were supposed to be my friends. Over the years I've tried to work out to what extent bullying is a product of environment and to what extent it's a natural stage of development. Children can go through a stage of being human beings that haven't yet learnt how to be people, with all of the responsibilities and empathy that are necessary to grow as a person. It's a fact that the abusers knew how much pain they were causing and I see it even today in the internet trolls that I encounter, for some reason there's an empathy disconnect. Most people grow out of it and become kind, supportive members of society and the one's that don't? Well they get Twitter accounts.

· · · · ·

When John Lennon was shot outside the Dakota Building in New York by a deranged fan, Mark Chapman, I cried. It was the first time that I remember the news having such an effect on me. It's happened innumerable times since, it seems that the older I get the more despair I feel that some things never change. Man's ability to hurt others or the injustice in the world, it's all made me weep on more occasions than I care to remember.

My favourite band growing up was The Jam, I owned every record they'd released and when Paul Weller announced that he was splitting the band up in 1982 I was heartbroken. There would be one more single and a final farewell tour. The single 'Beat Surrender' went straight into the charts at number 1, their fourth single to do so equalling the record set by The Beatles.

A local newsagents was selling tickets for the last gig at The Brighton Centre, for about £15 including the bus fare, I had to go I didn't care what anyone said. A friend and I managed to get tickets and that was it, we were on. The atmosphere on the bus was amazing, full of Mods, listening to the Jam and we even had Quadrophenia on video. A TV on a bus? Whatever next.

Outside the venue there were Mods everywhere, plus a few skinheads who seemed to be looking for trouble. The occasional scooter would cruise past us as we queued to get in, our parkas protecting us from the December wind coming off the Channel.

The Jam were arguably the best band to come out of England in the seventies, carriers of the torch left to them by The Who, the Small Faces and The Beatles. Paul Weller, the voice of a generation, well at least until he started the Style Council. I loved this band more than anything else when I was fifteen, they were the best, the coolest and they wrote great songs. I'd even had the Steve Marriott, from the Small Faces, centre parting hairstyle that Weller had sported when 'Start!' came out. I remember going into the barbers holding the front page from the NME or Sounds with a picture of Paul Weller and telling the guy that THAT was what I wanted.

The Jam's set went by in a blur, I was stood right at the front near Paul Weller, in awe of his presence. My parka that protected me from the elements outside had the opposite effect in this mass of sweating Mods,

I was beginning to wish that I'd left it on the bus, but no I wanted to be cool, a misconception if ever there was one.

A fight broke out at the back of the hall. In an effort to avoid trouble outside the venue the doors had been opened to allow everyone in and some of the skinheads started throwing pint pots towards the stage. This was long before the days of plastic containers for drinks at gigs and the heavy, dimpled glasses were likely to kill someone if they caught you wrong . Bruce Foxton looked at them and made his feelings clear: "we're all here to enjoy our bloody selves and if you don't like it you can fuck off!"

. . . . .

In the modern world of 24/7 TV, hundreds if not thousands of channels and high speed internet access bringing the entire world to our fingertips it's sometimes difficult to imagine quite how isolated and uninformed it was possible to be in the 1970s and 80s. There were only three TV channels and they only transmitted in the evenings, no daytime TV and we were all so excited when we got Channel 4, it was a 33% increase in the amount of TV available, and they were risky and rude.

Growing up in those days I had no idea what the hell was going on with me, we had no LGBT role models let alone any transgender ones. We had Section 28 outlawing the promotion of homosexuality in schools and the hatred directed at gay people was shocking. Trans women were purely seen as freaks and monsters. The world hadn't yet woken up to the idea that trans men could exist and non-binary wouldn't even be mentioned for another four decades.

The pain and isolation that I experienced was becoming increasingly unbearable, trapped in a body that meant nothing to me, a male prison of flesh containing a single, solitary prisoner, the small, frightened 7-year-old Jenny. I was finding it difficult to connect with other children my age. I wasn't interested in the same things as most of the boys, I was artistic and loved reading, and the girls were only interested in the company of the alpha males, the sporty showoffs, not in quiet bookworms like me.

. . . . .

I slowly lock the garage door, trying to stay as quiet as possible. I don't want anyone to know that I'm here, I don't want anyone to ever know that I was here, at all.

I turn, catching my reflection in the mirrored doors of an old medicine cabinet as I slump to the floor. I don't see me. I see someone else, someone that I am increasingly learning to despise.

I begin to cry, the tears rolling down my face before dropping to my chest that is shaking uncontrollably with the intensity of the sobs. I want to scream, but can't, I don't want anyone to know that I am here, hidden away. It doesn't matter anyway, if I was to cry out what would I say? I don't have the words to explain my pain, neither in magnitude nor understanding. All I know is that I am wrong, in some fundamental way, beyond my comprehension.

I curl into a ball, trying to make myself small enough to disappear, to cease to be, but I'm still here, the pain proves that to me.

Slowly I stand, pushing myself up against the rough breeze block wall. Still crying but with a purpose now as there, among the dusty, half used oil cans and old jam jars filled with odd nuts and bolts, my sight falls on a rope under the workbench. I reach for it, my hand brushing away the cobwebs that enshroud the blue nylon rope, frayed and rough in my hands. Looking up I see the joists traversing the space between the eaves of the garage and reach up to throw one end of the rope across the bare, wooden roof beam.

Fashioning two knots I first attach the rope to the beam and then tie another to create a noose. Standing on a toolbox I place the rope over my head and around my neck. The rough nylon scratches my neck and for a second my attention transfers from my emotional pain to the discomfort across my throat, I close my eyes and take a calm, measured breath, first one, then two.

Then I step off, into the void.

· · · · ·

"Are you ever afraid?"

The reporter leans forward to proffer the microphone to Donald Campbell as he sits, relaxed on the sponson of his azure jet boat.

"Of course, I'm afraid every time I get into the Bluebird. Courage is not being fearless. Courage is overcoming and smashing through fear."

2

FOR QUEEN AND COUNTRY

The pig's eyes fix on mine, oblivious to the mayhem surrounding it.

The blonde, wiry hairs on its snout pristinely clean save for a single spot of dark crimson to the left of its mouth which seems to smile wryly at me.

"Yes, I know it's bad, but at least you're not me", he seems to be telling me.

My eyes move slowly around the room, the white tiles stained with blood, the broken furniture and flooded floor, the possessions strewn amongst the blood and water, in the corner a pile of clothes covered in faeces.

I take in the sight of the pigs companions, lined up, one by one along the wall, all attentively looking to me for answers. I shake my head, trying to clear the fog, trying to come up with some explanation for them but failing.

I retch and fall to my knees in the fetid liquid covering the floor, water, mixed with blood, urine and shit. Still the pigs hold my gaze, not moving, their neatly decapitated heads staring blankly at me from the urinal bowls where they lay.

· · · · ·

The day that I completed basic recruit training in the Royal Air Force began as a celebration.

16 years old, at the beginning of a journey that I'd dreamt of since childhood having grown up with my Dad's and Grandad's stories of the RAF and the roar of Phantom jets flying low and loud above my school,

sheets of flame from the afterburners trailing behind them.

Both of them shared stories with me about aircraft and air force life, Grandad had been a wireless operator/mechanic in Burma during the Second World War, and I grew up obsessed with planes. I built Airfix kits, going into meticulous detail with the construction and painting of the 1/72nd scale models. I collected aviation books like some people collect stamps, I read and reread them, able to identify most of the world's aircraft by my early teens.

My declared aim from an early age was to follow in their footsteps and become an RAF aircraft engineer. At school despite showing a little talent in art, the subject was abandoned in favour of metalwork and technical drawing, much to the distress of my exasperated art teacher, Miss Guy. Some 3 decades later I'm still friends with her and there's a certain satisfaction that I did, eventually, let my artistic talents out through my photography.

I attested into the RAF at the Careers Information Office in Southampton on October 18, 1983 as an Apprentice Aircraft Technician Airframes/Propulsion this was the pinnacle of engineering trades within the service, a joint trade supertech and part of an elite that stretched back to 1920 and the then Chief of the Air Staff Lord Trenchard. The three year course was exclusively for males aged between 16 and 18 and apprentices emerged at the end of the three years with the nickname Trenchard Brats.

I'd grown a lot in the four years since I had tried to take my own life in the garage in Liss, the frayed rope had given way as it failed to take my weight, scraping my throat and causing a graze that I found hard, but not impossible, to explain away.

I was still struggling with my mental health and in particular my gender identity but the self loathing hadn't been enough to prompt a further suicide attempt.

Following six weeks of basic recruit training at RAF Swinderby in Lincolnshire, learning how to march, fire a gun, polish shoes, press uniforms and generally accept orders, my passing out parade featured two Lightning jets, their engines roaring as their flypast coordinated with our salute.

My parents had made the long trip up from the south coast and proudly posed for a photograph with me, my father in his best suit stood with me in my dress blues behind my mother sat in a chair, before I was bundled onto a service bus and shipped back down the A1 to RAF Halton in Buckinghamshire to begin my apprenticeship.

The Royal Air Force Halton Aircraft Apprenticeship was something like an English boarding school crossed with an American military academy. The boys were segregated into entries, I was part of 142 Entry and each entry had a sister entry 18 months ahead of them in the process. In addition to the technical, physical education and drill instructors that were part of the No 1 School of Technical Training the Apprentices had their own hierarchical rank system with senior boys being promoted to Leading, Corporal or Sergeant Aircraft Apprentice. These were totally internal ranks and had no sway over anyone outside of the apprentices but they gave the holder the power of unquestionable authority over their subordinates, an authority that was regularly abused.

Our sister entry was 139 and the arrival of a new entry was a big day for them, it was a right of passage, going from being a junior entry to a senior one and they intended to enjoy every second of that elevation.

Unbeknownst to myself and my fellow new recruits, fresh from our passing out parade at Swinderby, tradition dictated that the first night at Halton was a hazing night in which our strength and resilience would be tested to the full.

Arriving on the bus we were immediately required to go on parade and march with all of our luggage to our barrack block, a three storey building with bathrooms and toilets off a central staircase and four man rooms arranged off corridors on either side.

Rooms were allocated, kit bags dropped and the order came to change into PE kit for a cross country run. White t-shirt, stiff blue cotton shorts and white plimsolls were donned and we were outside, formed up in our ranks facing shouted orders, jeers, abuse and laughter as our sister entry took every opportunity to inflict on us the pain that had been theirs only 18 months earlier.

The course took us around the base and out into the woods where boys lay in wait to hurl further abuse at us, continually chipping away at our spirits and energy before finally leading us back to the barrack block some hours later, covered in mud, exhausted and ready for a shower and bed.

As we approached the building the noise levels increased to a roar as we ran the final few yards between the barrack blocks. People were hanging out of windows, shouting and throwing things at us, and then we saw it.

Whilst we had been conveniently out of the way our building had been ransacked, personal possessions, kit, furniture and even beds had been thrown out of windows. On entering the building we discovered devastation and filth everywhere we went, rotten food, shit, blood and dead animals. Not a single item in the building appeared to be untouched by the chaos.

I sank to my knees, shell shocked on the floor of the bathroom, surrounded by decapitated pigs heads as one of the Sergeant Apprentices walked in, surveyed the scene and said:

"Looks like you're going to have a late night, I want all of this spotless for a full inspection in the morning."

. . . . .

The 3 year RAF Apprenticeship consisted of everything from aeronautics and aircraft systems to mathematics, physics and metalwork and whilst I had no problem keeping up in the technical subjects when it came to filing aluminium to a tolerance of 0.05mm I struggled.

It wasn't all precision metalwork that I had difficulties with, apparently mild steel was ok for me, the harder material was more forgiving and I soon created, from scratch, a G clamp, cutting, filing, tapping, and treating the metal to the required accuracy. But the softer aluminium alloy proved troublesome and I never quite got the hang of it. Unfortunately this was a compulsory pass on the training programme and so, after almost a year, I was given a choice.

I could either drop back to a following course and try again or leave the apprenticeship and become an engine mechanic. There was no way that I could go back to the beginning and survive all of the hazing, bullying and abuse for an additional six months. The alternative meant that within four months I would be qualified and working on operational aircraft somewhere in the real RAF. This is what I'd joined for, I loved aircraft and wanted to work on them, I was stifled and uncomfortable in the overly regimented educational world of Halton. The choice was easy, leave the elitist apprentices and enter the real world.

The change drew immediate benefits, I went from struggling to being amongst the most gifted, helped by my extra year of experience and the level of training that I'd already received. Unfortunately, as is the nature with elitism, it also meant that many of my apprentice friends turned their back on me. I was no longer one of them and there was no way that they could fraternise with me, for my part, this just helped to fuel my rebellious nature and I soon became adept at playing the system. I could see the ridiculousness of unnecessarily harsh discipline and did everything that I could to reduce its impact on my younger colleagues.

Four months later the pain of the apprentice course was finally forgotten as my mechanics course graduated and our postings were read out.

"Cook, 27 Squadron, Marham."

"Brilliant, that's Vulcans!" I exclaimed to my neighbour.
"Hard luck Cook, they've just converted to Tornados."

· · · · ·

RAF Marham, nestled between the Norfolk village of Swaffham and the town of King's Lynn, had been used firstly by the Royal Flying Corps and then the RAF since it's construction in 1916 and was home to two Squadrons of Tornados and two of Victor tankers. The Victors had been part of Britain's V-bomber fleet of the 50s and 60s, alongside the Vulcan and Valiant, and had been converted for the tanker role when large nuclear armed bombers ceased to be part of the gameplay for any future war. I soon settled in to life on the squadron, loving the activity of keeping these dirty, noisy machines serviceable. The sheet of blue flame that shot out of the exhaust nozzle as the engines accelerated to max reheat for take-off, cone like shock waves forming within the efflux as the rumble shook the ground and your body.

My gender identity was still confusing me, I was no closer to understanding what my feelings meant and I began to keep a stash of feminine clothes, hidden away in a locker, out of sight, in the room that I shared with three others. The lack of privacy made it very difficult to experiment and I would regularly be beset by guilt and shame causing me to frequently purge my collection, vowing to never do it again but I always did.

In addition to my gender issues I was also the subject of various degrees of bullying, the fact that I was a Mod caused much ridicule for some and one day I returned to the barracks to find that all of my possessions had been trashed and my posters covered in graffiti. As upset as I was I was still relieved to see that my locked cupboard containing the hidden wardrobe of female clothes had gone undetected but it was a scare that I could have done without.

There are links between abusive behaviour towards people and animal cruelty, and a history of both is often found in those guilty of the most heinous crimes. The same was true of my tormentors. Not content with bullying me they were excited to discover that one of our roommates pet hamster had given birth. The dozen or so tiny creatures, pink, hairless and blind were huddled in a mass, buried slightly under the sawdust and newspaper that the mother had used to make a nest.

Pulling the babies out one by one the aggressors began by throwing the tiny creatures to each other, laughing and joking, especially if someone dropped their catch. This soon progressed into a form of tennis as a racquet was produced. After a while they tired of this activity and despite our protests, they threatened to force the creatures down our throats if we objected, they began thinking of further tortures. Kettles, light bulbs and cigarettes were all pressed into service as they enacted their sadistic lusts, all the while ridiculing and tormenting those of us that protested.

· · · · ·

A military airfield can be a place of intense peace and calm, the noise and commotion limited to the moments when the jets take off for sorties. Unlike a civil airfield where these are spaced out, on air bases the aircraft launch in pairs, often as formations that can include four or more aircraft. Between these periods of activity a calmness and quiet descends, the remote location devoid even of traffic noise and the sounds of civilisation. The tranquility was completed by the warm sun that shone down from a luxuriant blue sky, marked only by the occasional cumulus cloud floating high above us.

"When are you going to get rid of that hairdryer and get a proper bike?"

Corporal Craig Overend was your typical RAF engineer, scruffy, long hair and a biker, and he was always gently taking the mickey out of the Vespa which was my chosen form of transport. The good natured banter continues as we walk out of the Hardened Aircraft Shelter (HAS) where we'd just completed a pre-flight service on one of the jets in preparation for a sortie later that day. The half tube like buildings were built to withstand a direct hit from a 500lb bomb and housed two Tornados and ancillary support equipment in case of war.

As we walk we hear an explosion, the sound sharp and piercing came from another shelter nearby. Within seconds a young engineer stumbles out of the shelter screaming. We begin to run, uncertain of what we will find. Entering the HAS it is immediately obvious that something had gone horribly wrong. Images flash through my mind, blood, metal, flesh, more blood, my senses are under attack as the noise assaults my ears, the sound of gas escaping and the screaming, oh God, the screaming.

There, on the floor, beneath the nose of the aircraft, surrounded by an ever growing pool of blood is a dark haired youth, barely older than my 18 years. Where his right arm had been only seconds ago there is now nothing but ragged flesh, blood and bone.

"Put a tourniquet on it," Craig shouts to me as he runs into the portacabin office that houses the shelters telephone to call for an ambulance. I grab the first aid kit, rip it open, triangular bandage, crepe bandage, eyewash, plasters, nothing that seems adequate for dealing with the situation in front of me. My eyes search the area, the random detritus and equipment that is left over from exercises and the daily maintenance of the aircraft. Canvas webbing, the one inch wide heavy duty straps used for securing loads, but how to tighten it?

I search the aircraft's toolkit and decide upon the speed brace, a U shaped hand tool used with a screwdriver bit to take panels off in a hurry. I tie the webbing around the remnants of the airman's arm, insert the speed brace and begin to twist.

The blood forms a pool around us as I hold the tourniquet tight, trying desperately to stem the flow of life, the life that I now kneel in. I recognise him as Andy Harris, 19, from Hull, he'd been on the squadron little longer than I had and he was now delirious with pain.

I keep talking to him, telling him that he's going to be alright. I don't know if I believe this or not, I don't know what I'm thinking, if indeed I am thinking at all. I feel numb, nothing else in the world exists beyond this boy, that wound, this webbing and speedbrace and the effort that I exert to staunch the flow of blood.

Other people start to arrive now, they form an outer perimeter around us, separate, not part of us. Our boss, the Engineering Officer, arrives on the scene, he begins issuing instructions. One of the aircraft's two nose wheels has exploded, shattering the alloy hub and reducing Andy's right forearm to redundant flesh. He gives orders for the aircraft to be jacked up to relieve the stress on the remaining wheel. I can see now that he was worried about the other nosewheel exploding but at the time I screamed at them to fuck off, I was thinking about more important things than the bloody aircraft.

The ambulance seems to take a lifetime to arrive, Andy's lifetime. Subsequently I discover that the incident report puts it at about seven minutes but every second is an eternity when you're fighting for a life. Medics rush up to us, unpacking emergency kits, field dressings and morphine and I hand Andy over into their care. I stagger away and collapse, crying, into the arms of one of the Corporals. Shock sweeping over me and taking hold of my brain, I don't see or hear any of the commotion around me, until I hear someone shouting my name.

"Who's Cooky?" it's one of the medics, Andy is asking for me to go in the ambulance with him. The shock and tears are pushed aside, no time for them now. I climb into the back of the ambulance and stroke Andy's hair, talking to him all the time whilst the medic goes to work filling him up with drugs.

· · · · ·

It's 15 miles from RAF Marham to the Queen Elizabeth Hospital in King's Lynn, 15 miles on country lanes that on a normal day could take you around half an hour to drive.

Blue lights blazing and siren wailing the ambulance speeds along the rural roads clogged with traffic, it seems to gravitate towards us, stopping and then blocking the roads.

I scream at the other vehicles, are they blind? Can't they see what is happening? Why aren't they moving?

The road is blocked at a roundabout and we swerve in the opposite direction and travel the wrong way around the congested junction. Finally we arrive at the hospital and the doors fly open. Medical staff rush to get Andy out of the ambulance, through the swing doors of the Accident & Emergency department and into the operating theatre.

Andy disappears.

. . . . .

A young nurse comes up to me, clipboard in hand, and starts asking for Andy's details. I answer in a daze, robotic, emotionless.

As soon as she finishes talking to me I collapse into a chair, crying. My overalls, boots, hands and face are all covered in blood and in my hands I hold the speed brace that I'd used to tighten the tourniquet.

After a while one of the non-commissioned officers comes to collect me, they talk quietly to the medical staff and then help me to stand, walking me out of the building to a waiting Land Rover which takes us back to the squadron.

Outside the engineering control office, I sit at a picnic table, silent, surrounded by concerned colleagues. Hours pass before they manage to take the speed brace off me, needing to check all of the tools away before the work could be signed off. I'd just been turning it over and over in my hands, repeating a mantra of denial in my mind.

The sun is still shining, the airbase is once again quiet but nothing will ever be the same again.

That evening I go back to the hospital where I meet Andy's parents. Their 19-year-old son has just lost an arm, their lives will never be the same again, nothing will ever be the same again.

Andy's mother holds me, weeping.

Andy's father shakes my hand.

I saved their son's life.

They thank me, I feel nothing.

3
SCARRED

Why? Childhoods gone

Young men out drinking
One of their number is off
To do his bit for Queen and country.

They party, revelling in their youth
Proud of their comrades
A team, as one.

Early morning
God my head aches
Get up, go to work
A glorious August morning.

Suddenly, the silence is broken
Forever
Young men
Not young anymore.

One lies in his own mortality
His body broken
Help arrives, another boy
So old now
So far from the merriment
Of before.

The fury at the world
I explode, I scream
Anyone who comes near is the enemy.

The hierarchy with their rules and regulations
"Don't touch anything!"
Already the evidence for the enquiry.

"Where's the bloody ambulance?"
I hold tight the tourniquet
Trying to stop the loss of life
The life I now kneel in.

In the ambulance
Knuckles white, can't loosen my grip
I stroke his head
No longer my friend
Now a brother.

Anger
The traffic so thick, so solid
At last the hospital, he goes in
I wait, I cry
A young nurse, new on the ward
Tries to comfort me
I wait.

Time has passed, but not the hurt
The love of a comrade, who now is far away.

I dream
Of him
Of his family
His father, who shook my hand
His mother, who cried and embraced me.

Why are they now gone?
Our childhoods gone
Two teenagers
So young, so scarred
In different ways.

So old
So tired
So scared
So alone
But still a teenager
Why?

Steve Cook, Oct 1986

. . . . .

I knew that things were different, I was different.

Arriving in Germany in the winter of 1985 I had changed.

The trauma following Andy's injury had made me increasingly withdrawn, unable to deal with what I'd seen and done.

The disassociation only increased as more people praised my actions, the more people that said I'd saved his life, the more people that called me a hero.

Survivor guilt was first identified during the 1960s amongst Holocaust survivors and has since been recognised in people that have been through disasters, terrorist attacks, friends or family of murder victims and emergency service personnel. It can manifest itself in many ways but for me the question was "Why did this happen to Andy? It should have been me."

The feeling was totally illogical, I wasn't part of why the incident happened, I wasn't responsible for his injuries, I wasn't even there when it took place. There was nothing that I could have done to prevent the incident happening. There was nothing that I could have done to produce a better outcome for him. In fact I was the person that had saved his life, but that meant nothing to me.

The more praise I received, the greater the guilt.

. . . . .

Honours In Confidence
Recommendation for Commendation by AOCinC No 1 Group
Senior Aircraftman Steven Robert Cook
Trade: Aircraft Mechanic Propulsion
Unit: No 27 Squadron Royal Air Force Marham
Appointment held: Aircraft Handler No 27 Squadron
Period covered by Recommendation: 15 August 1985

Particulars of meritorious service:

On 15 August 1985 at RAF Marham, 2 tradesmen were inflating the nose wheel tyre of a Tornado aircraft when the tyre exploded causing one of the airman to lose his arm. Senior Aircraftman Cook heard the explosion and made his way to the scene, There he found the injured airman lying on the ground, bleeding profusely and screaming for help. Despite others being on the scene before him, it was Senior Aircraftman Cook who immediately took control. He located the first aid kit, found nothing of use therein, and so used lashing tape found in the vicinity to apply a tourniquet. He then instructed a corporal on the scene to find him a speed-brace which he used to tighten the tourniquet. Cook then comforted the injured man until qualified medical help arrived. The Medical Officer has testified that Senior Aircraftman Cook's impressive reactions were responsible for saving the life of the injured airman.

I recommend that this meritorious service be recognised by the award of Commendation by the AOCinC

Group Captain PC Norriss
Officer Commanding Royal Air Force Marham
7 November 1985

. . . . .

Sitting in the front row of the awards presentation alongside veteran service members being recognised for their long and distinguished service I'm numb, sullen and uncommunicative.

Following each commendation being read out by the officer conducting the ceremony the smiling recipient steps forward to receive their award from the station commander and pose for a cheery photo capturing forever the joyous moment.

I don't feel joyous. In fact I don't want to be here at all.

The pain and darkness inside me threatens to explode out of me in a torrent of abuse and recrimination. I want to scream at them "You did this! You broke Andy!"

"You broke me…"

Towards the end of the ceremony after all of the Long Service and Good Conduct Medals they come to me, reading the commendation that I've received for saving Andy's life. I just sit there, staring into space, oblivious to those around me and the words I'm hearing.

"SAC Cook, SAC Cook…"

I rise to my feet and walk numbly towards the station commander, he shakes my hand, I'm silent. I think he senses my mood, after all I'm making no effort to hide it, why should I? In contrast to all of the smiling images that the photographer takes that day mine is emotionless. My eyes dead, open but unseeing, looking through the viewer to some forgotten place before the explosion. The monochrome image mirroring my mood, devoid of colour and life.

. . . . .

I was struggling. I was alone.

Following the incident news of Andy's recovery was sparse and my suicidal feelings increased as my guilt grew. Why hadn't it been me? After all I wanted to die. If it had to happen to someone then I was a better choice, I was worthless and the whole world would be better off if it had been me.

When the Diagnostic and Statistical Manual of Mental Disorders IV (DSM-IV) was published, survivor guilt was removed as a recognized specific diagnosis, and redefined as a significant symptom of post traumatic stress disorder (PTSD). Three decades later it's hard to believe that the Forces were so unaware of the effects of trauma on mental health. I was offered no counselling, I was told that the Padre was always available if I needed to talk to someone but as an agnostic the idea of speaking to a priest about my emotional state seemed alien, after all, I didn't need spiritual guidance.

We seem to have been involved in a perpetual state of war, somewhere around the world, since those simpler times during the Cold War when there was the one perceived enemy, the status quo ruled and no shots were fired. I dearly wish that every single one of our service personnel could be brought home to their families and friends today and that no one ever again had to face the pain of losing their loved one through combat. I'm glad to see that things have progressed in the recognition of the psychological effects of trauma but know that things can be still be improved greatly. Around 250,000 British troops have seen active duty in Afghanistan and Iraq since 2003 with many experiencing mental health issues following their return home. They have a higher rate of being in prison or homeless than the general population and the continuing lack of adequate mental health support is a significant contributing factor. They are trained for war, experience traumatising events and yet no one prepares them for life after service.

. . . . .

Three months after Andy's injury I'm gone.

Given the lack of professional help for my unrecognised, unacknowledged and undiagnosed PTSD the RAF decide that a change is as good as a rest and ship me off to Germany.

I'm sure that someone, somewhere thought that they were doing the right thing, removing me from the site of the trauma, giving me a fresh start, but in reality what they were doing was separating me from my support network, the people that knew what I'd been through and the only support that I had.

Arriving in Germany I immediately felt isolated.

For the first few weeks at RAF Laarbruch I was accommodated in an ageing H-block barrack built during the 1950s and housed in a 32 man room, eight bunk beds lined the walls on either side of an aisle, privacy was at a premium and I didn't qualify.

20 Squadron and their Tornado bombers were located on the far side of the airfield dispersed around a central hub in hardened aircraft shelters (HAS) similar to those I'd worked in back in Norfolk, the difference was in the personnel.

In numerous war films across the generations there was always a rogue squadron, filled with all of the rejects from other units, the Dirty Dozen or the Wild Bunch, and 20 or XX Squadron felt like RAF Germany's equivalent. The younger members of the unit would have been more at home in University halls than a military unit, and the old hands leaned more towards disaffected insolence than obedient military service.

Amongst the flat top haircuts, bleached jeans and Smiths t-shirts I immediately felt out of place, with my nondescript short back and sides haircut and military issue moustache I gave the image of someone approaching middle age, not the 18-year-old that I actually was.

As numb as I was from my mental anguish this cultural rebellion seemed to be exactly the channel that I needed to release and direct my fury. The moustache went almost immediately and soon my hair had grown into a more acceptable style.

The Mod years were drawing to a close, since the demise of The Jam in 1982 the movement had been on borrowed time and whilst I still rode a Vespa my life had started to evolve.

In these 21st century days of constant connection to the internet and a smartphone, or sometimes two, in everyone's pocket or bag, it's strange to think how totally out of contact it was possible to be in the past. People find it impossible to go to the shops now without their phone where once it was usual to just arrange a time to meet back at the car.

When my parents waved me off from the family run pub in Winchester after new year 1986, on a fully laden 125cc Vespa, 18 years old and with no possible method of communication, to ride the 400 miles to Germany, no one batted an eyelid.

The ride down to Dover was easy enough, the winter sun shone bright and warm. Things were very different disembarking from the ferry in Zeebrugge at 2am to 3 inches of snow still with 200 miles to travel. I was colder than I had ever been before, warming my hands on the exhaust pipe outside a closed service station at 5am, very few places were open 24 hours a day back then. Eventually, around 7am I finally arrived at the camp gates, having narrowly avoided a spinning car on the autobahn, the guard looked with barely disguised pity at this idiot on a scooter and waved me through with minimal checks.

A year or so later I replaced the 125cc Vespa with an 1100cc Yamaha and the journey time shrank considerably.

. . . . .

My gender identity was still troubling me. Although I discovered that I wasn't alone in questioning my identity, the transsexual performers that I saw in the readily available explicit continental pornography were as far removed from my life and experience as were the lives of film stars. Their lives seemed to be a fantasy purely for the sexual gratification of men, what I saw spoke nothing to me about how I felt inside.

I'd also started to question my sexuality and had my first sexual experience with a German man who approached me in a bar. Not much happened but it was enough to tell me that there were possibilities outside of the heteronormative world I'd previously taken as read.

Needing to find a way to express my emotions I began to write poetry, I think that I looked at the works of the great poets of the First World War, Rupert Brooke, Siegfried Sassoon and Wilfred Owen and saw through them a way to channel the horror and pain that was eating me from within.

Over the space of a couple of years I produced a small book of my collected poems, typed on a portable typewriter, photocopied and bound in a pale blue card cover imprinted with the title 'Steve Cook - Selected Poems 85-87'. Once printed I distributed copies to family and friends. In recent years I rediscovered those writings and was horrified to read the painful, dark, introspective poems.

How could my family have not known how badly I was hurting? Why did they not immediately seek an intervention?Reading the words now they strike me as a 44 page long suicide note.

You were young
So young
Where oh where
Did it all go wrong.

A moment of error
Your youth is gone
Forever.

Steve Cook, c 1985-86

. . . . .

Night

The dark closes in
Constricts my mind
My throat
Life extinguished
A daylight atheist
Finds his God
As the terror
Descends.

Steve Cook, c 1985-86

. . . . .

Suicide
Gives a certain feeling
Sweet
Yet strangely stale.

How can your life
Be worth so little
That all you do
Is hurt.

Steve Cook, c 1985-86

. . . . .

How can a man who's seen so much
Still be so naive

You've seen the evil, that men can do
Why be so innocent?

Now that your time has come
Why are you not ready?

Death has seen you once
And been denied
He will not wait
Again.

Steve Cook, c 1985-86

. . . . .

Squadron life in Germany suited me, I loved the work and it offered various perks including the opportunity to travel and during the three years that I was on 20 Squadron I enjoyed detachments to Sardinia, Newfoundland in Canada and a rather eventful two weeks at Nellis AFB just outside Las Vegas, Nevada.

It was in Las Vegas that someone first pointed a gun at me.

The Vegas that I visited in the 1980s was nothing like the shining pleasureland that now awaits visitors to Sin City. Between the famous strip and downtown there was still an area of desert wasteland, and this is where the RAF decided to billet the engineers, in a hotel that had lost it's gaming license, whilst the officers were housed in the much more fitting surroundings of Caesar's Palace.

One afternoon when I was off shift I took the opportunity to visit a bar around the corner from our hotel. Like many of the bars in this particularly salubrious run down area of the city this establishment employed the talents of exotic dancers one of whom took a shine to the shy young airman from England. Having arranged to meet her for a drink when she finished work I was sat in a car outside the bar when two rather large men approached the vehicle, all tattoos and testosterone. It would seem that they were not best pleased with the potential match and producing a handgun made it very clear that I should move along and not come back.

Deciding that I didn't want to cause a diplomatic incident with our closest allies I decided to follow their advice and head off after making my case for transatlantic relations.

"Please don't point a gun at me, I'm from Bournemouth, we don't do guns."

· · · · ·

I've always believed that travel and experiencing other cultures helps us to grow and develop the empathy that is so important to all human relationships and it was on these detachments that I first started to see the very real effects of political actions and in particular poverty. Having grown up in a very nice, English village I was protected from some of the harshness that life presents but in these foreign lands I encountered children begging, I saw slums and the effects of failing economies and racial hatred.

The political awakening led to an interest in reading political science and I began reading about socialism and in particular the works of Karl Marx. Strangely enough these weren't available from the station library and it did raise a few eyebrows when I sat reading them in the squadron crewroom between jobs.

· · · · ·

Growing up I'd always had the strong family that my friends envied, at a time when divorce was starting to become more prevalent amongst my peers parents my parents marriage always appeared rock solid.

Thinking that I'd surprise my family with an unplanned visit I turned up on the doorstep of my parents pub in Winchester to find my Mum wearing a business suit deep in conversation with my Father. Something wasn't right about this scenario and it soon became apparent when I was informed that my parents had separated. Instead of spending a relaxing weekend with my loving family I had walked into my greatest nightmare, through all of my pain the stability of my home was the thing that had held me together. Subsequently I discovered that my Mother had a new relationship and I tried to help my Dad come to terms with this before my return to Germany.

A couple of months later he told me that he'd met someone and that she was helping him to recover from the break up but I still felt uneasy about the situation.

· · · · ·

I'd had no news from Marham about Andy's condition since I'd arrived in Germany. People discussed the incident, surmising on rumoured causes and outcomes without ever knowing that I was in any way connected to the events.

One day a group of guys were in the crew room, talking about what had happened when someone asked what had happened to the injured airman.

"Didn't you hear? He killed himself, he couldn't deal with his injuries," came the reply.

The news that Andy had taken his own life floored me, if he's done that then why did I save him? Why did I put myself through all of that pain for nothing?

Running out of the crew room I headed for the toilets and only just made it before vomiting, collapsing into the corner of the stall.

I felt responsible for his suicide, by saving him I'd cheated death and condemned him to a life without his arm, an injury so horrific that he could see no future.

Sobbing uncontrollably I began clawing at my skin, I wanted to remove my arm, I wanted to die, I wanted to go back in time and let him die when he was supposed to, then he wouldn't have been tormented enough to take his own life. If I'd never been born then this wouldn't have happened. I wanted to do anything that I could to change this but there was absolutely nothing that I could do.

I just sat, and sobbed, and prayed for death.

· · · · ·

Childhoods Gone - Suicide note

Can't believe the news
The world crumbles
Why did you do it?
I tried so hard
I gave you my youth
My innocence
My soul
I tried, oh God I tried
You threw it away, why?
Why should I bother?
Why should I try so hard
What gives you the right?

If you're gone
What have I got?
What?

Steve Cook, Oct 1986

· · · · ·

As I look around the bar the noise inside my head becomes unbearable, the pain washes over and engulfs me.

People's faces become pinpoints in the distance as I retreat deep within, trying to block out their voices.

I turn and head, unobserved, towards the toilets at the rear of the bar, skirting the pools of light thrown by the lamps above the tables laden with drinks.

Once inside I lock the cubicle door and slump down to the seat, the weight of my pain seemingly drawing me down, crushing me, diminishing me and making me smaller. I reach inside my jacket pocket and pull out my wallet, inside, hiding amongst the Deutschmarks, is the tool with which I will sate my pain.

The razor blade catches the light from the single, bare bulb above my head as I turn it over in my hand, feeling the symbolic power of release that resides within it.

I look down at my wrists, the skin looks so thin, diaphanous, barely covering the vein that lies beneath, so fragile, so vulnerable, so easy to defile with the blade's cold edge. I sense that the pressure that needs release does not reside there, the darkness lies deep within me, hidden, somehow impenetrable.

I move my gaze up my arm, coming to rest on my forearm as I carefully and deliberately roll up the sleeve of my shirt.

I bring the blade up, using it to caress the skin before bringing it down in a rapid pass across the flesh, I feel an instant burn of pain, then nothing.

A moment passes and then a thin, scarlet line appears, as I watch the line seems to swell outward and then spread slightly across my arm as the line becomes liquid and flows across the pale flesh of my arm.

I watch all of this as if watching an abstraction, I do not feel connected to what I see, this is not my arm, my flesh, my blood. I feel no pain from the wound, the physical pain is but an attempt to give form and meaning to the emotional and mental pain that is tormenting my mind.

The blade comes down for a second time, the red line makes a neat cross with the first, then again and again, two scarlet crosses mark the skin.

I close my eyes and take a deep breath, my nostrils and lungs filling with the stale smell of human waste and disinfectant. I rest, searching for a stillness within myself.

Feeling the release I roll down my sleeve, oblivious to the blood which is staining the dark material the deepest black and, standing to leave, I return the blade to its resting place within my wallet.

As I re-enter the bar, the world is exactly as I left it, the pool players deliberate over a shot, a couple, relaxed and intimate joke in a booth and my colleagues greet me at the bar with the refrain of "get the drinks in, it's your round".

4

THE KINGDOM

The silence is broken by a scream.

I'm worried, we need help, we need medical assistance. Where are they? Where is the ambulance?

"Get help" I say "try next door."

The boy runs out of the bedroom and towards the stairs.

There seems to be so much blood, too much, I'm deeply concerned about the blood loss but there's nothing that I can do to stop it.

Keep calm, be supportive, we should have medical help but there's none here. The nearest hospital is 10 miles away on country roads that can be treacherous even on a clear summers night such as this.

The neighbour arrives, a woman in her fifties, she's shocked but she does a great job of hiding it.

"We need towels, every one you've got", she says

· · · · ·

After three years in Germany it was time to move on. The RAF operated a system whereby you could apply for your desired posting and also list the places that you didn't want to go to. The joke was that if they couldn't send you to your positive choices they just carried on down the list and used one of your negative ones.

This time I hit the jackpot.

RAF Chivenor was home to a training unit operating British Aerospace Hawk aircraft. It was quiet, the aircraft didn't fly on weekends, exercises were virtually unheard of and it was situated by a beach on the North Devon coast, what was there not to like?

On top of all that I also had a great job, working on the Visiting Aircraft Servicing Flight. This effectively meant no maintenance work at all, purely seeing in any aircraft that happened to be visiting, whether it was a C-130 Hercules, USAF A10 Warthogs, Frank Williams private jet dropping off Nigel Mansell for his nearby golf club or a Jaguar pilot using his jet to commute at weekends to see his girlfriend.

Relatively close to my hometown of Bournemouth the location was perfect and I lived in a house near the beach, life was good, so of course it couldn't last. Within six months I was promoted and sent back to RAF Halton, the scene of my apprenticeship, for further training as a jet engine technician.

It was strange to see the boy apprentices once again on parade. After my time in Germany and all of the experiences that I'd been through in the four years since I'd left it was hard to believe that I'd ever been part of that world.

My mental health was being masked by a veil of indifference, post traumatic nightmares and survivor guilt still haunted my low points and my gender identity tormented me with feelings of shame.

During my training course I would spend weekends visiting my Mum and her new husband in Southampton and it was on one of these trips that I met a woman that would soon become my wife. Tracey lived in a council flat in the Harefield area of town and had previously had relationships with sailors from the nearby Royal Navy docks at Portsmouth. She was used to having a partner that was away with the Forces and we fell in love and married within months. She already had a 9 year old son, he was a wonderful child, polite, intelligent and friendly and I was overjoyed that we got on so well.

At the end of my training course we moved into married quarters at RAF Coningsby in Lincolnshire where I would service the Spey engines from the few remaining Phantoms based in the Falkland Islands, the same aircraft that my Dad had worked on a decade or so earlier.

After all of the pain that I'd suffered it was nice to feel part of something more, part of a family, I loved Jason like my own son and a few months later I was overjoyed at the news that Tracey was pregnant.

· · · · ·

"Dad! Mum's on the toilet and she's asking for you."

I'd just opened the doors of my Austin Allegro, the bronze coloured car that I'd bought when it became obvious that a family of four wouldn't fit on an 1100cc Yamaha motorbike. The overnight bag full of birthing essentials was on the back seat and I was heading back into the house to take Tracey, who was going into labour, to the hospital in nearby Boston.

As I bounded up the stairs, two at a time, it became clear that Tracey's waters had broken and that the baby was on the way. Helping her out of the toilet I led her to the bedroom as I flicked the lights back on.

We should be in a hospital, I thought, as I tried to make her as comfortable as possible. I'd previously had a relationship with a nurse and was horrified to hear how many women still died in childbirth, until then I always thought that it was something from the past but at this moment it felt very real, and very scary.

"How long have you been having contractions?" I asked.

"A couple of hours" she said, "there was no point waking you up earlier."

The plans of a nice comfortable, safe, delivery room all flew out of the window. This was happening here and now and we'd need as much help as possible. I rang the midwife and she reassured me that everything would be OK, she was on her way and so was the ambulance, they'd be here soon.

We'd become friendly with the couple next door and I sent Jason to wake them up and ask for help until the medical staff arrived.

Thirty minutes later, with just her mother, myself and the next door neighbour for company my daughter, Victoria, was born.

Later the ambulance arrived and attended to the aftercare and an hour after that we were joined, eventually, by the midwife.

For all of the fear the birth had proved to be straightforward and without major drama, although my nerves would have been much calmer with the presence of midwives, doctors and machines that go ping. This was my wife and my baby, they were the centre of my world, and I'd been terrified at the possibility that anything might go wrong to either of them.

The medical staff left having decided that mother and baby were well enough that they didn't need to go to hospital and I spent the day cuddling my new daughter whilst watching the motorcycle grand prix on TV, I couldn't have been happier.

Everything seemed perfect in my life.

For a second.

. . . . .

In the years since the Cold War, during which Iraq had been an ally of the Soviet Union, there had been a difficult relationship between the Gulf state and the US. The Americans were concerned with Iraq's support for the Palestinians against the occupying Israeli forces but assisted them in the Iran-Iraq war as they were considered useful in the battle to stop the spread of Islamic fundamentalism.

Iraq had long claimed neighbouring Kuwait to be an Iraqi territory. It had been a part of the Ottoman Empire's province of Basra until the British took control of the area as a protectorate in 1899 and when the border between the two countries was redrawn in 1922, making Iraq virtually landlocked, it created lasting resentment.

A key part of ensuring prosperity throughout the countries of OPEC were the quotas for oil production, if they were exceeded then the price would drop below the desired price of $18 per barrel. Kuwait and the UAE were consistently overproducing and the price began to fall, sinking as low as $10 a barrel leading to a $7 billion per year fall in revenues for Iraq, the equivalent of its 1989 balance of payments deficit.

Further aggrieved by the Kuwaitis slant-drilling across the border to access oil from Iraq's Rumaila oil field, an act the Iraqis described as economic warfare, on August 2 1990, two weeks after Victoria's birth the eyes of the world turned to the Persian Gulf as Saddam Hussein ordered the invasion of Kuwait.

. . . . .

It became clear that my modest RAF income which had been adequate for a single man with very few financial responsibilities was going to struggle to support a family of four. The bills began to pile up whilst the cupboards were frequently empty. As happens in so many relationships the tensions grew in proportion to the debt and my new wife began to pressure me to find better paid work outside of the service.

Since the early 70s the most lucrative of post-service career paths for RAF engineers had been in the desert kingdom of Saudi Arabia where BAE Systems and its predecessors, British Aerospace and the British Aircraft Corporation had supplied the Royal Saudi Air Force, first with BAC Lightnings and Strikemasters and later the Panavia Tornado and Hawk.

The Al Yamamah project, named after the arabic word for 'The Dove', was Britain's largest ever export agreement. In 2005 the then CEO of BAE Systems, Mike Turner, said that the deal had earned BAE £43 billion in twenty years and that it could expect to earn another £40 billion with the ongoing commitment to the new Eurofighter Typhoon aircraft.

The exact details of the deal have never been made public but in 1988 the Financial Times described it as "the biggest UK sale ever of anything to anyone" and consisted of the delivery and support for 96 Tornado ground attack aircraft, 24 Tornado Air Defence Variants (ADVs), 50 Hawks and 50 Pilatus PC-9 trainer aircraft, naval vessels, and infrastructure.

Over the years there have been many allegations of bribery and corruption involved in the signing of the Al Yamamah deal, and in 2007 the BBC's investigative programme Panorama alleged that BAE Systems had "paid hundreds of millions of pounds to the ex-Saudi ambassador to the US, Prince Bandar bin Sultan."

As far back as 1992 the National Audit Office (NAO) investigated the contracts but its conclusions have never been released, the only NAO report ever to be withheld. The Serious Fraud Office also carried out a high profile investigation until it was forced to drop the case by Prime Minister Tony Blair who justified the decision on BBC News saying: "Our relationship with Saudi Arabia is vitally important for our country in terms of counter-terrorism, in terms of the broader Middle East, in terms of helping in respect of Israel and Palestine. That strategic interest comes first."

In 2018 Tony Blair's relationship with Saudi Arabia came under scrutiny when it was confirmed that the Tony Blair Institute, an NGO set up in his name, had received donations of up to $12 million from the Kingdom. A revelation that raised many questions about the former Prime Minister's decision making regarding the region.

The corruption in the deal was finally, partly, addressed in 2010 when the US Department of Justice sentenced BAE through a plea bargain to pay a $400 million fine, one of the largest fines in the history of the DOJ. In sentencing the judge said that the company's conduct involved "deception, duplicity and knowing violations of law on an enormous scale".

Interestingly BAE wasn't convicted of bribery which conveniently avoided them being blacklisted from future contracts.

$$. . . . .$$

During the 90s BAE Systems employed in the region of 5000 personnel in the Kingdom to support the Royal Saudi Air Force and despite my misgivings about leaving my wife and young family I applied to join them.

To leave the service early I had to buy myself out of my contract and the RAF Form 1680A 'Bills for services provided' lists the 'Type of supply' as 'Discharge by purchase' - cost £250 and duly paid by cheque.

Joining BAe Systems the first thing that they insisted upon was sending me on six months of courses, effectively retraining me for the job that I'd spent the past five years doing. My time was spread between the various manufacturers of components of the Tornado, BAe in Warton, Lancashire for systems, Rolls-Royce in Bristol for engines and KHD in Frankfurt for the gearboxes. While I was sat in a classroom the war was going on without me in the Gulf. My former RAF colleagues had been deployed there as part of Operation Granby, the British element of Desert Shield, and my BAe colleagues were maintaining the Saudi Air Force jets.

I was stuck in the run down and dated monolithic Norbreck Castle Hotel on the North Blackpool coast, seemingly sentenced to an eternity in these inauspicious surroundings that in 1988 had been the venue for the birth of the Liberal Democrats as the Liberal Party and Social Democratic Party merged. Writing in the New Statesman at the time Jonathan Calder said: "Blackpool's Norbreck Castle Hotel does not lift the spirit at the best of times, and its Soviet ambience was enhanced by the trams and melting snow in the streets outside." I do not disagree.

· · · · ·

Finally arriving in the Kingdom of Saudi Arabia in September 1991 I was struck by the wave of hot, humid air as the door of the Saudia Lockheed L-1011 TriStar opened and the aircraft's cabin immediately became a sauna as a result of the 50°C heat coupled with 60% humidity.

On the minibus journey to our residential compound we passed large blue freight containers with rough holes cut in their sides by Oxy Acetylene torches. These were homes to migrant workers from the Indian subcontinent and Far East. Housed in inhuman conditions and employed as construction workers, street cleaners, gardeners or maids with no workers rights or health and safety protection. Tied to their employer by the kafala system, their passports were held by their sponsor and only released when they deemed it acceptable.

A 2008 Human Rights Watch report described the kafala system in Saudi Arabia, "an employer assumes responsibility for a hired migrant worker and must grant explicit permission before the worker can enter Saudi Arabia, transfer employment, or leave the country. The kafala system gives the employer immense control over the worker."

The report went on to say that "some abusive employers exploit the kafala system and force domestic workers to continue working against their will and forbid them from returning to their countries of origin" and that "the combination of the high recruitment fees paid by Saudi employers and the power granted them by the kafala system to control whether a worker can change employers or exit the country made some employers feel entitled to exert 'ownership' over a domestic worker" and that the "sense of ownership... creates slavery-like conditions".

· · · · ·

I immediately felt uneasy in the Kingdom, the work and my colleagues were ok, after all much of it was the same as I'd experienced in the RAF and indeed I regularly bumped into people that I knew from the service, but I was missing my new family.

I missed Tracey and Jason, and Vicki was only 14 months old, it broke my heart not to be with them and I immediately regretted being so far away. I wanted to go home, to be with them but Tracey kept telling me to stick it out and that everything would be ok.

Throwing myself into the expat life I settled in at work servicing the Tornado ADV jets of the Royal Saudi Air Force's (RSAF) 29 Squadron. The majority of the technical personnel were British with a few Australians and Kiwis thrown in, all ex-Forces, all male. My job title of Technician Trainer showed how I was working towards Saudization, a plan to reduce the RSAF's reliance on overseas contractors and eventually make them a self-sufficient service.

Saudization had been a goal of the Saudi government since the mid-1980s, officially known as the Saudi nationalization scheme, it requires Saudi companies to employ certain numbers of Saudi nationals. During my time in Saudi Arabia in the 1990s it was rare to see a Saudi man employed anywhere other than with the government and to put the scale of the problem into perspective the 2003 goal that 30% of employees at companies with 20 or more workers should be Saudi natives was dropped to 10% in 2006 due to pressure from business executives.

As of 2018 the unemployment rate amongst Saudi men is 12.8% rising to 33% for Saudi women who are barred from many areas of employment. The economy is dependent on state spending, and social and cultural issues make change unlikely. 45% of private sector jobs in the kingdom are in construction, a sector that has little appeal for Saudi men and is virtually banned for Saudi women who make up about 85% of job seekers.

My contribution to Saudization was to teach my RSAF trainee, Adel Al-Ghamdi, to service the RB199 engines of the Tornado. Having seen my colleagues fail to bond with their Saudi trainees I thought that looking for some common ground might ease the working relationship.

"So have you always been interested in aircraft Adel?" I asked.

"No."

"Do you enjoy engineering? Fixing your own car?"

"No, why would I?"

It was true, why would he? As in all other jobs imported labour kept the motor vehicles of the Kingdom running long past their safe to use date.

I tried a different tack, I'd loved the travel opportunities that the RAF had given me, he couldn't serve abroad but he might want to see a bit more of his own country.

"Are you interested in getting posted somewhere else in the Kingdom? Khamis or Tabuk?"

"Why would I? My family are here, I have no wish to go there."

Adel showed no interest in the aircraft or the work and it was difficult to work out his motivation for joining the airforce. He hadn't been conscripted but for a young Saudi man there were very few 'acceptable' avenues of employment and societal pressure to have military service on his CV had obviously played a part.

. . . . .

As is the case in a lot of expat communities around the world boredom and loneliness were a problem. I was missing my family terribly and my old demons made their presence felt. The PTSD that had begun to subside as my relationship grew returned together with the discomfort about my gender leading to an increased emotional detachment, and for solace I turned to alcohol.

Alcohol is totally illegal in Saudi Arabia.

Saudi law comes from a strict interpretation of the Koran and as the home of the two holy mosques of Mecca and Medina the Kingdom is the centre of Islam. That said the Saudi authorities turned a blind eye to all but the most blatant of infringements by the western contractors upon whom their industry and defence were reliant.

The walled compound on which I lived together with hundreds of other BAe employees, Al Gosaibi, was home to numerous bars and even nightclubs. Once these had been prefabricated villas like the one in which I lived but over the years the occupants had extended them, building bars, brewrooms, stages and dancefloors. The illicit night time economy of Algo, as it was affectionately known, was thriving and any bar owner or booze baron could expect to make many times their legitimate income through meeting the needs of the expat community although the risks were high and over the years a few of them served time, and received lashes, in Saudi prisons.

The majority of the alcohol was home brewed, plastic dustbins were filled with non-alcoholic malt beverages, Kaliber or Moussy, and combined with sacks of sugar and yeast to put the alcohol back into these alcohol free 'beers'. Wines and Jeddah Gin were produced in similar fashion just by varying the ingredients but my drink of choice was Sid.

Sid or Siddiqi, from the arabic word for 'friend', was a clear rum-like moonshine, the product of sugar and water and yards of copper tubing. It could be of varying quality and its strength could be as high as 90% alcohol. It was commonly drunk as a double measure with coke or juice but I soon found myself filling a pint glass with seven measures and topping it up with a splash of cola.

My relationship with Tracey had begun to deteriorate from the moment I arrived in Saudi and suffered a further setback following the death of her father. She withdrew from me and on my four monthly trips back home she would tell me that she didn't love me any more as she headed out of the door to spend time with her friends.

I loved her and adored my children who were growing up without me, I wanted to leave Saudi and return home to them but it became increasingly clear that I just wasn't welcome.

· · · · ·

I threw myself into life in Saudi, working, drinking and motorbike racing.

The last two definitely don't go together very well but I wasn't exactly thinking straight.

Within the expat community there was a fledgling Saudi National Motocross Championship. Made up of all nations, French former Paris-Dakar riders, Australian and Kiwi farm boys that had grown up with dirt bikes, an ex-supercrosser from the US and a handful of Brits raised with road bikes and off-roading for the first time.

Beginning with a 1980s air cooled Yamaha YZ250, the oldest and heaviest dirt bike in the region, I took to the dirt and soon established a reputation for crashing as my exuberance far outweighed my ability. The advanced age and unrideability of my bike certainly didn't help me and it soon became known as 'The Beast' a title that I embraced by adopting 666 as my race number to replace the slightly less prophetic 13 that the bike had previously worn.

It quickly became evident that I needed an equipment upgrade and the Beast was replaced by a former Grand Prix bike imported from the UK, my results improved but the limiting factor remained my lack of talent and my inability to separate my drinking, which was increasingly becoming a problem, from my racing.

This period also saw my first foray into writing as I launched a satirical fanzine directed at my fellow racers. Pieced together manually with a typewriter, scissors, glue and a photocopier this predated desktop publishing and featured interviews, rumour, innuendo, jokes, photos and race results. It soon became a popular diversion in the pits at race meetings where I could be found scribbling notes between races, hungover with bloodshot eyes from the previous nights partying.

My greatest success on the track saw me take 3rd place in the Novice category at the Jeddah National despite a total lack of feeling in my right hand as my carpal tunnel tightened up due to the punishing desert track, pinching the nerves and reducing my brake control to a simple on-off action.

· · · · ·

The engine revs rise as I accelerate up the ramp, the wheels leave the ground and the vibration stops as I momentarily feel weightless at the apex of my flight.

A second later I'm back on the ground, bike bucking as noise, dust and heat assault my senses. I open the throttle and shoot towards the next corner throwing the bike on its side as I extend my left leg to support the machine as the back wheel spins and searches for grip.

Adrenalin courses through my body as sweat stings the corners of my eyes which are fixed on the entry line to the hairpin ahead of me and the climb to the highest point of the track. As I crest the peak the ground and bike drop away from me, again feeling the freedom of flight, repositioning myself for the next corner and tapping the back brake to bring the front wheel down for my landing.

A red Honda flashes into my peripheral vision to my left and I take the faster wide line around the corner, tyres digging into the raised banking as I accelerate towards the six foot drop at the corners exit. The Honda brakes sharply, spinning its back wheel as it attempts to cut under me and force it's way past.

I maintain my line, ensuring that the other rider has space, the wide line allows me to keep my speed and, hopefully, exit the corner before him. As I accelerate the red bike begins to drift across in front of me, encroaching on my piece of track, shutting the door on me and taking the lead. I try to adjust my path but I've nowhere to go as the Honda's rear wheel whips across striking my front wheel.

Time slows, the front end of my bike folds from under me.

Falling forward and to my left the bike launches off the six foot drop, engine revving and rear wheel spinning, searching for traction. My left shoulder hits the ground, instantly dislocating and shattering under the impact as the upended Yamaha pushes me into the ground before arcing down to crush my left leg under its frame.

I lie on the track, immobilised by my injuries, eyes and face contorted as the pain overwhelms my senses and a darkness descends on me.

Help arrives and a four wheel drive is brought onto the track as I sit up, a hollow under my race jersey where my left shoulder should be. Nausea and pain engulf me and I'm helped to my feet to get into the vehicle, my left leg giving way as the broken bones scrape together.

"By the way, I've broken my leg as well."

5
BROKEN

The leather strap closes around my left wrist, tight enough to restrain but not uncomfortably so.

Next the strap passes around my naked thigh, holding the arm close to my body, restricting all movement. Lying back on the bed I try to relax but a wave of apprehension washes over me. I've done this before but I'm still anxious, the pain can be unbearable and this is supposed to be a time of rest.

I close my eyes, trying to remember happier times, times when the pain didn't consume me, trying to find peace but it eludes me. The heat of the room brings beads of sweat to the surface of my skin, slowly sliding across the scars before being absorbed by the bedding.

Darkness and pain envelop my mind as my demons return to torment me and Morpheus welcomes me to the land of dreams.

· · · · ·

My recovery from the injuries that I sustained in the crash was a long process, the left shoulder was broken and required screws to reassemble the shattered bones, and the muscles and tendons of the rotator cuff that hold the head of the humerus into the cartilage cup of the labrum had been severely damaged.

The result was that my shoulder joint became highly unstable and prone to dislocation at every opportunity. I'd already damaged my right shoulder in another crash and I could pop that back in following a dislocation quite easily but my left shoulder would drop 4", leaving a strange empty hollow in my body where my shoulder should be, an injury that always required a trip to the operating theatre and a general anesthetic to reattach my errant limb.

I would regularly wake with my arm lying, unattached, on the pillow next to me having dislocated in my sleep. I would swear, pick it up gently with my right hand and call for an ambulance. The situation got so bad that I resorted to tying my left wrist to my left thigh in order to restrict its movements whilst I slept and for months this became the only way that I could guarantee that I would wake up with my shoulder still in its joint.

The following year saw further surgeries, continued racing, more crashes and my list of injuries began to mount. Two broken shoulders, numerous dislocations, broken arm, broken wrist, broken leg, two broken thumbs. Each time I crashed the medics would plaster cast me and two weeks later I would be sat in the pits at the racetrack using shears to remove the cast in an effort to allow me to go racing again.

The damage to my body meant nothing to me, the real damage had been inflicted on my mind and mental health. My drinking was continuing unabated, my relationship with Tracey was deteriorating by the week and my self hatred was reaching new levels. I was tormented by my PTSD, my shoulder injury brought back the thoughts of Andy losing his arm. The frequency of dislocations got so great that I contemplated cutting the 'bloody thing' off as the limb seemed useless and a curse. My gender confusion and sexuality compounded the problems as guilt and shame added their own voice to the demons already chipping away at my fragile mental state.

Eventually the tally of injuries got too great, and with the patience of my employer reaching breaking point, I reluctantly decided to retire from racing. The bike was sold on, the helmet hidden at the back of the wardrobe and my body was given a chance to mend. Unfortunately the damaged shoulder continued to trouble me and even after further surgeries would dislocate whenever it wished for another decade and to this day, more than twenty years later, I'm still anxious about lifting that arm into the unstable position above my head.

Robbed of my adrenalin fix and main method of whiling away the endless hours of an expats life I started to spend more time with my old friend Sid, as my drink problem became worse.

· · · · ·

In an effort to fill the void left by my retirement from racing I turned to music. It had always been a big part of my life, I'd fallen in love with listening to records as a teen and still enjoy this today, getting great pleasure from the fact that I still own every record that I've ever bought.

During my childhood I'd had a brief stint in the village brass band playing the trombone alongside my Grandad on cornet and flugelhorn. I lasted a good year or so, despite the fact that I couldn't actually play it, due to my ability to watch the player next to me and follow their movements of the slide.

I became the singer in a band, Fazed Out, belting out Neil Young and AC/DC covers, singing in the illegal bars and drinking establishments on the various western compounds. But quickly internal tensions within the band began to surface, the lead guitarist and bass player were married and had their own difficulties that would manifest as arguments and name calling on stage. The bad feeling increasingly pushed the rhythm guitarist, a Yorkshireman called Ian Stacey, and myself to the fringes of the band and further affected my mental health.

As the final song of another particularly vitriolic performance ended I dropped the microphone, walked off stage, out of the venue and straight into another bar where I ordered a large drink and, despite being a non-smoker, a pack of cigarettes. My thinking was that they must do something for you, otherwise why would people smoke. A few coughs later and I handed the full pack to someone else realising that even nicotine couldn't lift my mood.

Back at the bar I sat on the edge of the stage, head in my hands, ready to break. I missed my family, I hated myself and all I really wanted to do was to die.

· · · · ·

Being in a band is supposed to be fun and eventually the stress of being in Fazed Out got too much for Ian and myself and we quit to set out on our own. Originally just him on guitar and me singing I soon picked up the bass guitar and helped to flesh out our sound.

One of the most exciting, but potentially conflict inducing jobs for any new band is the all important discussion where you name the band, this was our first band on our own and we had to come up with the goods. After much wordplay we finally settled on a tribute to 80s pop duo Mel and Kim and named our fledgeling band Melon King.

The setlist was unlike any other band on the Saudi circuit, gone were the Eagles and Clapton, instead replaced by the new sound from America, Nirvana and Green Day, as well as songs from our youth, punk, Bauhaus' 'Bela Lugosi's Dead' and The Jam.

A particular highlight came when I discovered that with a single finger and the disco rhythm on our keyboard I could play New Order's 'Blue Monday' with Ian taking my bass guitar and me covering Bernie Sumner's laid back vocals. I even tried rap in the form of the Beastie Boys 'Sabotage' and these numbers always went down well with an audience bored of middle of the road rock.

I also began writing again and this time the poetry became lyrics. With Ian and I working on the tunes, these songs soon became favourites with our growing group of loyal fans. One in particular, an angry punk song about the life of a Saudi expat, beholden to corporate greed, travelling back to the Kingdom from Heathrow soon became our anthem.

Terminal 4

Going nowhere fast
Journey back into the past
I don't need this shit
Can't always handle it

Terminal 4, you corporate whore

I'm gonna rip it up
Destroy all the stupid fucks
Gotta be a better way
For me to earn my pay

Terminal 4, you corporate whore
Terminal 4, you terminal bore

Steve Cook, 1994

· · · · ·

Melon King better than sex - Official

A recent survey into the bizarre sexual fantasies of post-menopausal women showed that most women in the 75-99 age group found listening to Dhahran punk group Melon King preferable to sex. This shocking finding caused the band no problem whatsoever though, said bass guitarist and singer Cooky, "We've always realised that there was something special about our blend of late 70's punk and 90's grunge. The way the old girls start panting and throwing their foundation garments at us has always been a trademark of our gigs."

Meanwhile guitarist Ian Stacey was unavailable for comment, choosing instead to remain silent behind the gates of his Scottish castle.

Melon King rose to prominence in 1994 after their very public split with their former band, Fazed Out, as Stacey said at the time "We had musical differences, they wanted to be musical and we wanted to be different." Well the boys certainly managed that with a number of high profile gigs, notably their debut at Manhattan's last August. "We made the cock ups that we'd always been making, some even worse, but we just laughed about it and the crowd loved it!"

Not everything has been rosy for the pop twosome though. The financial flop of their ambitious Rockfest 94 and the poor performance at Riyadh B (both occasions being notable for the dream team double bill with Purl Nekless) caused the band to take stock and re-evaluate their musical aims.

The December 29, 1994, the Delta Club. Melon King rock back to form with the gig of the year. A new light show and a more positive attitude payoff as the boys blast their way through old favourites like 'My Girl', 'Sort It Out' and the classic 'Terminal 4'. Joined by their latest hit 'Winter Sun' and remarkable covers of Oasis' 'Supersonic', Green Day's 'Basket Case' and 'Longview' and Therapy's 'Trigger Inside' these were but the brightest stars in a repertoire as bright as the Milky Way.

Two days later and Melon King were at it again, this time rocking the Rugby Club into the New Year in a Townshend-esque display of sheer bravado. Due to disband in April, Melon King plan to go out in style, with 2 headline shows at the Delta Club on March 16 and April 13. This may be the end of the story, or it could be a new beginning, we'll just have to wait and see.

The King is dead, long live Melon King.

Melon King Fan Club Flyer, Early 1995

· · · · ·

One of the unavoidable facts of expat life is that people move on and just as Melon King was coming together, building a following and becoming fun Ian reached the point where he had to return home to Edinburgh.

Just before I went home for Christmas '95 Jeff Sanders, whom I'd known since my RAF days, and I were talking about starting a band. I'd done nothing since Ian went home and Jeff had just started learning the bass. Since we were both bassists it seemed like a good idea for one of us to take up the guitar, Jeff had just bought a gorgeous Rickenbacker 4001 bass so it looked like I was going to be the guitarist.

That Christmas Tracey and the kids bought me a Rickenbacker 330 copy, a cheap Encore version of the guitars that Pete Townshend, John Lennon and Paul Weller had used. With that and the chord book for Oasis' 'Definitely Maybe' I was ready.

· · · · ·

"My guitar playing is coming on OK, I've now mastered the all important barre chords. It's funny how much easier it is to learn to play Oasis songs than it was to learn 'She'll be coming round the mountain' or 'Tie a yellow ribbon round the old oak tree' at school. Maybe it's got something to do with being motivated, perhaps someone should point this out to all of the boring old folkies that write guitar books.

Jeff Sanders and I have started up a band, he's on bass, I'm on guitar, we've got a couple of new guys with us as well (a guitarist with no guitar and a drummer with no drums), Martin (the voice) Anderson on occasional and non-committal vocals (well he's got the P.A.) and Jim Robertson on keyboards.

The set list is pretty good since I chose them all. Most of the songs I can play and sing on my own, which is a bloody good thing, 'cos it's a pain in the arse trying to get a five piece band off their backsides to do anything."

Letter to Ian Stacey, January 13, 1996

· · · · ·

Only a few of us turned up for the first band practice, we got drunk, I played some Billy Bragg songs, and the drummer, asked us to buy him some drums, the answer was no.

Apart from that one meeting the band did nothing, Jeff and I continued practising together and the band gradually fell apart if you can say it ever existed, all we had was a name, thanks to a promise that Jeff had made when he bought his bass guitar off a Scotsman called Andy Robb that if he started a band it had to be called 'Taggart'.

That was that until one evening when I was out drinking with my regular brother in booze Jim Robertson in the Rugby Club, it was the early hours of Thursday morning, and we were slightly inebriated. I was giving the owner an ear-bashing about the poster he had on the door which read, 'Live Music Every Thursday'.

"I've said it to you before, any week when you're stuck give us a shout, you've got nobody on tomorrow just a horse racing night, if you'd said we could have come down and played as well, no charge, just beer."

Next thing you know I'm booked to play a gig the following night, and it's now 3am. Jim agreed to do sound, operate the drum machine and provide moral support and that was it.

Up at eight, I learnt 20 songs by lunchtime when my hangover finally began to subside and then it was time for me and Jim to set up the gear. We needed to sort out some drum patterns to flesh it out a bit, and this is where my vision stayed true to the ideals of Melon King. Every song used exactly the same 4/4 drum beat, just at different speeds. Jim would put the drums on, I'd try playing a bit then just tell him if it needed to be faster or slower.

As the evening grew closer my nerves started to get to me. I was due to start at 9pm, but the horse-racing started late meaning that I didn't go on until nearly eleven.

The place was packed with over three hundred people, and there I was sat at the side of the stage, all alone and with only two months experience of playing guitar. Why the hell had I got myself into this? Eventually my time came and the disco introduced me as 'The Melon King' and I was off.

Walking up to the mic stand, eyes fixed on my feet, avoiding looking out front at the packed bar, I said a quick "Hi" and went straight into the easiest song I knew, 'Stepping Stone.' I sang the whole song looking at a point about three feet in front of me and at the end was amazed by all of the clapping and cheering. I looked up and everyone was on my side, I couldn't believe it. "Thanks," I said, still taken aback.

I played the rest of my songs OK but managed to screw up my own song 'Terminal 4' when the audience insisted on it even though I'd never played it on the guitar. I think I did alright and, as it happens, so did everyone else.

I continued playing solo gigs throughout the first half of '96 and even got a residency in the Rugby Club playing every other Wednesday for fifty quid a time. Jim was doing the drums for me and the set list grew, I even wrote a song specifically for the Wednesday night Rugby Club crowd.

· · · · ·

Have a go

You think I'm pretty crap
I know you talk about me like that
You say that I can't sing
I don't know about anything.

But I know
Oh yes I know
Anyone can play guitar.

You say just play guitar
Then maybe I'll be a star
Maybe I should forget the words
Then you wouldn't be so bored.

But I know
Oh yes I know
Anyone can play guitar.

I'm nearly at the end
Time for your ears to mend
I'll tell you what to do
Buy a guitar and do it too.

But I know
Oh yes I know
Anyone can play guitar.

Steve Cook, 1996

·····

It really was the typical three chord wonder that anyone can play, it even had a lead break in it, which was in fact 'Hey Joe' as if to prove that if I can do it anyone can, even left-handed people.

The solo shows were alright, they were a laugh, if I didn't like something I could change it at will. They were hard work and they made me a bit of a target for piss-takers but what the hell, I enjoyed doing it and Jim got to get drunk, so we were all happy.

About this time our friend Paul Turnbull, who had always wanted to sing for us, recognising in us the kind of fun that he used to have with his band 'Purl Nekless' introduced us to a singer. We all knew Roly Hindle already, but none of us knew that he could sing, and on numerous occasions in the future we would joke that he still couldn't.

Paul brought Roly along to a rehearsal and we gave him a try-out. We were amazed when we gave him some Oasis songs to sing, not by his ability, but by the fact that he'd never heard any of them. It didn't matter though, he could sing reasonably, and he knew even less about music than the rest of us and was therefore easy to bully into what we wanted to do. We now had a proper line-up for the band, me on guitar, Jeff on bass, Jim on keyboards and Roly singing. My villa on Al Gosaibi was used for the rehearsals and we started to get some songs together, a mixture of Oasis, The Jam, the Sex Pistols, and some old Melon King songs. All we needed now was a decent name.

It took a lot of brain power and and even more beer but eventually we got there. My suggestion of 'Chilli Jalapeno and the Rocking Burritos' got voted down, I still don't know why because it certainly wasn't the worst suggestion that anyone came up with. Eventually Roly came up with the only good idea he's had in his life, 'Beef', it was us, British, mad, the lot.

I was still doing the solo shows in the Rugby Club and they became the perfect way to gradually give the boys some experience. I was the only one of us who'd ever played live and so I'd end up playing for two hours or so, then the rest of them would get up, do a handful of songs with me and grab all of the attention, typical.

· · · · ·

Rehearsals generally consisted of me playing a song and trying to get everyone else to learn at least some of it before we were all too drunk to continue and headed off to a bar. Following one such attempt at bashing the band into shape I was enjoying a cheeky Sid or three when a woman queuing for the bar turned to me and sarcastically commented on my, albeit dodgy, LA Gear basketball boots.

"Nice shoes."

Dawn was a secretary for Aramco, the Saudi Arabian Oil Company, one of the largest companies in the world by revenue and, according to Bloomberg News, the most profitable company in the world.

Saudi Aramco had been responsible for discovering oil in the Kingdom back in 1938 at their seventh attempt with a well that became known as Dammam No7. In 1951 they discovered the Safaniya Oil Field, the world's largest offshore field and six years later discovered that the Ghawar Field, the world's largest onshore field. Aramco were responsible for Saudi Arabia's wealth and power.

Dawn and I became friends, she would take the mickey out of me and I acted as her unpaid taxi service, women couldn't drive in the Kingdom and relied on the assistance of friends to get them around.

We had a lot in common, from our love of Mod and soul music to our sense of humour and her friendship really helped me at a time when my marriage to Tracey was deteriorating by the day. From the outside it may have looked like we were in a relationship but we were, in fact, just really close friends, supporting each other through the stresses of life 3000 miles from home.

· · · · ·

Leading up to Christmas '96 I was excited about a number of things. We were about to play our biggest gig yet and I was feeling really positive about the bands progress, then 48 hours later I would be at Earl's Court watching The Who before spending the holiday with my wife and children.

I nearly got to see The Who in 1982 but at the last minute we couldn't afford it. "Never mind", my Dad said, "just wait until next time they tour" and that was it, for fourteen years. The Who split up and I thought that my chance was gone forever. After such a wait I could barely believe that I was going to see my favourite band perform my favourite album, 'Quadrophenia', live.

In the week leading up to the gig we were practising pretty much solidly. On the day before the gig, we had a last practice and the pressure was starting to show.

Jeff was always annoyed with Roly turning up late for practice and then leaving early to meet his girlfriend, Roly in turn would complain about Jeff's unreasonable attitude and upset by the arguing I retreated into myself, introverted and silent.

It came to a head when Jeff and Roly almost came to blows about the inclusion or not of a particular song, the animosity in the room was palpable and I felt the receiving end purely for not expressing an opinion. That night the band came close to splitting up, and maybe if we hadn't been playing the next night we would have dwelt on it longer, as it was we all decided to put it behind us and put everything into the gig.

· · · · ·

A lot of effort had gone into ensuring that this was the most visually stunning gig that anyone had ever seen in Dhahran, I'd been creating backdrops for the band and produced an 8' x 14' montage of newspaper headlines and photos of the Mods v Rockers riots of the early '60s. Jeff had got hold of three 1000W halogen flood lights which we connected to a footswitch.

Opening the show with the sampled helicopters and feedback of Oasis' 'Morning Glory' Jeff hit the switch as the guitars came in, bathing the whole room with 3000W of blinding light.

The gig was the best we'd ever played, there was no shortage of bands around Dhahran, many of which were infinitely better technically than us, but we understood rock n roll, posturing, shouting, drinking, fighting and I was still the only guitarist that could do a decent Pete Townshend windmill.

There was, however, one of my songs that felt a little too much like tempting fate. 'Been and gone' referred to my missed opportunity to see The Who back in my teens. I wanted to drop the song, but it was one of our best and remained on the setlist despite my reservations.

Been and gone

Pete Townshend on the dodgem cars
Sniffing the smell of the electric stars
Cool black angel jumps up beside
Sorry Elvis Presley it's the end of your ride

Never ever got to see The Who
Saw The Jam in 1982
I'll never ever get to see Nirvana
Just Springsteen in a sweaty bandanna

Pete Townshend with naughty Mrs. Mills
Trying to play twister with a head full of pills
In comes John Lennon and he says Veronica
May I accompany on my harmonica

Never ever got to see The Who
Saw The Jam in 1982
I'll never ever get to see Nirvana
Just Springsteen in a sweaty bandanna

Pete Townshend met Freud in a dream
Selling stop me and buy one Mr. Whippy ice cream
Siggie says you ought to call your stories
Knickerbocker Splits and Banana Glories

Never ever got to see The Who
Saw The Jam in 1982
I'll never ever get to see Nirvana
Just Springsteen in a sweaty bandanna

Steve Cook, 1996

. . . . .

The following night I flew back to Southampton via Amsterdam, travelling all night before arriving at 10am. Tracey and Vicki met me at the airport and took me home.

I tried talking to Tracey and was checking the plans for getting to London to see The Who that night, but she said that she didn't feel well and wasn't up to it.

I wasn't sure what the matter was but I knew that we were going to have to talk, I couldn't go on forever like this.

Sat together in the bedroom she told me that she still didn't love me, in some ways it was a relief getting it straight out in the open. I asked her what she thought we should do about it, and did she want a separation? She wasn't sure but that's what we decided, we both had a good cry and a cuddle, and to tell the truth we felt better together than we had for years.

I got some stuff together and headed off into town to catch the train to London.

Walking away from the house I felt a great sorrow that things hadn't worked out, I still loved Tracey and nothing was more important to me than my kids.

Our marriage had failed, we'd been apart for far too long and it seemed that we didn't know each other at all. At the same time a great weight was lifted off me, for the first time in my adult life I was free of all restraints, I had no home, except for my villa in Saudi, and I had nowhere to go.

After the events of the past two days, the gig, splitting up with Tracey and three days without sleep, the train journey took on symbolic overtones as I listened to The Who on my walkman.

. . . . .

Why should I care?, why should I care?,
Girls of fifteen, sexually knowing,
The ushers are sniffing, eau-de-cologning,
The seats are seductive, celibate sitting,
Pretty girls, digging prettier women.

Out of my brain on the 5:15,
Out of my brain on the train.

'5:15' by Pete Townshend, The Who

Jimmy, the schizophrenic mod from Quadrophenia, was me, the
mental health issues, the extroverted introvert, the hopeless romantic.
My life had been turned upside down, I had no idea what I was going to
do with it. My thoughts for the future didn't extend beyond the moment,
I was on my way to London, to see The Who, playing the music that had
shaped my teenage years.

Checking into a seedy hotel in King's Cross I sat on the bed and began
to cry. I was alone, isolated, no wife, no family, no home and no direction.

That night at the concert I lose myself in the music, haunted by the
empty seat next to me, a constant reminder of the failure of my marriage.
The Who are amazing, everything that I'd ever dreamt of, and more.
Roger Daltrey swinging his microphone, still fit and lean with blonde
hair and that powerful, cutting voice. John Entwistle, the Ox, the Quiet
One, like a statue, but with fingers of steel, the great swooping bass lines
carrying you along. Then there was Pete Townshend, leaping around,
doing windmills and basically just being Pete Townshend, only two days
after I'd done my best to emulate him three thousand miles away.

I take my time getting back to the hotel, it doesn't seem like I should
be rushing to get anywhere. Outside Earl's Court there's a crush trying to
get into the tube and police officers everywhere. A few people break into
choruses of "We are the Mods!" I can't, I don't feel part of it, I'm numb,
alone, an outsider.

I start walking, neither knowing not caring where I'm going. The
further I get from Earl's Court the thinner the crowds, unlike me they
have somewhere to go. Eventually I find myself in Soho, in a cellar club
playing dance music, I get a beer and stand in front of the speakers.
Closing my eyes I feel the music, crashing through me in an assault
of decibels. My mind races, the previous 48 hours have been the most
hectic of my life, and without a doubt the most far-reaching. Tracey, the
kids, Beef, The Who, the rest of my life, I don't have a clue what I am

going to do. The stress and exhaustion take its toll and I fall asleep, stood against a wall in a noisy little club in Soho, time to go.

$$\cdot\ \cdot\ \cdot\ \cdot\ \cdot$$

Below me the landscape slowly changes from the verdant green of Europe to the bleached white of the Arabian desert. Staring from the window of the Airbus A320, still feeling the effects of four days hard drinking in London, I feel lost.

Christmas is still two weeks away, I should be at home with my wife and children, yet here I am flying back to Saudi Arabia to spend the holiday alone. My plans for the future extend no further than the bottom of the glass in which I am intending to spend the next few weeks.

Self hate and loneliness fill my thoughts as the darkness tries to envelop me.

"They'd all be better off without you. You're nothing. You don't deserve love. You don't deserve happiness."

I'm confused, not knowing who I truly am or if I will ever be loved again.

On my Walkman the haunting voice of The Who's Roger Daltrey echoes my melancholia.

"Love… reign o'er me…"

6

NEW DAWN

December 25th in Saudi Arabia is just another day for the expat community except, of course, it isn't.

The drink flows freer, the parties are a little more raucous despite it being a work day, the homesickness bites a little deeper and the focus for many is elsewhere, 3000 miles away.

Waking on Christmas morning, not with my wife and children in our home in Southampton but in my villa in Saudi, I felt isolated. My marriage was over, I had no one to answer to, I had no work to do as I was still on leave and I had every intention of retreating into the bottle.

Over the following weeks Dawn and I began to spend more time together, after years of being in a marriage where I was constantly told that I wasn't loved it felt great to be with someone that seemed to enjoy my company. Our friendship grew and eventually developed into a relationship.

This new love helped to alleviate my loneliness but did little to quiet my demons. The post traumatic stress still haunted me and whilst the alcohol numbed the pain it brought with it a melancholy and sense of nihilism that left me empty and without direction.

My diary illustrated the problems my drinking caused:

October 16, 1997 - Cooky's Laws of Drunkenness

Dawn invited a few people around last night for some pre-party drinks before we moved on elsewhere. I got very drunk, then in my second stage of drunkenness I decided to call Biggran and Grandad.

According to Cooky's Laws of Drunkenness:

- Stage 1 - Pleasure, the subject, me, feels the immense joy of the moment, a euphoric high.
- Stage 2 - Affection, the subject feels a need to communicate his feelings of well-being to his family and loved ones.
- Stage 3 - Introversion, the subject withdraws into himself and becomes silent and sullen.
- Stage 4 - Depression, a suicidal despair falls upon the subject, self-destructive, not to be left unsupervised.

I dread to think how long the call was, but I got all mushy and told Grandad how much I loved him and Biggran and how much I missed them both. I was about to tell him that whilst I was away all these long years my biggest fear was for something to happen to them before I could say goodbye. I'm glad that I didn't tell him this, as with 15 weeks to go I could have been tempting fate, and that is my other biggest fear.

$$\cdots\cdots$$

How much of my life had I missed? How much had disappeared due to the drink?

When I met Dawn I was in the depths of an alcoholic, depressive low, I was drinking pints of Sid and Coke quicker than my mates could drink a small one. It gets you drunk, but more than that it makes you forget, you end up with black spots in your memory, your life just stops for hours at a time. It doesn't solve any of your problems but it makes you forget that you had them.

I never worried about being an alcoholic, after all I could easily go without during the week. Everybody knows that if you don't drink during the week, then you can't be an alcoholic, it wasn't until I spoke to Jim that I realised that there was a name for what we did.

Jim drank like me, we could both go days without a drink, but when we started we couldn't stop until we were comatose. Jim and I used to get into the serious drinking at a bar called Jamaica Joe's on one of the compounds every Wednesday night. Pints of Sid and Coke until we dropped.

Our drinking was beginning to take its toll and one evening as I headed home Jim jumped into his Camaro.

"Are you good?" I asked him.

"Just gonna have a little kip before I head home", he replied.

The following day Jim didn't arrive to set up for a gig and fearing that he might be lying dead in a pool of his own vomit we kicked the door to his villa in. He was nowhere to be found but eventually surfaced attached to a drip in the medical centre.

In his drunken state he'd fallen asleep in the car with the air conditioning on full power. This resulted in him earning the dubious honour as the only person to ever get hypothermia in Saudi Arabia at the height of summer.

Jim was a 'binge alcoholic' and so was I.

I went through a phase of not wanting to go out at all, Dawn would moan at me for being boring, and not wanting to play. But I knew that if I started drinking, then there was no way that I could stop before I passed out.

She kept trying, I kept getting pissed and fucked up. It was always the same, but at least she learned what I was like. Tracey always treated me like a pariah, my moods were always me being fucked up and fucking everyone else up. I was a stereotype. The fucked up veteran, self destructive artist, self hating poet with no sense of self esteem or worth.

I was becoming increasingly depressed about being in Saudi Arabia, the isolation compounded the ability of my demons to torment me. The drinking, to a certain extent, numbed me to the pain but the self hatred and despair still found ways to manifest themselves with plans to take my own life and self harm.

· · · · ·

November 20, 1997

OK, so life isn't always a bowl of cherries. I've just used a Stanley knife to write prophetic statements in my forearms for the first time in six or seven years. In a way it's almost nostalgic, bringing back, as it does, those heady days of my youth. My teenage years, in particular, were perforated, if that is the correct self-mutilatory term, with my words of protest. Tonight it is…. well… I've just tried working it out but I can't be sure… blob… scratch… scratch… blob. Well, I know that whatever it's supposed to say… it must have been very relevant at the time. Knowing me, it probably says something as astute as "Arsehole." Maybe? I've got a luverley bunch of arteries…

· · · · ·

The separation was proving hard on both Tracey and I despite the fact that we'd only really been together for two years before I left for Saudi.

I missed her and the children terribly but after six years isolated from them in the Kingdom I was, in some way, used to being on my own.

. . . . .

I'd wanted to leave Saudi Arabia since the day I arrived back in '91 and the only thing keeping me there was the need to provide for my wife and family back home. Now that Tracey and I had separated I was set free to the possibility of returning home, albeit alone. Knowing that this was probably going to be my last chance to see a bit of the world, I used the next year to travel, finally experiencing the lifestyle that my single friends had enjoyed throughout their time in the Kingdom.

. . . . .

A thick layer of haze blanketed the city, shrouding the top floors of the 88-storey Baiyoke Tower in smog a thousand feet above me. Construction workers busied themselves on the site, many, like the commuters below, wearing dust masks to protect them from the toxic cloud.

Upon completion later that year the skyscraper hotel would become the tallest building in Bangkok, a title it held for the next 20 years.

The noxious smog, a result of sulphur levels in the fuel being burnt by the vehicles gridlocked on the city's streets being 200 times higher than modern fuel, together with the stifling heat gave the city a diabolical feeling.

The traffic was at a standstill on Sukhumvit Road, the commercial street that leaves the city and runs all the way along the coast from Bangkok to Cambodia. As I pass Soi Cowboy the neon signs of the gogo bars illuminate the pavements which swarm with tourists and ladyboy prostitutes eager to catch the eye.

Commonly referred to as 'katoey' these transgender woman are believed by many Thais to be a third gender, although most trans women in Thai society see the term as pejorative and prefer to describe themselves as 'phuying', or 'women', and a minority use the term 'phuying praphet song' which translates as a 'second kind of woman'.

Entering one of the gaudy clubs I order a Singha beer and take a seat at the bar as the cheesy pop music assaults my senses. One of the hostesses approaches me and introduces herself as Bella. She is genuinely one of the most beautiful women I have ever met, her black hair, olive skin and large dark eyes taking my breath away. Her english is perfect, with barely a trace of an accent, and as we talk I open up to her about my own gender identity.

I tell her about Jenny, the girl I felt I truly was at age seven, I share my continuing struggle to come to terms with how I see myself and my desperation to understand how I can ever resolve this.

Sensing a kindred spirit she opens up about her life and tells me how despite the seeming openness of Thai society transgender people still faced much prejudice, it was to be another two decades before they finally gained legal recognition, and how many Buddhists believed that they were born with a disability as a result of sins committed in a past life. She told me about discrimination in the job market, and how bullying and low salaries affected her self-esteem leading her like so many others to see sex work in the ladyboy gogo bars as the only option. Here she found a sense of community and validation of her gender identity.

The conversation did nothing to ease my continuing gender confusion. I still saw no way in which my identity could ever be resolved, I saw only despair and a lifetime of denial and pain ahead of me. As we talk I become acutely aware of the activity around us, older western men pawing the bodies of young Thai women, it makes me feel sick, dirty and depressed and on the way back to my hotel I enter a travel agents to book myself a ticket out of Bangkok.

I had no idea where I wanted to go, I just knew that I couldn't stay in that place. I needed clean air, I needed to get away from the city that seemed so exploitative, I needed to be surrounded by beauty not pain and I found it in Koh Samui.

· · · · ·

White sands and azure lagoons pass beneath my window as the engine tone from the twin turboprops flattens and actuators whine, extending the flaps as the Bangkok Airways ATR 72 makes its final approach to Samui International Airport. Flying low over the single storey villas, their red roofs pinpoints in the lushness of the coconut groves of the island.

Departing from the aircraft I'm immediately struck by the beauty of the island, the runway fringed with a verdant forest filled with purple blooms a stark contrast to the grime and smog of Bangkok. As I enter the open-air terminal, it's roof supported by wooden pillars rather than walls I feel myself relax, the fresh air blowing away some of my negativity.

During the 90s Koh Samui had rules which forbade the building of any structure higher than the coconut trees that cover the island although all of that was to soon change and I count myself lucky that I had the opportunity to visit before the developers moved in and destroyed the unique atmosphere of this island paradise.

Staying in a beachside hut at Lamai Beach I spend my days reading, relaxing and walking on the beach whilst the evenings are spent in the small, makeshift bar drinking Thai beer and watching the news on a 14" black and white portable TV mounted on the wall.

Like many countries that I visited during the 1990s the sole viewing choice for English speaking visitors was the American news network CNN. As I watch the small flickering screen the studio cuts to the familiar view of 10 Downing Street where Tony Blair, the newly elected Labour Prime Minister of Great Britain stands making his victory speech.

"I have just accepted Her Majesty the Queen's kind offer to form a new administration and government for the country.

"I know well what this country has voted for today. It is a mandate for New Labour and I say to the people of this country, we ran for office as New Labour, we will govern as New Labour.

"It will be a government that seeks to restore trust in politics in this country. That cleans it up, that decentralizes it, that gives people hope once again that politics is and always should be about the service of the public.

"It shall be a government rooted in strong values, the values of justice and progress and community, the values that have guided me all my political life. But a government ready with the courage to embrace the new ideas necessary to make those values live again for today's world, a government of practical measures in pursuit of noble causes. That is our objective for the people of Britain.

"Above all, we have secured a mandate to bring this nation together, to unite us, one Britain, one nation in which our ambition for ourselves is matched by our sense of compassion and decency and duty towards other people. Simple values, but the right ones.

"For 18 years, for 18 long years, my party has been in opposition. It could only say, it could not do. Today we are charged with the deep responsibility of government. Today, enough of talking, it is time now to do."

As I leave the bar, walking barefoot onto the white sands of the beach I feel elated, after 18 long years we were finally free of the Conservative Government that had decimated our working class communities, waged war on the Trade Unions and indulged in sabre rattling at the behest of a Republican American President.

We were free of Margaret Thatcher, John Major and the profits before people doctrines of Thatcherism. As the lyrics to the D:Ream song adopted by Tony Blair's campaign as their anthem promised: "Things can only get better."

"Hyud hyud!"

An elderly Thai woman sits on a stool under a coconut tree. She is shouting at me, breaking my reverie, but I neither understand her words nor what I've done to offend her.

"Chlām hyud plā chlām!"

She's waving now, pointing at my feet.

"Chlām chlām."

My eyes follow her extended finger to a point on the sand, barely a yard from my bare feet, there lays a dead and decaying grey corpse. Its jet black eyes stare blindly through me, and the open wound on its head erupts as a myriad of flies, disturbed by my presence, take to the wing.

Crimson blood stains the eye sockets and line the mouth, a row of razor sharp teeth forming a deadly smile on the remains of the 7 foot long Bull Shark that I had almost stepped in. My stomach turns, I'm fascinated but nauseated, staying just long enough to examine this wonder of the oceans from a distance, thankful that I'd neither met it in its habitat or placed my foot in its lifeless mouth.

"Thing can only get better," I whisper to myself.

. . . . .

Sitting in the Mercedes 250CE taxi I can feel a broken seat spring stabbing me through the broken velour of the rear seat. The radio playing cheesy electro pop songs, a blend of western and eastern influences evident in both the composition and choice of instruments. As the battered, faded green car bounces along the potholed roads the suspension creaks in syncopation to the music.

Passing an apartment block, its floors collapsed, one on top of the other in one corner while people move around their makeshift homes on the opposite side of the damaged structure, their children playing happily among the washing lines and rubble.

The car lurches to the right as it hits a particularly large pothole turning into Omar Daouk Street, throwing my head painfully against the window frame as the pockmarked remains of a 26 storey building come into view.

The famed Beirut Holiday Inn had once featured a revolving restaurant on the top floor, a nightclub and 400 guest rooms as part of a complex that included a cinema, offices, shops, restaurants, and a supermarket when it opened in 1974, back when the city was the most glamorous destination in the region - 'the Paris of the Middle East'.

Barely a year later the Lebanese Civil War broke out between the Israeli Defense Forces supported by the South Lebanon Army, a surrogate militia that they armed and financed, and the Lebanese and Palestinian resistance groups of which Hezbollah, the Party of God, was the largest.

By October 1975 the hotel was a war zone as over 25,000 combatants fought for control of the high ground of a group of towering luxury hotels that included the Holiday Inn, perfect for snipers and of strategic importance due to their proximity to the coast. Over the space of six months, the 'Battle of the Hotels' resulted in over 1000 deaths, many of them people that were thrown from the roof of the Holiday Inn.

Even after the Civil War there was no peace for this building. Stripped by scavengers it once again became a battleground after the 1982 Israeli invasion of Beirut, leaving it as a bullet-riddled testament to the destruction of the 15 year civil war.

A black Land Rover screeches to a halt in front of us, quickly followed by three more, as its doors open disgorging four men, wearing grubby black fatigues, combat jackets and the traditional black and white keffiyeh scarf, onto the busy street. In their hands they each hold an AK-47 assault rifle, with battered and scuffed wooden stocks and the distinctive curved magazine attached.

They begin shouting, waving vehicles away and pointing their weapons at anyone they feel isn't complying quickly enough. In the back of the cab, Dawn and I try to sink deeper into our seats as our driver does the unthinkable and begins to shout at the armed men.

Turning towards the shouting one of the men raises his weapon and aims at us, our driver continues to hurl abuse, gesturing madly at the gunman. I too am screaming, but sensibly mine stays inside my head.

"Stop, shouting, at, the man, with, the gun," my inner voice screams silently.

I have my camera in my lap and desperately want to photograph this situation but common sense tells me that pointing a camera at an angry armed man in Beirut probably isn't the brightest idea.

A motorcade of black limos rushes past us and as quickly as it began the armed men are back in their Land Rovers and speeding off to the next intersection.

Like many other wartorn countries I visited including Vietnam, I found the Lebanese people to be very friendly and welcoming, perhaps seeing westerners as a sign of normality and peace after the years of conflict.

Just a few month earlier the Israeli military campaign 'Operation Grapes of Wrath' had left 154 Lebanese civilians dead and 351 injured.

During the same period three Israeli civilians were seriously injured in Hezbollah rocket attacks.

Unfortunately for the people of Beirut their fragile peace was to be broken again very soon after we left as the American built F-16 military aircraft of the Israeli Defence Force, that we had seen patrolling the skies above the city, dropped laser-guided bombs destroying electrical stations around the city as part of a campaign against civilian infrastructure in violation of international humanitarian law. With each attack, large parts of Lebanon were plunged into darkness, and electricity had to be rationed throughout the entire country.

In 2000 Human Rights Watch stated that "any state has the right to procure weapons for its legitimate self-defense, but maintains that it must also respect international humanitarian law. Human Rights Watch urges the U.S. government not to go forward with the sale of any U.S. air-to-ground missiles to Israel until the U.S. receives assurances from the Israeli government that it will not use those weapons to attack power plants and other civilian structures in Lebanon."

Two decades later it appears that the western arms industry is still free to supply governments across the globe, regardless of their human rights record, leading to untold suffering for the sake of international trade and profit.

But as D:Ream said, "things can only get better".

· · · · ·

There's a story that expats tell about how when you first move abroad you are issued with two bags, one for money and one for shit. The implication being that you know it's time to go home when one of the bags is full.

While my money bag was suspiciously empty my shit bag was overflowing.

It was time to go home.

7

WHO ARE YOU

After seven long years away I finally returned to a country locked deep within a damp and cold British winter. Single, alone and lost.

I spent my first few days staying with my Mum and her husband. It wasn't ideal, I'd left home when I was sixteen and I really wasn't used to living with my Mum. My brother, on the other hand, couldn't understand what the problem was, as far as he was concerned living with Mum and having my washing done and my food cooked was his idea of nirvana.

Having separated from Tracey and not having the sort of family ties that dictate geography I began to think about where I could settle. My new home had to be far enough away from Southampton that I wouldn't bump into her on the street and close enough to see the kids easily. Despite having left Bournemouth when I was 10 the seaside town had always felt like home and so I began looking for a flat.

After viewing a selection of slums and damp ridden former student digs I finally found a flat barely a few hundred yards from my old Infant School and the road that I'd grown up in. The two bedroom flat had no central-heating, instead storage heaters and a log fire provided the warmth during those first cold February days and when it rained water ran down the inside of the windows pooling on the sill before falling like a waterfall onto the floor. It had been left empty for a number of years, it was a tip, but it showed promise. Gradually the place started to get more like home thanks to my credit cards as I furnished the place, a new stereo, tables, shelves, washing machine, and a new bed.

I decided to do a bit of job-hunting. Flight Refuelling were advertising for aircraft fitters at their Wimborne factory, I gave the agency a ring to enquire. Twenty minutes later they rang me back to ask me if I'd faxed them my CV yet, "it's about to go in the machine now" I replied. "Well get a move on because there's a job starting tomorrow if you want it." I didn't even think, I just said yes automatically.

The job was refitting decompression chambers for the Ministry of Defence at a factory in Hamworthy over near Poole. The morning was cold and fresh and the factory was an industrial unit specialising in autoclaves for the manufacture of carbon-fibre assemblies. I spent the morning drilling holes in alloy brackets for use inside the chambers, had a cup of coffee for my lunch and then spent the afternoon drilling holes in alloy brackets for use inside the chambers. At four o'clock I said enough. I couldn't do it anymore, it was driving me mad. I didn't need the money, I hadn't even received my pay-off from BAe yet. I rang the agency and told them that I'd had enough, could I hang on till the end of the week? They begged me. Yes, I suppose so. I went back and told the foreman that they'd talked me into staying on. "You don't want to do that, do you?" he asked me. I had to admit that I didn't, "well go back and bloody tell them."

They didn't like it, but then again they didn't really have a lot of choice. My first experience of agency work, and unfortunately it was a good indication of what to expect in the future. A crap job on crap pay.

Other agency jobs followed including as tint fitting fuel systems to refuelling pods for Flight Refuelling and a week of nights at the Ryvita factory in Poole. Arriving for my first shift in the large factory unit that seemed to be permanently shrouded in a fine mist of dust I was directed to three pallets in the middle of the shopfloor.

"We need you to take a pack of Original crispbread from that pallet, tape a sample pack of Rye to it from the second pallet and then pack them for despatch on the third."

Needless to say that if drilling holes in brackets bored me, taping crispbread packets together was almost coma inducing, I think I stayed three days, or maybe even a week, but it wasn't long.

$$\cdots\cdots$$

My ambition when I came home was to become a photographer and I immediately set out to capture some great images but the reality was that I had no idea whatsoever about how to earn a living from my camera.

Still struggling with my identity and my mental health the last thing that I wanted to do was to have to photograph people but it quickly became apparent that for someone just setting out in the industry this was the only possible way to make money.

One of the first regular gigs that I got was working with one of the country's biggest schools photography firms, Oxford based Gillman & Soame. On the training day I quickly became popular with the boss as I already knew how to use a camera unlike some of my colleagues. Within weeks I was being sent out to schools across the country and could, with a finely honed routine, photograph a school of 1000 pupils in a morning, packing away the last of the 25 rolls of 35mm film as the dinner ladies began laying out the tables for lunch.

I also realised that weddings were going to be a must if I hoped to be able to pay the rent but I'd never shot one before and this is where I came up with a cunning plan.

For generations all wedding photographers pretty much had the same, classical, portrait style executed with greater or lesser skill, the key elements of which were:

- Shot on medium format colour film, probably a square format Hasselblad
- A touch of soft focus filter whenever the bride was in the image.
- 12 group shots shot outside the door of the church, a square format 6x6cm film has 12 shots on a roll and many photographers would shoot an entire wedding on a single roll of film.
1. Bride
2. Bride & parents
3. Bride & bridesmaids
4. Groom
5. Groom & parents
6. Groom & best man
7. Bride & groom
8. Bride & groom & parents
9. Bride & groom & best man & bridesmaids
10. Bride & groom & his family
11. Bride & groom & her family
12. Bride & groom & both families
- Presented, one image to a page in an overlay, in an ivory leather album.

This staid, artificial record of what was supposed to be the happiest day of your life said nothing to me. I wanted to do things differently.

I had a love of action and news photography, my photographic heroes were Don McCullin and Frank Capa, the war photographers who captured raw human emotion in a dramatic yet intimate style.

I'd already started shooting football matches for the local paper. Shooting the first half and then dropping off the film at their offices for processing and scanning to be used in that evenings Pink Paper, the late edition sports news that was staple reading in the pubs and working men's clubs on Saturday evenings before the internet.

Putting together a portfolio of my sports, music, news and fashion shots I sat down with my first couple. "I'm going to be honest with you. I've never photographed a wedding but I want to photograph it like this…"

For young couples already bored by visiting five different photographers that all showed them the same formulaic 12 images in the standard issue ivory album my images were a revelation. Action, drama, life, passion, saturated colours and grainy black and whites. They had seen nothing like it before and they were inspired, I booked ten weddings before I'd even shot one.

Over the coming decade I would go on to shoot over five hundred weddings and at the height covered eleven in one month, Friday, Saturday, Sunday each and every weekend. I captured the passion and love, the drama, the tears and the laughter. The arguments and fights I left unrecorded and certainly made myself scarce the time that a best man was caught in a cupboard with a bridesmaid by his wife.

Now everyone with a digital camera can set themselves up as a 'reportage' wedding photographer, again with greater or lesser skill, but twenty years ago it was unheard of.

· · · · ·

Effectively being free for the first time in my life, not living with parents, or in the RAF, or married, or in Saudi, allowed me to finally explore my gender identity. Dawn was still in Saudi Arabia at this point and while I'd raised the subject tentatively with her before my return I hadn't known myself how deep the feelings ran so it was impossible for me to express more than vague feelings of unease about my gender.

I began to fill out my wardrobe, underwear, clothing, shoes, dresses and skirts. Most came from charity shops or Evans, unlike now very few women's clothes shops stocked larger sizes around the turn of the millenium and being a size 20 my options were limited.

Growing up all women have to find their own style which is often a road fraught with fashion faux pas and inappropriate outfits. For young cisgender, meaning identifying as their birth sex, women this period in their development usually coincides with that of their peers meaning that they all either look ok or disastrous at the same time. For trans women, often transitioning later in life, they go through the same revelatory process but this tends to be in isolation the same fashion mistakes can lead to ridicule and abuse.

For my part, I found my style reasonably quickly, although I may have had slightly too much fondness for bedazzled denim than was good for me, but hey it was the 90s, I'm sure Jennifer Aniston was wearing it as well.

Finally unleashed I needed to know more about the person inside of me.

· · · · ·

The lady answering the door to the unremarkable suburban terrace house is in her mid-50s, dressed in a floral print dress with shoulder length blonde hair and neat, subdued makeup.

"Hello, come in, I'm Susie and what would you like me to call you?"

The question catches me off guard and this confusion adds to my nervous look.

"What's your femme name?"

"Oh, um, Sophie" I reply anxiously.

"Lovely to meet you Sophie, come on through. I hope that you don't mind dogs", she says as a small wiry terrier excitedly paws at my legs.

She leads me through the house and into a converted garage in the back garden filled floor to ceiling with clothes, from sexy lingerie to fabulous evening gowns, wedding dresses, maids outfits, business suits and fetish wear. On one wall dozens of polystyrene heads display a wide range of wigs, red, brown, blonde, long, short, straight and curly. A makeup table and large mirror dominate the space alongside a small home photographic studio setup.

"So Sophie, what would you like to do today? Any particular style or look that you're going for?"

"I don't know really. Sorry, I'm just a bit nervous," I reply, "I've never done anything like this before."

"Don't worry love, come on let's get you out of those nasty male clothes and into something a bit more comfortable."

"I've brought my own clothes" I say, unpacking underwear, tights, a knee length black pencil skirt and red top.

"I'm just going to pop and make us a cup of tea while you slip into those, make yourself at home and I'll be back in a minute to do your makeup."

I turn to take in every inch of this Aladdin's Cave of femininity as I slowly begin to undress.

Over the next two hours she slowly transforms Steve into Sophie, applying makeup and explaining the use of each of the cosmetics. The finishing touch is when she takes me over to the wall of wigs and together we select a style, typical of the day, all brash auburn curls, very much like Angie the much loved landlady of the Queen Vic pub in Eastenders.

"You'll need shoes", she says handing me a pair of black high heel court shoes.

Finally Susie leads me over to the full length mirror that had, until this point, been covered by a thick cloth.

"Are you ready?"

"As I'll ever be," fear tinged with excitement.

There before me, as the cloth drops from the mirror, is someone that I thought I would never meet. At the age of thirty-two, twenty-five years after I'd spent the holiday in Wales as Jenny, looking back at me from the mirror is a woman, Sophie. Hidden for all of those years, silent, unseen.

I catch my breath, unable to speak, a hammer blow to my chest forcing all of the air from me. My heart breaks, just a little, as the realisation of who I truly am overwhelms my senses.

Standing there, in a converted garage, surrounded by hyper stylised femininity, I meet myself for the very first time as a tear begins its slow journey down my powdered cheek.

"Hey, don't cry," Susie says gently, "you'll ruin your makeup."

· · · · ·

I knew at that moment that something had changed. I no longer saw the broken man in the mirror, I saw the real me shining brightly. But much as Pandora found it difficult to close her box of troublesome mixed blessings, once released the feelings would only increase my torment over the coming years.

And like the mythological Pandora all that remained in the box once the lid was replaced was the blessing of hope, and for me that hope was to one day be whole.

"Looking good," Susie says breaking my reverie.

"Thank you so much," I choke out through the tears.

"What are your plans now? Are you going out?"

"No, I couldn't possibly, I'd be too scared."

"If you wanted I could call someone to see if they'd take you out. They're lovely and they'd be delighted to take you out and show you around town."

"Uh, ok," I reply, not entirely convinced but knowing that I don't want this moment to end.

Within an hour I'm being introduced to Christine, she's a 6' tall trans woman, around ten years older than me, with long, curly, red hair and a cleavage to die for. She introduces herself with a broad west country accent and offers to take me out that evening around the LGBT venues of Bournemouth.

In her black mesh top, leather mini skirt and stilettos she's dressed much more provocatively than myself but I'm happy to hide in her shadow on my first trip into the big wide world.

The first stop is The Queens, a gay bar with a notorious sauna upstairs that has long since closed to be replaced by a Co-op. Christine shows me off and introduces me to the regulars. This is followed by a few drinks in Bournemouth's most popular gay pub The Branksome, now also closed but ironically replaced by another gay sauna, before ending up in The Xchange.

The Xchange was, and still is, being the only venue we visited that night that is still open, a tight, claustrophobic gay club come bar. Popular with drag artistes and with a dance floor at the back it was the number one pick up spot in the town for gay men in those pre-internet days before everyone started using Grindr and Squirt. The clientele ranged from cute young twinks, to bears, to guys that looked like geography teachers sneaking off from supervising a school trip, all nervous and furtive, to a handful of trans people like ourselves.

I'd finally taken Sophie public and it felt amazing, no longer imprisoned inside my head, she was set free to drink, dance and talk to others who, for one reason or another, had always been treated like outsiders.

Over the coming months I would venture further afield to visit Trans clubs including one that met in the cellar bar of a hotel in Lyndhurst and, oddly, the Conservative Club in Totton, Southampton. Whilst the members of the local Conservative Association drank their pints of bitter and G&Ts in the lounge and public bars the function room was packed with all manner of gender variant from transgender women to transvestites and crossdressers, happy to be men during the week but needing a release come the weekend, or in this case on a Thursday evening.

Every trip out en femme was fraught with worry, the ever present fear of being stopped by the police, not because of anything that you might have done wrong but due to the fear of being outed. The shame that would have accompanied any interaction with the police would lead to vilification as a pervert in the local press and potential ruin both of relationships and career.

The situation caused enough concern to warrant The Mayflower Club of Southampton to include a legal notice of rights on their membership card, for possible use during any altercation with the custodians of law, order and moral outrage.

· · · · ·

The Mayflower Club, Southampton

This is to certify that
Name: Sophie Cook
Membership number: 180
Is a practicing
Cross-dresser / Transgenderist / Pre-op/Post-op Transsexual
(*Delete as applicable)

To whom it may concern…

Transvestism is a lawful practice and the fact that this person is wearing the clothing of his/her opposite gender DOES NOT IMPLY any sexual impropriety. Please accord the person identified above the rights and dignity afforded to any and every citizen of the United Kingdom.

The Mayflower Club expects its members to behave in accordance with the laws (actual and implied) of the UK. The Club does not condone nor support any action by this member that would be regarded as unsociable or unlawful.

Signed for Membership Committee

· · · · ·

Dawn and I had been continuing a long distance relationship during this period and as the time approached for her return to the UK I knew that I had to open up to her about who I really was.

The feelings were too strong, too undeniable, to ignore and bury for much longer. I knew that I was Sophie and I knew that, after decades of mental anguish, self harm and suicide attempts, this was the only way to save my life.

· · · · ·

Walking along the seafront, still quiet before the days sun brought the hordes of visitors, Dawn and I held hands and laughed. The months apart had been hard for both of us but now we were ready to start our life together.

Above Boscombe Pier the seagulls swooped, constantly searching for scraps of food dropped by clumsy hands or pulled from the bins by their confederates.

"Thank you for coming from Bournemouth," Dawn said as she turned from the view to me, our arms instinctively going around each other as we kissed.

She was from Stevenage in Hertfordshire and while the town had its charms, it certainly didn't have a beach.

"I've got to talk to you," I said, feeling anxious, "do you remember when I told you that I was confused about my gender?"

"Yes, why? You know that I'll love you whatever", she replied.

"Since I got back from Saudi I've been trying to work it all out, once and for all, and I now realise that I'm transgender. I was born in the wrong body. I've always been a woman inside and denying that has been causing me so much pain for all of these years."

I held her hand tight, afraid that I was about to drown in my words. I told her about the dressing service, my trips out and how they gave me a peace that I'd never experienced before.

"I need to continue exploring this, to find out what it all means", I continued.

"And I'd love it if you were by my side helping me."

Dawn squeezed my hands and my tears burst forth like a dam that had been breached.

"Hey, don't cry. It'll all be alright. We'll be alright. I told you that I'd love you whatever and I meant it. Come on, let's get you home missy."

· · · · ·

At home I showed Dawn my wardrobe and over the coming months she showed me how to apply makeup and we went shopping together, working hard to refine my personal style. She began to accompany me to some of the bars and clubs and the whole thing seemed to be proceeding painlessly but that was all to change.

Having always been cursed with a surfeit of body hair I decided that waxing would help with my self image and reduce some of the dysphoria that I was feeling about my body. Through the local freeads we found a lady that worked from home who was willing to carry out the epilation and an appointment was made.

Lying naked on her massage table I immediately began to question my decision. Her constant fussing about the correct temperature for the wax made me wonder about her proficiency. Applying the first strip the wax appeared to be clumpy rather than molten and when she attempted to remove it the hair stood firm.Putting her back into it she tried again, eventually removing the strip, my hair and a fair amount of skin, and as the blood began to flow from my leg I immediately regretted going for the full body wax.

I'm no medical expert but when someone starts shivering uncontrollably, feeling cold to their core, nauseous and crying I tend to see it as a sign of their body going into shock. Beauty really is pain.

· · · · ·

Hurrying through the cemetery I slip, after a lifetime in jeans and trainers I seem ill equipped for walking at pace in high heels, tights snagging and bra pinching.

Hundreds of lifeless stone eyes watch me through the early morning mist, without emotion but still seemingly judging me as I negotiate the uneven path trying not to make eye contact with the homeless man waking from his sleep on a rusty and paint peeled bench.

I check my watch, horrified to see how late it is but despite the fear I find it impossible to walk any faster as the new shoes are rubbing my already blistered and bleeding heels causing pain with every step. Emerging from the gates of the Victorian Margravine Cemetery I look up to see the white monolithic structure of Charing Cross Hospital, the concrete and steel impervious to my suffering.

The receptionist looks up at me disapprovingly as I rush through the doors of the Gender Identity Clinic, dishevelled, hobbling and out of breath.

"Sophie Cook, I've got a 9 o'clock appointment," I manage to gasp between breaths.

"You're fifteen minutes late," she replies, "the Doctor may not see you."

"But I've come all the way from Bournemouth, please." I feel the tears of pain and despair start to form at the corners of my eyes.

"Take a seat and I'll check if he's prepared to see you."

I look around the waiting room and choose a seat away from the desk not wanting to be under her watchful gaze any more than I had to be. Thirty minutes later she called my name and directed me to an examination room.

"What makes you believe that you're a woman?" the consultant looks at me clinically from above his glasses which perch on the end of his nose.

Was this a trick question? Was he trying to catch me out?

"I just know it, I feel wrong. There's just something, not right, about me, I've always felt wrong and that only ever stops when I'm Sophie."

"But how does it feel to be a woman?"

Surely a biological woman would struggle with this question.

"It feels like me. It feels right."

"Well make sure that you arrive on time for your next appointment Miss Cook or we will be removing you from my patient list."

. . . . .

Many myths existed around the way in which the Charing Cross Gender Identity Clinic (GIC) treated their patients. So great was their prevalence that as recently as 2010 the GIC sought to dispel these stories but like many myths they had at least some basis in fact.

. . . . .

West London Mental Health Trust (WLMHT) GIC myths

The WLMHT ("Charing Cross") Gender Identity Clinic has existed in one form or another since the early 1960s, and clinical practice is constantly evolving.

It is perhaps inevitable that, in that time, a number of false beliefs and misconceptions have arisen.

Not all these beliefs are "myths" in the sense of having always been untrue – some stem from the way the GIC operated in the past, or the approaches of previous clinicians – but all are outdated, and unreflective of current treatment protocol.

The following, then, are examples of commonly held beliefs about the WLMHT GIC which are untrue:

- You have to wear a skirt to the GIC - Perhaps the most widely cited misconception, this is not the case. As part of the Real Life Experience (RLE), male-to-female transitioners are expected to present themselves in female role 100% of the time, and sometimes it is relevant to discuss this in clinic appointments. However, the range of feminine apparel is, obviously, wide and varied, and cannot simply be reduced to "wear a skirt". A less common variant holds that female-to-male transitioners must wear a suit and tie to be taken seriously at the GIC. This too is without basis.

- You have to be living "in role" - Not the case. We see people who experience gender related distress: some are pre-transition, some do not undergo transition at all. All are valid referrals to our service.

- You have to want surgery - Not at all. Not everyone needs or wants gender related surgery.

- You have to be suicidal - On the contrary, it is important that those undergoing transition be stable, physically and psychologically. It is not unusual for us to see people who have, as a result of their gender distress, been depressed – sometimes to the point of suicidality – but we would hope that, as transition progresses, this gradually improves.

- You have to be heterosexual - We have heard health professionals say this of the clinic, but it is patently ridiculous. It would be grossly unethical of us to insist on heterosexuality in our patients.

- You can't admit to doubt - Transition is, for many, a major life change and it would be unusual to have no doubts whatsoever. You should feel comfortable discussing feelings of doubt with your clinicians.

- You have to give a standard trans narrative - As the UK's largest gender clinic, we see a huge diversity of people, and neither wish nor expect you to tailor your own experiences to a set of clichés. Just be honest.

- The GIC will start you at the beginning again - This was our practice in decades past. In the last decade or so, it has been standard practice to acknowledge previous time spent in the preferred gender role. Typically, we "back date" the start of transition to the start of living in role full time as well as making an official name change or equivalent.

- They deliberately play Good Cop/Bad Cop - Different clinicians have different approaches, and will form different therapeutic relationships with their patients. Choice of clinician is determined by availability of appointment slots, not by any sort of organised Good/Bad Clinician policy.

Charing Cross GIC, November 2010

. . . . .

As they say above: "Not all these beliefs are 'myths' in the sense of having always been untrue – some stem from the way the GIC operated in the past, or the approaches of previous clinicians – but all are outdated, and unreflective of current treatment protocol."

Unfortunately, when I visited the GIC in 1999 many of these 'myths' were still standard operating procedure and the brutal attitudes of some clinicians bordered on transphobic mental abuse.

To put it into perspective here's the 1990s equivalent of the modern mythbusting.

· · · · ·

West London Mental Health Trust (WLMHT) GIC myths 20th century edition

The following were examples of commonly held beliefs amongst clinicians at the WLMHT GIC in the past:

- You have to wear a skirt to the GIC - It seemed that the GIC had an exclusively binary view of gender plus a good helping of university educated snobbery. Twin sets and pearls were definitely in and anything considered too 'tarty' could imply that you were a fetishist rather than a woman proud of her body. Likewise a full face of makeup was essential, as were heels and wig. Heaven help you if you were androgynous and didn't fit their misogynistic view of womanhood.
- You have to be living "in role" - The slightest break in role was seen as a lack of commitment to the process. If you wanted to be taken seriously then you had to be out and in role long before you were ready or able to handle the constant abuse and prejudice that faced every trans person in the last millenium.
- You have to want surgery - It seemed, again, as if any kind of reticence towards gender related surgery would show a lack of commitment and proved that you couldn't be taken seriously.
- You have to be suicidal - On the contrary, any mention of mental health issues, particularly suicidal feeling and self harming were seen as red flags which would cause the immediate cessation of any treatment. The Trans Mental Health Survey 2012 showed that almost half (48%) of trans people in Britain have attempted suicide at least once and that 84% have thought about it. More than half (55%) have been diagnosed with depression at some

point. In 1999 no one cared enough to carry out this kind of research but I don't think that it's unrealistic to assume that the figures were higher due to less awareness, understanding and treatment and increased prejudice and discrimination.

- You have to be heterosexual - The gender binary extended to patients sexuality and when asked about your choices of sexual partner there appeared to be no 'right answer'. If you admitted that you liked men, then they'd suggest you were actually a homosexual man who was trying to fulfil some sort of effeminate stereotype 'to please your gay lover'. If you said you were attracted to women you were living out some lesbian fantasy and if you enjoyed penetrative sex, they'd suggest you 'weren't transgender enough', because trans women were supposed to despise their penis.

- You can't admit to doubt - Doubt was the reason to delay any and all treatment, if you weren't sure then how could you possibly go ahead with any treatment. You either wanted this more than anything else in the world or you didn't want it at all, in which case you should just go home, pack away your female clothes and stop wasting everyone's time.

- You have to give a standard trans narrative - Ah, you mean the one where you've always known that you were trapped in the wrong body, played with girls toys as a child, despised your penis, but not to the extent of feeling the need to self harm or think about suicide, and wanted full surgery to match you body to your inner self and finally feel whole. Yes, definitely, whatever you do, never go against the grain or rock the boat, there were so many ways to kick you off the patient list.

- The GIC will start you at the beginning again - This was our practice in decades past. Indeed it was, the slightest break in your two year real life test, living in role and it was straight back to the beginning. No, not the beginning at Charing Cross, all the way back to your GP and the endless rounds of referrals and psychological evaluations required before you even got anywhere near the GIC. Do not pass Go, do not collect £200.

- They deliberately play Good Cop/Bad Cop - Different clinicians have different approaches, and will form different therapeutic relationships with their patients. In my experience during the late 90s they were much more likely to play Bad Cop/Bad Cop.

· · · · ·

The role of the GIC was as gatekeepers to the Holy Grail of surgery and they would use any trick in the book to test your resolve and commitment to transitioning. If they could talk you out of it then they felt justified in their bullying as you were obviously never a suitable candidate for surgery in the first place.

I don't recall ever having an appointment at the clinic that didn't leave me in tears as soon as I was free of their judgemental gaze. There was one occasion where the clinician had mockingly informed me that he was going to recommend that I should wait eight years for my surgery.

"I can't," I thought. "I can't wait that long, I need to be a woman now, not when I'm bloody 40."

· · · · ·

The hatred was all around me, everywhere I went. On days out I would be abused, shouted or spat at and on one occasion I even faced the hatred in my GP's waiting room.

A man in his late thirties was staring at me with unbridled disgust, I looked away, trying desperately to avoid eye contact.

"Fucking freak, fucking disgusting, your kind shouldn't be allowed out, fucking paedo!"

He spat the words, the hate and vitriol evident in every single syllable.

When I was finally called into the consulting room I told my GP of the incident but rather than express sympathy or regret he looked at me with only marginally less disgust than my abuser in the waiting room.

"Well, you chose to do this," he said, "so you're going to have to get used to it."

I reeled at his words, shocked that he knew so little about being transgender, you certainly didn't choose it, and dismayed at his total lack of empathy.

· · · · ·

Dawn walked into the kitchen where I was in the process of making a cup of tea.

"I've got a surprise for you," she said, "hands together and eyes closed."

I dutifully clamped my eyes shut and held my hands out flat in front of me, unsure of the nature of the surprise. I felt a rectangular object around 5 inches long and half an inch across placed on my upturned palms. I turned the object over in my hands, trying and failing to find familiarity in the form.

"No idea," I said, "can I open my eyes now?"

"Yes."

My eyes blinked as they adjusted to the light and there in my hands was an instantly recognisable white plastic bar, at its centre was a window containing two blue lines.

"Surprise!" she said, smiling uncontrollably, "we're going to have a baby."

8

CRADLE TO THE GRAVE

"Push your chin down, harder, harder."

"That's it, keep pushing, you can do it."

Dawn's hand squeezes mine, her nails digging into my palm.

"Fuck, fuck, fuck!"

"Breathe love, you're doing great, keep going," my words seem inadequate but they're all I have to offer.

Sweat covers Dawn in a fine film, her hair matted and her eyes screwed shut against the pain as a low, guttural cry escapes her lips. She takes a large gulp from the gas and air and calms momentarily before the next contraction hits bringing forth a further stream of expletives.

I'm terrified, childbirth brings mixed emotions, the joy of a new arrival tempered by the horror of seeing your loved one in so much pain.

"We've got a head, with lots of beautiful black hair," announces the midwife as Dawn lets out another scream. "That's it, push, push, keep pushing."

"I can't push any more. Get it out of me, please," Dawn begs between contractions reaching for the calming relief of the Entonox.

"Yes, you can, keep going, you're almost there."

"But…"

"You've done the hard part, just the last bit to go."

"You can do it love, just a few more pushes," I try to comfort her but struggle to hide my concern.

With one almighty push the baby's shoulders are suddenly free and he slides, unceremoniously into the hands of the waiting midwife who immediately wipes the child's face, wraps him in a blanket and places him on Dawn's chest.

"Well done Dawn you did great, congratulations, it's a boy."

Dawn and I look at each other and then at our beautiful baby boy, so small and perfect as he fills his lungs and begins to let out a tiny, croaking cry.

His face creased and eyes clenched tight against the light.

Slowly his blue grey skin starts to gain some colour as his crying intensifies.

He's not the only one crying, tears fill both of our eyes and in a small, exhausted voice Dawn says: "He's so beautiful, our beautiful baby boy."

I agree wholeheartedly he's the most beautiful thing I'd ever seen, despite looking vaguely like an alien, or Radiohead's Thom Yorke, with his thick shock of black hair.

Our beautiful baby boy, Travis, or Harrison, we weren't sure yet, definitely, maybe one or the other.

As the medical staff tidy up, cutting the umbilical cord and preparing mother and baby for the return to the ward, Dawn and I realise that in all of the excitement we'd forgotten to play our birthing music compilation tape so I head over the stereo and inserting the tape hit play.

· · · · ·

Slip inside the eye of your mind
Don't you know you might find
A better place to play
You said that you'd never been
But all the things that you've seen
Will slowly fade away

So I'll start a revolution from my bed
'Cause you said the brains I had went to my head
Step outside, summertime's in bloom
Stand up beside the fireplace
Take that look from off your face
You ain't ever gonna burn my heart out

And so Sally can wait, she knows it's too late as we're walking on by
Her soul slides away, "But don't look back in anger," I heard you say

Don't Look Back In Anger by Noel Gallagher, Oasis

· · · · ·

The song fills the small room, bringing so many memories flooding back, the gigs I'd played in Saudi Arabia, playing the Oasis song as Dawn watched from the audience, the countless times that I would just pick up my guitar at home and start strumming away at the chords to the song, C, G, Am, E, F, G.

"What do you think of the name Noel?" I ask looking up from our tiny son to Dawn's face.

"Yes, yes I think so," came the reply.

· · · · ·

Noel was small, scarily so, he was two weeks premature, labour having been induced after the paediatricians had become concerned about his lack of growth in the womb, and we were both concerned about his safety. Despite the fears the birth seemed to have gone smoothly and now our boy was here, fully formed, ten tiny fingers, ten tiny toes, we thought that the worst was behind us.

Our local hospital was the Royal Bournemouth but due to labour being induced Noel was born at Poole Hospital and a few hours after his birth it was decided to transfer mother and child back to Bournemouth for monitoring while I went home to grab a shower and contact friends and family.

Noel even had a shout out on Simon Mayo's Radio 1 breakfast show.

"Steve and Dawn, still in awe of their new son, born at 5am this morning in Bournemouth. That was only four and a half hours ago it's just as well that you're still in awe of him really, he's going to be around for a while, although you'll have your down moments."

Little did we know quite how prophetic the DJs words would be.

· · · · ·

The following morning I'm woken by my phone, Dawn and Noel had been kept in hospital overnight for monitoring and I was keen to see them.

"Something's happened, you've got to get back here!" Dawn can barely talk, the fear in her voice terrifies me and it feels like a truck has just hit me in the chest.

"It's Noel, he's really ill, they don't know what's happening."

"I'm on my way," I say pulling on the nearest clothes to hand and rushing for the door. I'm frantic and it shows in my driving, speeding, pushing every single red light until the last possible moment, just doing everything that I can to be back with my partner and baby. Arriving at the hospital I abandon my car near the entrance, oblivious to parking regulations and run towards the maternity ward.

"He wasn't feeding and I was getting worried about it but they kept saying that he'd feed when he was hungry, but he didn't," Dawn sobs.

Noel's blood sugar levels have fallen rapidly leading to a seizure, our beautiful boy was fighting for his life and there was nothing that we could do to help him.

"We're going to transfer Noel back to the Neonatal Intensive Care Unit at Poole Hospital," explains the consultant, Dr Hussey, "he'll be blue lighted in an ambulance, are you ok to drive?"

"Yes, yes, please help him," I cry, my heart breaking.

Noel looks so small in the travel incubator no bigger than a pet carrier but surrounded by oxygen bottles and monitors, their sensors and intravenous lines attached to his tiny limbs, as the staff rush him out of the ward and to the waiting ambulance.

Dawn and I follow in my car as the blue lights and sirens scream into life, sticking as close as we can, allowing the emergency vehicle to cut a path through traffic big enough for both of us. We're both frantic with fear and nausea threatens to overwhelm me. I have never felt so powerless in my entire life. The person that I loved most in the entire world was in mortal danger and there was not one thing that I could do to help him. The impotence formed a boling mass in my chest, threatening to crush my heart and force all air from my lungs.

Arriving in the Neonatal Intensive Care Unit (NICU) Noel is immediately hooked up to more machines, sensors are taped to his body, a tube goes up his nose, a needle into a vein. This looks more like some inhuman torture than medicine but we put the life of our child into these people's hands. My heart is breaking, never before, or since had I known such fear and pain.

Once Noel has been stabilised they leave us to watch over him in his clear perspex incubator surrounded by machines measuring his respiration, his heart rate, his blood oxygen saturation and various other parameters that mean even less to me but which keep track of which side of the wafer thin line between life and death Noel is on. A nurse approaches and offers us the use of a polaroid camera, this terrifies me. In the days before camera phones in everyone's pockets, this camera seems important. Was this to ensure that whatever the next few hours hold for our tiny family that we would get a photograph of our son, alive.

· · · · ·

Over the coming days Noel slowly began to improve, getting stronger each day. We spent our days and nights beside his incubator, occasionally retiring to the anteroom that the staff had made available for us to try to grab some rest.

Twelve days after he was born Noel was visited in NICU by Santa Claus who left a small knitted cap on each of the incubators containing the doll-like premature babies, their translucent skin, red and raw, their tiny limbs barely formed and so small that you could fit them in the palm of your hand.

Looking around the ward, a place full of fear but also of hope, I took in the sight of the amazing NHS staff, calmly, professionally and caringly going about the work of saving our children's lives.

We all owe the staff of the NHS so much, we were born in the NHS, they care for us and our loved ones throughout our lives, from the cradle to the grave, free at the point of use. There are many things wrong with the National Health Service but most of these issues are the makings of politicians rather than physicians. The NHS is the greatest social achievement of the last century and we cannot allow it to be destroyed, underfunded, broken up and sold for profit, and all for the want of the political will to save it.

That year we had our first Christmas dinner together as a family, in Poole Hospital's Neonatal Intensive Care Unit. Noel had his nutrients and electrolytes supplied by intravenous drip and Dawn and I treated ourselves to microwave curries from the petrol station up the road, the only place open.

As I looked down at Noel in his plastic world full of cables and tubes a tear threatened to spill from my eye and I gently told him, "Happy Christmas son".

. . . . .

Two days later we were finally able to take Noel home and while we were relieved that he was improving we also feared that there was more to come.

Dawn and I were besotted with our new son but the future was now looking uncertain and fraught with concerns. We'd discussed what was going to happen with my transition after he was born and the plan was for him to have two mothers from day one.

Nowadays it's not unusual to see rainbow families and many of my gay or lesbian friends have families, but it wasn't until December 2005 that a change in the law allowed same sex couples to adopt. When the

UK's first online sperm donor service for lesbians launched in 2002 pro-family organisations described it as "revolting". Lynette Burrows from the Family Education Trust told the Telegraph that: "These are designer babies for alternative lifestyles. It's a wicked and selfish idea subjecting the child to a lifetime of psychological difficulties, starting with having two mothers, which they know is not possible, and no father, and what their peers are going to say about that abnormal situation."

We didn't feel abnormal but we were certainly made to feel it.

On family days out I would occasionally be able to spend time with my son as Sophie, one of his pair of Mum's. Picking Noel up to feed him in a cafe by the seafront in Weymouth my life felt complete. I was my true self, I had the love of a woman that I cared about deeply and in my arms the only man that I needed in my life.

But not everyone shared the love for our unconventional family and the disapproving looks and sniggers seemed to follow me everywhere. Sometimes these manifested themselves as snide remarks, sometimes as outright abuse and hatred.

I had been shocked to the core by Noel's illness and it led me to re-evaluate my priorities. My transition didn't seem so important now, the life of my baby boy trumped everything and I'd nearly lost him. When the pediatrician informed us that Noel had epilepsy and learning difficulties I realised that his life was going to be difficult enough without having a transgender parent.

The abuse, the bullying from the GIC and concern for my son's welfare all contributed to me making a momentous, and life-changing decision. I would discharge myself from the GIC, stop taking female hormones, and halt my transition which had become both mentally and physically exhausting. I just didn't have the strength to fight for myself at the same time that I was fighting for Noel.

Dawn and Noel had been through enough trauma and I couldn't add to that.

I took Sophie, my inner true self, and I murdered her.

I buried her, and I tried to forget that she'd ever existed. I would not be looking back. For the sake of my family Sophie was dead, buried and gone forever.

9
KEEP CALM AND CARRY ON

The trees flash past my open window creating a strobe effect on my face as the rays of the setting sun are momentarily blocked by their leaves. Ahead of me the road meanders gently through the villages of the New Forest to home.

Primal Scream come on the stereo, asking the existential question.

"Just what is it that you want to do?"

Indeed, what do you want to do? Where do you see yourself in five years, five months, five weeks, five minutes...

"We wanna be free, we wanna be free to do what we wanna do,

And we wanna get loaded and we wanna have a good time,

And that's what we're gonna do,

We're gonna have a good time, we're gonna have a party."

The horns of the song fill the car with joyous music, celebrating life and love, and getting loaded. It all sounds great, today has been a good day and now I'm on my way home to my family.

I sing along to the song, "I'm gonna get deep down, deep down".

"Do you now? Do you really want to get loaded?"

I don't look but I know that he's there, my ears don't hear the words but there they are inside my head. I feel his dark presence beside me, there but not there, a black void that swallows all hope and joy.

"But you're not really happy are you? They would be so much better off without you."

His sibilant speech cuts through me like a diamond on glass, destroying my will and draining my strength.

"You don't deserve to be happy. You don't deserve love, and you certainly don't deserve them."

He has always been with me, reminding me of my worthlessness, keeping my feet grounded in quicksand every time that happiness tried to enter my life. From that day in my parents garage at age 12 when I first tried to take my own life. He was there, beside me, encouraging me to tie the knot. On the flight back to Saudi after the break up of my marriage, sat next to me in seat 26B. When I cut myself in the toilets of the German bar he was in the next cubicle, whispering to me under the partition, asking me if Andy would have been better off without me saving his life. Asking me if life really was better than death.

"The pain is too great for you to carry," he makes a compelling argument. "Don't you wish that it would just end?"

I do, I do want the pain to end, it seems like I've carried this weight of pain inside my heart since before I can remember. I'm tired, so tired, of fighting to survive.

"To die, to sleep;

To sleep: perchance to dream: ay, there's the rub;

For in that sleep of death what dreams may come

When we have shuffled off this mortal coil."

Quoting Hamlet is a low blow I think but he has a point, the dreams that elude us in life may be possible in death, and only then might I be free.

"You don't even need to do anything," he suggests, "all you have to do is not do".

"Take your hands off the steering wheel, close your eyes and be at peace."

The words are persuasive, offering a way out, a respite from the pain, a salvation.

As the forest speeds past the window, the sun beginning to set to the west, I close my eyes and take my hands off the steering wheel immediately feeling the release.

Seconds stretch to minutes then hours and years, each breath lasts an eternity.

Suddenly the demons hypnotic words are gone, replaced by the giggling smiling face of Noel, my baby boy, my love, my world, my everything.

Fear returns, as does pain and my eyes snap open, hands grasping at the wheel frantically searching for control of the vehicle. The car swerves, narrowly missing a road sign, careering from one curb to the other before I can bring the car to a halt in a layby, wheels skidding and gravel flying as I force the brake pedal to the floor.

My demon has left me, for now, returning to the deepest, darkest corners of my mind where he lives, glorifying in my despair and pain, waiting for his next opportunity to torment me.

I begin to cry, deep, painful sobs, coming from deep within my soul as I grasp the steering wheel. Knuckles white, clinging to life, a drowning man holding on to a lifebelt by his fingertips. My head slumps forwards onto the top of the wheel, exhaustion washes over me, I don't know how much longer I can do this.

Instinctively knowing that I'm being watched I turn my head and there beside my open window is a large, black eye inspecting me, asking questions of me. The calm, inquisitive face of a pony, his muzzle inches from the window, showing real concern for me.

"Thanks," I say, "yes, I know, time to go home".

· · · · ·

Imagine what it's like to take something that's so intrinsically a part of you, your sexuality, religion, love of music or, in my case, your gender identity, and not just stop doing it but deny that it ever existed.

In killing Sophie that is what I tried to achieve.

Whilst I concentrated on my family and business I was oblivious to the tumour that was growing, hidden deep within my soul.

My mental health was deteriorating and I was becoming increasingly emotionally withdrawn. I no longer self harmed in the ways in which I had previously but instead used food to damage myself, developing an unhealthy emotional reliance on calories to fill the void inside me. When people think of self harm they tend to think of deliberately causing injury to yourself, cutting or other activities, but many destructive behaviours can be a symptom of self harm and over the years I exhibited many of them.

Alcohol abuse, substance abuse, over or under eating, partaking in unsafe sex, staying in an abusive relationship, all of these activities have the potential to damage your body but are not traditionally seen as self harming activity, and are often portrayed as antisocial or immoral behaviour.

For me, as for many others, self harm was the relief valve. The way of turning emotional pain that I had no explanation for, or control over, into a physical pain that I could both see and therefore comprehend.

When I looked in the mirror I could only see my eyes, the rest of my body a prison of flesh to which I had no connection and therefore no empathy.

· · · · ·

Over the months following Noel's birth it became clear that he had suffered some form of brain injury due to the seizure, he had epilepsy and would experience learning difficulties growing up. He would have terrifying seizures, often in his sleep and it became so bad that I mounted a CCTV camera on his cot so that we could monitor his condition constantly.

We were living three streets away from Poole Hospital in a Victorian terrace house and when I discovered Noel's lifeless and limp body one morning I didn't even think about calling for an ambulance. Scooping him up in my arms I immediately left the house and began running to the hospital barefoot. I was desperate, I was crying, he was naked save for a nappy and his limbs hung loosely as I ran, struggling for breath. I wasn't using the paths, I was running down the middle of the road and when a woman in a small red Vauxhall Astra approached us I flagged her over and begged for a lift the rest of the way. Seeing the despair on my face and the unconscious baby in my arms she complied and got us to A&E in minutes.

Once again disaster was averted but it felt like we were living on borrowed time with our son, the regular seizures and as yet unknown medical issues haunted us and we soon became regulars with the ambulance service and medical staff. Visits to the hospital were always traumatic, fear of the unknown and the constant stream of tests that Noel underwent took their toll.

As a parent you want to do everything that you can to protect your child and losing that ability can leave you feeling impotent and useless. Having to restrain your beautiful baby boy so that nurses could stick needles into his veins was heartbreaking, we knew that they were trying to help him but all he could understand was the pain they were causing him.

At one point the doctors prescribed him steroids and immediately our beautiful, little boy ballooned up to comic book proportions, a condition that thankfully reversed when he was taken off the drugs returning him to his natural size and to this day he is still slim, only now, at 18 years old he's as tall as me.

. . . . .

On Christmas Day 2003 we were back in the maternity unit at Poole Hospital as our little family grew again when Noel was joined by a sister.

When you have had a traumatic experience with the birth of a child it leaves fears for future pregnancies but our new daughter arrived without drama, although she has made up for it since. Her birth wasn't without controversy though, for the first few hours of her life she was called India, a name which was greeted with resistance by certain family members that didn't seem to have received the memo about political correctness. As I drove to collect Noel from a friend that had kindly allowed him to be part of her family's christmas celebrations, The Beatles came on the iPod, 'Sexy Sadie', by the time I got back to Dawn she had been renamed, I'm just grateful that it wasn't 'Lovely Rita'.

A wonderful bond immediately formed between our two babies that survives to this day, and they can exhibit overwhelming kindness and support for each other, although as teenagers they both try to deny it and sometimes their relationship descends to open warfare.

· · · · ·

As a photographer in the Premier League I was always getting emails from aspiring photographers asking if they could shadow me at the match against Manchester United or Arsenal so that they could learn how to be a sports photographer. Well apart from the massive licensing and accreditation issues with shooting a Premier League match, it isn't where you learn your trade.

There are 24 levels of football in England containing an estimated 7,000 teams, of which the top 160 teams make up the National League, 3 divisions 68 clubs, and the Football League, 4 divisions 92 clubs. The twenty Premier League clubs represent the top 0.2% of football clubs in this country.

This means that there are roughly 6980 football clubs outside of the Premier League, many of whom would love to have a photographer come along to a match, allowing them much greater access than the Premier League can offer and giving them the opportunity to hone their skills and build a portfolio of work.

For me that club was Wimborne Town.

Established in 1878, the Magpies greatest glory came in 1992 when they won the FA Vase at Wembley, and as a Dorset Premier League club they attracted crowds in the low, sometimes very low, hundreds.

Like every other non-league football club throughout the country money was always an issue for the club and they were always looking for new, innovative ways to raise the funds needed to maintain their ground, The Cuthbury, and pay for players with the talent to push for promotion. To this end they employed an amazing piece of lateral thinking. Instead of approaching local companies begging for shirt sponsorship they decided to run a raffle, £250 a ticket and first prize was the opportunity to have your logo on the players shirts as club sponsor.

The idea intrigued me, and despite having no connection to the club I purchased a ticket. I'd recommend this approach to any small sporting team, that year the club raised over £15,000 with the raffle, a sum that they would have found impossible to match by simply selling the sponsorships. When former AFC Bournemouth manager, and local legend, Harry Redknapp pulled my ticket from the hat I was ecstatic, my business, Seeker Photography, would be the main shirt sponsor for the coming season.

I knew that this was a once in a lifetime opportunity and feeling the need to maximise on the exposure it would give my business immediately offered my services as club photographer, both filling a need for the club and ensuring that the local press would be adequately supplied with images featuring my branding on the team's shirts. And that was where I learnt my trade as a football photographer, shooting matches, kit launches, team groups, events. It was unpaid but I learnt a lot there, not least of which was that you don't need to be in the Premier League in order to take football photos, and if I hadn't spent my time at Wimborne then I'd have never joined AFC Bournemouth.

· · · · ·

One rainy September afternoon in 2008 I had just received a call from the club informing me that the bottom corner of the wildly sloping Cuthbury pitch was waterlogged and as a result that evening's match was postponed when my phone rang again.

It was my friend Suzy Wheeler whom I had known for years and who I had supported with photography when she helped to set up the Dorset Music Forum, a link between local talent and the wider music industry.

"Are you doing anything tonight?" she asked.

"Not now, the footy's just been cancelled, why? What are you up to?"

"We're holding a press conference tonight with Pete Doherty, do you want to come along and take some photos for us?"

Now at this point I feel that I need to hold my hands up. I could say that I'd been a massive Libertines fan since their debut 'Up the bracket' was released in 2002 but for some reason they'd escaped my attention, I'm just guessing that I was distracted with a new family and was in one of those periods when you're not really paying attention to new music, just going through the motions with the same old familiar albums of your youth.

My main knowledge of Pete was the lurid tales so beloved of trashy tabloids and outraged social commentators but I had nothing better to do and so I acquiesced to attend.

That evening I found Pete to be open and friendly, if a little distracted, but I managed to get some great unguarded images away from the crowds. Moments of solitary reflection as the world revolved around this artist that had been at the centre of a maelstrom for so long. Even today, a decade later, I still cherish those images as some of the finest that I have ever taken and was honoured when one of them, depicting a thoughtful Pete, eyes closed and relaxed, was used as part of the original artwork that he produced for the cover of his 2016 solo album 'Hamburg Demonstrations'.

Over the next fortnight I photographed him on three separate occasions, the final time being a gig at Boscombe's Opera House, now the O2 Academy, during which I captured a series of images of Babyshambles drummer Adam Ficek that would cement my reputation as a music photographer.

One of the interesting features of digital images that you never got with film is the ability to know the exact moment that you took an image, down to the second. Taking Adam out of the stage door and into the back alley behind the venue I immediately accessed the area for potential shots. He didn't have long, he was due back on stage at any second, and I had to work quickly.

Using the security lamps as my only source of illumination I began to direct him as I released the shutter, '"over here please Adam, yes that's it, look up a bit, thanks, perfect". Over the course of 60 seconds I captured a series of dramatic images that he would use as publicity stills for years to come including one that was strangely reminiscent of da Vinci's 'L'Uomo Vitruviano', The Vitruvian Man, arms and legs extended, back to the camera with the high spotlights casting dagger like shadows across the wall.

The work that I did that night and the friendships that I made would, eventually lead to standing on stage photographing The Libertines as they headlined Hyde Park. For now it was the start of a career in music photography that would see me capturing images of so many artists that I admired from Oasis to Dolly Parton, from Blondie to Madness.

$\cdots$

I suppose that if you were going to take one lesson from those stories it would be to seize every opportunity that comes your way. You never know when the opportunity will come again, indeed many never will. Our lives are journeys with numerous forks and turns, once we start down one path we may never find the way back to the turning that we missed.

I've always chosen the difficult path, the well trodden path holds little interest for me. The untrodden route may be overgrown with brambles, it may be painful to navigate, but it leads to a place that few ever see. Sometimes it leads to personal growth and relationships, for me it also led to working in the Premier League and standing on stage in front of 75,000 people at the Reading Festival.

Ultimately, if I had never become the photographer for Wimborne Town I would never have worked in the Premier League, I would never have had any of the opportunities that I had because of that and you wouldn't be reading this book. Life really is an amazing journey.

. . . . .

My experiences following Noel's birth instilled a sense of gratitude towards the work of those that care for us, the NHS workers and the charities that give so much support to those in need. I'm also someone that is always much more likely to immediately say "yes" to any request for help than to start weighing up the pros and cons and this led to a series of increasingly unusual fundraising challenges over the next few years.

The first was a charity cycle ride the length of Vietnam from Saigon to Hanoi during which I learnt the power of the global language of football.

. . . . .

One of the first mistakes that you can make with a charity cycle ride is to assume that everyone is going to be of a similar ability to yourself. For me that meant well meaning, out of shape but eager. Arriving in Vietnam I soon discovered that my expedition mates were all much fitter than me, much more proficient and included international triathletes. The result was that for the next week I would say goodbye to them in the morning and then spend the rest of the day cycling on my own through the towns and villages of this beautiful country.

Like Beirut I found the people of Vietnam to be extremely friendly and welcoming. Perhaps there is something about people that have to endure war which means that they celebrate peace with an openness that manifests as hope and a hospitable welcome for travellers prepared to stray off the familiar path to more popular destinations where locals might be jaded by too many tourists, drunken hen and stag parties and food outlets selling full english breakfasts.

Having left the beautiful city of Dà Lat, high in the mountains of Lâm Dong Province, 5000' above sea level on the Langbian Plateau I found myself, once again, cycling alone on the twisting roads that wind their way through the woods that led to it being called the 'City of thousands of pine trees'. A fine mist shrouds the valleys, adding to the sense of isolation, the only sound my breathing and occasional swearing at my exertion.

Reaching a small village of rough dwellings built from a wide range of natural and recycled materials I'm greeted by the children running alongside me, obviously bemused by the strange European cycling alone through their home. Smiling, they laugh and skip as they keep pace with me. I know no Vietnamese with which to communicate save for "xin chào", "hello" but it would appear that they can trump my two words of Vietnamese and reply with their three words of English.

"Hello, David Beckham."

Even here, 6500 miles from Old Trafford, it seems that the children of Vietnam know of the midfield maestro who can bend it like, well you know.

Vietnam is a truly beautiful country and travelling through it at such a slow pace allows me to soak it in, my mind emptying of so many of the issues that afflicted my mental health at home.

As the day grows longer I begin to feel a sense of unease that I should have rendezvoused with the rest of our party by now, morning becomes afternoon, afternoon threatens to become evening, and still I cycle. My water is running short and I haven't passed a village in hours, this might actually be an issue, I begin to think.

In these days of 24/7 global internet and mobile phone connectivity it can be difficult to remember the time before the iPhone but I was on the other side of the world with no communications and very little idea of where I was. A plan begins to formulate in my mind, but it won't be easy and it certainly won't be quick.

The first step is to find a telephone, that means continuing to ride until I come across one, somewhere, ahead of me on this road. Stage 2 is to try to call, with limited funds on me, Dawn in England, she also doesn't have a mobile phone so with the six hour time difference it could be a case of trying to catch her at home and awake. She then needs to call the charity in England and hope that they had a contact number for the guides in Vietnam, also problematic as it relies on the local guides being in touch with some central office here in country, also from a random landline somewhere along the route.

Easy, no problem, I feel confident that I can expect to see a rescue at some point during the next three months, maybe, if I was lucky.

Luck can be a cruel mistress but on this day she is on my side. Just as night begins to fall an aged Honda 50 moped comes to a halt alongside me, engine popping and straining under the load as the rider and his passenger, our tour guide, dismount.

"We've found you, I was about to give up and turn back," he says excitedly.

It transpires that I'd missed the lunch stop and continued to cycle all afternoon unaware that I had left the party behind. They in turn had no idea where I had disappeared to and after failing to find me on the roads that we had already covered set out to search the road ahead of our destination, reaching me just as the Honda threatened to splutter out of life due to a lack of fuel.

Reunited with my group, my body aching, hungry and dehydrated I heartily tuck into my dinner that evening despite the ever present rats watching our every move, hoping to scavenge any food left unattended for more than a second.

· · · · ·

I was desperate to repay the debt that we owed to the staff at Poole Hospital that had saved Noel's life and hatched a plan to photograph 1000 people in a day for a charity community artwork. After a few moments consideration and calculations on a scrap of paper I realised that I would need to shoot 125 people an hour for eight hours straight in order to achieve that, or one every 30 seconds. It was doable, if you had them all lined up at the beginning and could pull them in, capture their image and send them on their way immediately. It allowed no time for finding the people to shoot, no time for people fussing about their hair, no time for uncooperative children, no time for a loo break.

In the end I set a target of 500 people to create an artwork entitled 500 Faces of Poole. That was still one a minute for nearly eight and a half hours. After much cajoling and numerous cups of coffee the feat was finally completed and I'm honoured to say that the final 16' x 8' montage featuring 504 faces is still on display in Poole Hospital and to this day nearly a decade later is a popular stop for visitors. To me it was one of those projects that gains more significance with the passage of time, it features people that are no longer with us, there are children, including my own who have grown up, there's even me, or a former version of me, hiding in there among the men, women, children, dolls and soft toys that had their likeness captured on that August day back in 2009.

On a recent visit to the hospital the Chief Executive, Debbie Fleming, welcomed me and thanked me for my fundraising efforts all those years ago. "We're very grateful for everything that you've done for the hospital", she told me.

"No, my pleasure, thank you for everything that you've given me", I said putting my arm around Noel.

. . . . .

I stand behind the screen, listening to the noise of the audience.

The room is packed with people, all seated around the walls facing the centre of the room, watching… and judging.

With no previous experience and only five hours training I'm about to do the unbelievable, the alien and new. A step into the unknown.

I look within myself and concentrate on my inner strength.

"All I need is within me now.

"All of the strength I need is within me now.

"All of the confidence I need is within me now.

"All of the focus I need is within me now.

"All of the knowledge I need is within me now."

The mantras keep repeating in my head, taking my total attention.

I barely see the other competitors come and go, barely hear the audience's response to them, my entire focus on my own mindset.

And then my time comes.

My name is announced, and together with my partner I step on to the dance floor.

The occasion is a Strictly Come Dancing event, and I, along with other prominent business people had been paired with professional dancers to compete for a local cancer charity.

Whenever I am asked to do anything like this my immediate response is always "yes", I've never shied away from the opportunity to push myself and take myself out of my comfort zone. So there I was, with only five hours training and no previous dance experience, performing the Paso Doble to a packed room.

After numerous errors and mistakes in training, the adrenalin of performance and competition focuses my mind and it is the only time that I ever nailed the routine.

It's still the same now, I know that my performance in practice runs is never anywhere close to what I can deliver in front of an audience, and I don't have any problem with that. Knowledge like that frees you from the stress associated with bad rehearsals and allows you to concentrate on your focus and mindset ahead of a performance. This was a different life, a different person, but that strength and focus is still part of me, perhaps even more so.

I've always felt drawn to the concepts of Buddhism, the idea that meditation helps to clear the mind of distractions allowing you to find your inner strength. I particular identify with the idea that Buddha is within all of us, he isn't a divine being to whom we pray in the hope that he will intervene and cure our ills. Buddhism teaches us that all of the skills, knowledge, compassion, bravery and strength that we need are within us and by quieting our minds we can find peace and our own ways to face all of our challenges.

"All I need is within me now."

. . . . .

The day before he died, my Grandad told me of the dream he'd had the previous night, a night that we didn't think he'd survive.

"Last night I dreamt that I was playing cricket, and at my feet were all of these words, mixed, random words, and I knew that if I stepped on the wrong one whilst playing my stroke then I would die."

The following morning he passed away, it was typical of him that he saw death as part of life's game.

Last week new statistics were released that said the average life expectancy is now 80, Grandad was 88 - I guess that's a good innings. So officially he was 10% above average, although we all know that he was so much more than that.

I loved my Grandad.

Like all children that grow up I didn't tell him often enough.

It's not until we have children ourselves that we realise how much love the older generations have for the young.

How much hurt is caused by the inevitable process of children growing up and creating their own lives and families. As we each, in turn, have our own children they become the focus of our love and the older generations take a back seat. Love flows downhill, from the old to the young and the young take it for granted.

My Grandad meant the world to me, he helped shape me, I told him on his last day that it was his fault that I'd joined the RAF and subsequently become a photographer. I also told him that I wouldn't swap a single day of it.

He gave me my thirst for knowledge, he was the only person that I ever met that had as many useless and random facts in their head as I did.

Growing up in a four generation household with my Great Grandmother, my brother, parents and my wonderful grandparents, Biggran and Grandad was a loving, nurturing environment for a kid with a thirst for knowledge.

Biggran and Grandad were a pair, to me they were a single unit and I will forever be grateful for the unconditional love that they gave me, no matter how far I travelled or how infrequently I visited.

I miss them both terribly and can only hope that they are, once more, together somewhere in a loving, kind place where pain and the passage of time don't exist.

I know that they will watch over us all and that they will live on, forever, in our hearts.

Grandad, thank you so much for everything you gave to me of yourself, my life would have been so much poorer for not having known you. I love you.

Without you, my life wouldn't have been the same
You gave me so much, of the man that I became.

We never believe, that time will fly by so fast
Always believing that this time won't be the last.

As a boy, the hours spent, a compensation
We travelled the world, in our conversation.

You gave me the thirst, for knowledge and for the world
An ever present, in my life as it unfurled.

How can you measure a life after its last laugh
Or can I capture your life in a photograph.

Steve Cook, Eulogy for Bill Moody, March 21, 2011

10
THE SEEKER

"Right guys, I've got a great idea."

It wasn't the first time that I'd walked into the office and announced this. I'd developed a bit of a reputation for coming up with audacious plans, seemingly impossible given the size of our team, and then applying ludicrous deadlines to the project.

Most of the year I fell into the trap that many business people find themselves in, constantly fire fighting any issues whilst tied up with the work of just producing any output required by the clients and never really having any time to develop new ideas or products. Today was the first day back after Christmas, a time when the nation overindulged with family and friends but also a time when I, with my mental health issues making me feel more isolated than usual, could focus on business ideas away from the everyday grind.

The previous year we had diversified into public relations with the recruitment of a journalist, adding words to my images, and offering a complete service to small businesses. Local newspapers had been downsizing for years and this left a lot of talented journalists available in the job market.

PR however was a very different business to photography. As a photographer I was used to being judged on the quality of the work that I produced, as a PR agency we were judged on whether or not some unseen editor decided to publish our story or not and I found this reliance on someone else for my reputation to be annoying.

"We're going to launch a magazine, and we're going to print in two weeks time."

My excitement was evident but not entirely matched by my team.

"We've got the skills, we've already got a lot of the content, all we need to do is pull it all together and get a designer on board."

Within the hour I had mocked up the cover for the first issue of Seeker News featuring images that I'd already taken of a local business guru, James Sale, who had just won a battle against cancer, I knew that he'd make a great feature interview. I duly printed numerous copies of the cover and stuck them all over the office, immediately making the new publication a real, physical thing.

Over the next week we found a designer, sold advertising space to pretty much every company that we'd ever done business with, found a printer, built a limited distribution network and assembled the stories and features that would fill our first issue.

The first issue was unlike any other magazine available in the area at the time, and my editorial reflected that.

· · · · ·

Seeker - Work/Life

Seeker News stands as a testament to the power of just getting on with it and not procrastinating. A month ago it didn't exist, except in some dark corner of my imagination, but now you're holding it in your hands.

All too often we lose time and inspiration by prevaricating, putting off the things we'd love to do in favour of the things we feel we should so. But sometimes the only real course of action is to get up and get on with it.

The best magazines are made of great words, great photos and great design. Seeker News won't settle for anything less in its mix of informative, well-researched news, profiles and features from the region's business community.

It's nearly 20 years since I wrote, produced and distributed a motorcycling fanzine from an airbase in the Saudi Arabian desert. It was made with a sand-filled camera, a typewriter, scissors, glue and blind enthusiasm. Seeker News is driven by the same commitment to delivering a publication that people are excited to read and advertisers want to be associated with.

Steve Cook, Seeker News Issue 1, February 2012
This magazine is dedicated to Bill Moody (1922-2011).
Thank you for the thirst for knowledge.

· · · · ·

The rest of the magazine featured news, columns, the arts and sports plus, as you might expect, some great images and it was my editorial goal that every issue would educate, inspire and inform our readers and to that aim we always included thought provoking articles. The first issue asked the question 'Did the media talk us into the recession?' with constant negative reporting affecting confidence and a feature looking at the lessons that I drew from my time in the RAF, lessons that I still apply in everyday life to this day.

· · · · ·

What I learnt in the Cold War

For those of you that were born in the 80s there was a time before Russian oligarchs owned Premiership football clubs. A time when the East and the West were involved in an ideological nuclear standoff, and a 16 year old from Southbourne joined the Royal Air Force to work on Tornado bombers. The lessons that I learnt locked in a bomb shelter, wearing a gas mask maintaining the readiness of a nuclear armed bomber have stood me in great stead for the rest of my life and business.

- Be prepared - "In peace prepare for war, in war prepare for peace." - Sun Tzu, The Art of War. In the same way that a Formula 1 team will endlessly practice pit stops, we would spend days fine tuning the refuelling and re-arming of our aircraft to make the operation as smooth and quick as possible. Throughout the Cold War we constantly prepared for a war that never came, although we did for some reason practice dropping bombs on deserts.
- Plan to succeed, but don't overplan - "A good plan violently executed now is better than a perfect plan executed next week." – George S. Patton. Some people won't put a plan into action until every single detail has been examined, refined and re-examined. Preparation and planning are good, but if you overdo it you may well miss the opportunity. A month ago this magazine didn't exist, we had a plan even if it was very basic. We could have spent weeks or months perfecting the plan and exploring every possible eventuality. If we'd done this we'd have lost the power and energy of momentum. Our plan was executed immediately and with vigour, you are holding the result
- Where's your head at? - "Victorious warriors win first and then go to war, while defeated warriors go to war first and then seek to win." - Sun Tzu. You have to have your motivation right, if you

are demoralised and demotivated it comes across and people will notice. You must believe in yourself and your service or product in order to sell it to others!

- Skills - You never stop learning. Be the best you can at what you do but be prepared to ask for help. Go to seminars, read books, practice your core skills but don't be scared to call in a specialist to help with skills gaps.

- Honesty and integrity - When you're servicing a £20 million bomber (1980s prices), honesty and integrity are essential. Everyone makes mistakes, the key is to spot them, rectify them, and be honest, better to lose face and fix the problem than to risk the lives of the crew by covering the mistake up. If you are honest and conduct yourself with integrity you will earn the trust of others, this adds to your credibility and people will be more likely to do business with you.

Steve Cook, Seeker News, February 2012

· · · · ·

Over the following months the magazine continued to grow, attracting a lot of attention including that of investors who saw it as a potentially franchisable business launching regional editions throughout the UK. One investor representing a consortium of funding sources even went as far as telling me that "within five years we'll make you a millionaire".

For me the focus was on producing a great publication that made a difference to people's lives.

· · · · ·

Throughout this period I'd been splitting my Saturday photographic duties between Wimborne Town, who by now had been through numerous new sponsors but I was, by this point, part of the team, and AFC Bournemouth, at the time struggling at the bottom of League 1. On Wednesday evenings I could be found on the infield at Poole Stadium shooting our Elite League speedway team, the Pirates. This gave me unprecedented access to the two most popular local sporting teams and a plan was hatched to launch a second magazine, Seeker Sport, with the first issue being released in September 2012.

· · · · ·

Bringing you all the very best in local sport

Sport is a family.

Whether it's the team you play for or the people you watch with, it's all about belonging – it's all about family.

As a child I'd regularly visit Dean Court with my family to watch Ted MacDougall and Phil Boyer, Wimborne Road for the high octane thrills of Malcolm Simmons and Neil Middleditch and Dean Park to marvel at the majesty of Barry Richards and Andy Roberts.

Like many in our country, and indeed the world, sport has always been a big part of my life. It's where we go to seek refuge from the stresses of our everyday lives, it's true escapist entertainment and the one place where tribalism is still accepted.

Locally, we're blessed with a diverse range of sports and whether you're a Cherries supporter or a Pirates fan you'll find Seeker Sport is packed with the interviews and news that really matter, together with some great photography.

We'll also be covering the wider world of sports in Dorset, from non-league football, to rugby, athletics, basketball, judo, sailing, hockey, tennis, badminton, showjumping – in fact, if there's a contest and it involves people and teams from Dorset, we want to hear about it. So don't hesitate to tell us!

Seeker Sport will be watching with you, taking part where we can and loving every minute of it... just like you!

Steve Cook, Seeker Sport Issue 1, September 2012

· · · · ·

That issue featured an interview with Cherries legend Steve Fletcher, twenty years at AFC Bournemouth and approaching the end of his playing career, football and speedway photo features and posters. I wanted the magazine to appeal to fans of all ages, including the kids, and the posters were a big part of that. Where else could young fans find images of their favourite local League 1 footballers to put on their wall? I loved walking out of the ground after a match and seeing players being asked to sign the pictures of them that I'd taken and that we'd published in the magazine.

We were now a multi-title publisher with a team of five and very limited resources, but we were getting noticed.

· · · · ·

Down the road at AFC Bournemouth things weren't going as well, by October we'd only managed to register one league win all season and were languishing at 21st in the table. The club was beginning to look like certainties for relegation and manager Paul Groves looked hopelessly out of his depth.

With the team showing no signs of improvement Chairman Eddie Mitchell decided that it was time for a change, sacking Groves and approaching former manager Eddie Howe about a possible return to Dean Court.

Eddie Howe had been a Bournemouth player from youth and had kept the Cherries in the Football League in his first season in charge. With only three months of the season left the club was ten points adrift at the bottom of the table, in danger of dropping into non-league obscurity and with the very real possibility of going out of business. In a massive turn around of fortunes under the fledgling manager's leadership which included a run of only one defeat in seven matches the club ensured safety with a match in hand when Steve Fletcher sent the Dean Court faithful wild, scoring his 100th career league goal 10 minutes from time against Grimsby to pull off a feat that is still known as the Great Escape.

The following season Howe led the team to promotion despite a very limited budget and many at the club were heartbroken when he left for Burnley in January 2011. When Mitchell approached Howe the Lancashire club were 16th in the Championship and it was inconceivable that he might want to return to the bottom of League 1.

For personal and family reasons the time was right for Eddie to return home and when he walked out onto the Dean Court pitch alongside assistant Jason Tindall before the home match against Orient he was met with rapturous applause. Walking in front of him, capturing the prodigal son's return I immediately felt a lift in spirits around the ground, the despair that afflicted us all was suddenly replaced with optimism and hope, in Eddie we trust.

Sitting in the press seats doing a live interview on BBC Radio he spoke about the changes at AFC Bournemouth in the two years that he'd been away at Turf Moor. The club had invested millions of pounds in improving the stadium and training facilities, as well as investing in new playing talent, but despite expectations he told the press that he wasn't thinking about promotion.

The image that I captured at that moment of the smiling, ever youthful manager, headphones on and microphone clasped in his hand proved prescient, framing Howe above a section of advertising hoarding which read simply 'The Champ'.

Six months later at a sunny Prenton Park, AFC Bournemouth would secure promotion to the Championship, for only the second time in our history, with a win against Tranmere Rovers and Eddie wasn't finished yet.

. . . . .

The path to promotion wasn't without its wobbles though, the club was still struggling financially and a month earlier following a run of bad results the Chairman had been forced to balance the books by dismissing a number of members of staff, Club photographer Mick Cunningham included.

Mick was Mr AFC Bournemouth, he'd been at the club for twenty years, and was one of the nicest guys that you could ever meet. We'd sit alongside each other at the undeveloped southern end of the Dean Court pitch, we only had three sides on our ground at the time, swapping stories about our time in the RAF and sharing our mutual love for the Cherries.

Rob Mitchell, the Commercial Director of the club called me and asked me to go in for an urgent meeting, "they've sacked Mick, and we need a photographer urgently," he told me.

I'd dreamt of being the club photographer but not like this, not with Mick going. There was no money available but like Mick before me I loved the club and wanted to do anything that I could to help them, and so I agreed to be the club photographer for the rest of the season without pay.

I initially experienced a lot of hostility from some of the fans who had the belief that I had pushed Mick out but I was as upset as they were, especially when Mick took the dismissal so badly that he stayed away from the club that he loved so much for the rest of the season.

Mick would eventually return to the club, photographing matches for the local newspaper and again we would sit on the touchline swapping stories of aircraft and football. He got to see his beloved Cherries play in the Premier League but tragically collapsed whilst photographing them play at Stoke City in 2015, passing away in hospital the following day at the age of 55. His loss was felt greatly at the club and fittingly his photo graced the cover of the programme for the next home match against Watford, a programme that he'd put so much love and effort into over the years.

. . . . .

The magazines had continued to grow and we'd made a couple of important additions to our team including former Daily Echo editor Neal Butterworth who had retired and moved to Spain after thirteen years with the paper before being diagnosed with cancer and returning to the UK for treatment. He felt that he still had more to give and it was great to have such a talented and experienced journalist join our small team.

We'd also attracted the Echo's former advertising manager, who joined us to help with commercial development and one day he surprised me with a question.

"Do you realise how much cheaper it is to produce a newspaper?".

I didn't, and over the next ten minutes he showed me cost projections and comparative costs for newsprint versus the glossy A4 magazine that we currently produced. The numbers made perfect sense, we could increase distribution and frequency whilst also cutting costs, and so the decision was made to transform our monthly magazines, Seeker News and Seeker Sport into a free newspaper retaining the Seeker News name. Initially to be printed fortnightly the plan was to switch to weekly as we grew.

The newspaper made an impact as soon as it was released and within months had a higher circulation than our competitor that had been in existence for over a century, hit by declining print sales and finding it hard to compete in the internet age, despite much greater resources, against the increasingly common free newspaper business model.

Despite our popularity with readers due in part to our great design, photos and positive editorial policy, refusing to include any stories that were in any way voyeuristic or divisive, we were struggling to achieve the required advertising revenues. A string of recruitment failures in this area, appointing seemingly great sales people who talked the talk but never actually delivered the results.

After letting one sales agent go due to abysmal sales figures I was shocked to discover that his computer had games installed on it, links to porn and dating websites and that he'd been messaging escorts in Thailand from work throughout the day. Another sales manager was a former family member and I trusted them completely, giving them advances on their wages to help over Christmas. In turn she took a few weeks off work to look after a family member, forgetting that being family we were connected via Facebook and posting about her new job that she'd started that morning despite supposedly still being on our payroll. When I rang her she continued to pretend that she was visiting a relative in hospital despite the Facebook post.

Every time we thought that we'd found the right salesperson something would stop it from happening. A lovely lady who seemed the perfect fit approached us as she worked at a competitor and she was struggling with them being supportive of her commitments looking after her disabled child. I told her that there was no way that would be a problem with us and so she gave in her notice only to spend the following weeks being called into meetings where they tried everything to persuade her not to leave, eventually giving her a payrise just so that she wouldn't join us.

Investors however, saw our fledgling newspaper as a unique opportunity a local property developer wanted to buy 51% of the company, a figure that I was uncomfortable with but the time was rapidly approaching when I might not have the choice.

We had numerous meetings, discussing the future direction of the publication, he even invited me down to his building that overlooked the beach, showing me the offices that we would be moving into, complete with sea views.

"That's great," I told him, "but we need to get this deal completed first. We need the investment to continue to grow the publication."

I'd gone as far as I could, with no resources, based purely on the talents of my team and willpower, we desperately needed the cash injection that he had been promising for months.

"We need the money now, we need ten grand this week in order to put out the next issue."

This represented a fraction of the investment that had been promised and he promised to see what he could do. The following morning I got an email from his PA saying that he'd decided to invest in other opportunities.

I was destroyed, I'd put everything into this business and there had been no warning that he was about to pull the plug on us. I called Dawn into my office and told her the bad news, appointments were made with business advisors and accountants. By the end of the day I was informed that I was left with no option, I was going to have to close the business and they told me exactly how I had to do it and it left a bad taste in my mouth.

I'd poured everything I had into the business, my life as well as everything I owned. I was deeply protective of and loyal to my team and I desperately searched for any solution that would keep them in work, including relaunching as a digital news service but despite my best efforts this wasn't to be. I'd made mistakes, I'd overstretched, I'd underestimated the opposition and I'd definitely put too much trust in the some of the wrong people.

My mental health imploded, after months of pressure and endless hours focused on the business I was cast adrift, with neither purpose or drive. The pain of the loss and feelings of failure drove me into myself, becoming increasingly reclusive, just wanting to hide away from the world. Venturing out only to photograph football matches, trying to find solitude locked away inside my own world, I would sit on the touchline avoiding all human contact.

·····

It had been six years since I first photographed Peter Doherty and Babyshambles, shooting them at venues across the UK, the highlight of which was a Teenage Cancer Trust gig at the Bristol Academy with special guest Roger Daltrey.

Having been a Who fan since my youth this was always going to be special. Standing there on stage during soundcheck as the band learnt the ten Who songs that they would perform that evening, capturing the interaction between the legendary Daltrey and Pete, playing a white Rickenbacker so evocative of the image of a young Townshend in the early days of The Who, I thought, "you might as well retire now, it's never going to get better than this".

When The Libertines announced their reunion gig at Hyde Park in 2014 I wondered if that would leave me out in the cold, they were bound to be using the talents of Roger Sargent, the photographer who had spent years at Rough Trade and the NME and had been with them from the start.

Arriving backstage Roger was one of the first people that I met, he was there to film the show, having diversified into documentary making and directing music videos. Our relationship was professional but detached at first however we soon warmed to each other.

"It would have been too easy to dislike you," he later told me, "but you were so open and friendly that I couldn't help but like you." For my part I found Roger to be gracious and supportive when he didn't have to be.

He later asked me to shoot the stills for the video he was directing to accompany the release of The Libertines' single 'Heart of the matter' and to say I felt honoured would be understating it.

·····

From the stage the scenes at the front of the 60,000 strong crowd resembled a warzone. As the boys took to the stage, launching into the first chords of 'Vertigo' the crowd had surged forward crushing those at the front against the barriers.

Security were trying their best to pull those affected out and into the photographers' pit but the weight of the mass was proving too much for them and some of the bodies hauled over the barrier appeared limp and lifeless. This looked serious and I was immediately reminded of previous incidents at gigs and sporting events where there had been serious casualties.

"Well tell me, baby, how does it feel?
I know you like the roll of the limousine wheel
And they all get them out for
For the boys in the band
They twist and they shout for
For the boys in the band…"

Boys in the band, The Libertines

Halfway into the second song, 'Boys in the band', security appeared on the stage, halting the band and asking for the crowd to move back.

Peter steps up to the microphone and pleads, "we can't carry on if you don't calm down a bit", while motioning for them to move away from the stage. After another false start the show eventually got underway again, luckily I don't believe that anyone was seriously injured but for a while it had the potential to turn very bad. Later in the show the band had to stop again as fans began climbing the relay towers supporting the speakers further back into the crowd. The fans hunger to see The Libertines was evident and it was just the beginning of a period that saw them release their third album 'Anthems for Doomed Youth' and become bigger than ever.

"You caught me in the middle dazed on the carpet
I was following the lines, that move like more snakes thinking
Something ain't quite right
You got the devil on your side, standing to your right come on

I get along singing my song,
People tell me I'm wrong...
Fuck 'em!"

I get along, The Libertines

As the final notes of 'I get along' die in the air, the four Libertines, Barat, Doherty, Hassall and Powell assemble at the front of the stage, hokey cokeying, hugging and jumping on each other, the love and excitement evident on each and every face, fan, crew, band.

Drummer Gary Powell grabs the microphone shouting, "you are all amazing and you are all Libertines."

Carl Barat and Pete look at each other and turn to the audience beginning to recite the words of Siegfried Sassoon's 1918 poem 'Suicide in the trenches'.

"I knew a simple soldier boy
Who grinned at life in empty joy,
Slept soundly through the lonesome dark,
And whistled early with the lark.
In winter trenches, cowed and glum,
With crumps and lice and lack of rum,
He put a bullet through his brain.
No one spoke of him again.

You smug-faced crowds with kindling eye
Who cheer when soldier lads march by,
Sneak home and pray you'll never know
The hell where youth and laughter go."

Siegfried Sassoon, Suicide in the trenches, 1918

· · · · ·

I close my eyes, feeling the pain threatening to burst from them in a torrent of tears. I am so tired, the guilt and self hatred that has accompanied me throughout my life washes over me. The doubt and confusion about who I am. The survivor guilt from Andy's accident in the RAF and the resulting PTSD. The years of self harming and suicidal feelings. The loneliness of being emotionally disconnected even within my marriage. The stress and hurt of losing my business, of letting people down.

"It's time," he says, his insidious words weaving their web of deceit around my heart.

"I'm so tired, I can't do it anymore," I reply.

"I know, it's been so long and you really need to end it."

"I can't, the kids, Dawn, my family."

"They won't miss you, they'll all be better off without you. Imagine their lives free of your influence, finally set free from your negativity and pain."

I feel the black void beside me growing, mist like tendrils reaching out to engulf me, embrace me, pulling me towards its dark, cold heart.

"Don't be scared," he says, "it's time".

2ND HALF
FOUND

"Perfer et obdura, dolor hic tibi proderit olim."
"Be strong and patient, someday this pain
will be useful to you."

Ovid, 16-15BC

11

THE GIRL FROM MARS

The dark clouds hang low over the skyline of Victorian sandstone houses, mirroring the rock of the homes blackened by generations of pollution and wear. Sleet falls mingling with the remnants of snow bordering the roads and railway lines as people make their way to work. The two main stands of Bradford City's Valley Parade stadium dominate the view across the city towards Daisy Hill and the west.

I stare from my window, numb, my mind searching the horizon for something, anything. The void between me and my home and family 300 miles to the south seems so much further than the physical distance of tarmac, the roads and motorways that I had travelled a few days earlier in order to photograph a brace of Cherries fixtures in our race for promotion to the Premier League.

Back-to-back matches against Rotherham and Leeds United meant that it was both economically prudent and time sensible for me to stay in the Ibis Budget hotel in Bradford rather than endure two 600 mile round trips in the space of a few day. The clean, adequate but uninspiring room is a prison cell for the condemned man, a feeling intensified by the forboding black clouds and unwelcoming weather outside the window.

My demon is an ever present companion, never straying too far, constantly ready to undermine me. I don't know how much longer I can do this, I feel exhausted, ground down by pain and his continual destructive, abusive love.

My mind searches for release, an answer, why? Why can I not get beyond this moment? Why can I not release the pain? Why?

The happiness that surrounds me, family, friends, love, always seems to elude me, passing close enough that I can hear its mocking laughter but never inviting me to partake of the joy.

There is something broken inside me, something that makes it impossible for me to be happy, content, secure, at peace. It's been broken for such a long time and I really don't believe that it would ever be possible to fix it.

Something has to change. My life cannot continue like this.

I must either change my life, or end it.

There is no other path left, no way out, no excuses, it's time.

Looking in the mirror I am filled with revulsion at the person staring back. Who is it? I don't recognise them but I know that they're not me. The self hate and depression has led to food abuse, self harming through eating, ballooning up to 23 stone. I hate myself so I eat, with no thought of what it might do to me, seeking the mood modification that comes with eating, seeking comfort and solace in calories. The more I eat the more weight I put on, the more weight I put on, the more I hate myself. It becomes the perfect cycle of self hate, food and weight gain. One feeding the other and consuming me as quickly as I consume the calories.

The only place that I see myself, reflected in the mirror, is buried deep within the lonely, frightened and tired eyes. Their blue irises like two cold pools of icy water in which to drown myself.

I'm struck by a thought, a realisation, a revelation, a moment of clarity through the fog.

"That's why you hate yourself so much," I tell myself.

"But it can't be, that's gone, dead and buried, years ago. It will destroy everything."

"Will it?"

"I can't do it."

"Why not?"

"I can't, Dawn, the kids, my family, work…"

"You may not have a choice. This is the only way, you can't put this off any longer, it's time, choose… life or death?"

There it was, the million dollar question, life or death?

Which was I most scared of? The unending void of death or the pain of living?

And so, I'm sure, like many weary travellers before me, I sat in the Hotel Ibis Budget in Bradford, and wondered where my life had gone wrong.

Except that I had the answer, and as painful as it was, I had no choice.

I choose life. I choose Sophie.

· · · · ·

A couple of hours later I return to the hotel room after a shopping expedition that saw me purchase makeup and a beautiful 1950s style floral dress with tight black top and flared floral skirt. There was also a brown, shoulder length wig that had taken an age to choose under the helpful guidance of a young Asian lady, who did an amazing job of keeping me at ease despite the bemused attention of some of the other customers.

After a close shave I begin to apply the heavy foundation that I'd used in a long forgotten life, powder, blush, eye shadow, eye liner, mascara and lipstick. Nerves threatening to overwhelm me, I check my reflection in the mirror noticing for the first time that my once lifeless and dull eyes now glow with a fire and radiance that has been absent for decades.

Sophie had been dead and buried for 15 years and the resurrection wasn't going to be painless. Far from being a zombie rising from the grave she had a thirst for life, finally escaping from the emotional wasteland in which Steve had been lost for so many years.

There were some difficult conversations ahead of me but I felt sure that my family would continue to love and support me, after all Dawn had been prepared to stay with me when I tried to transition all those years earlier.

• • • • •

"We've got to talk," Dawn and I were stood in the kitchen, the kids were still at school but would be home soon. "I've really been struggling lately."

My depression and detachment had been growing for a number of years and I was beginning to spend as many nights crying myself to sleep on the sofa downstairs, feeling lost and alone, than I was in our bed. We still cared for each other but for some reason the gulf between us seemed to be getting wider all of the time.

"I've been having bad thoughts, thinking of suicide, and I think the only way to stop it is for me to transition," I said, trying to hold back the tears.

"I always knew that it would come back," Dawn replied, gazing absently out of the kitchen window.

"I'm sorry, I tried, I really did. This past fifteen years has been so hard, I love you and the kids but if I don't do this then I think that it's going to kill me."

• • • • •

Over the coming weeks I began to dress a little when the kids were at school and whilst she was supportive to a point I could tell that Dawn was going to struggle with my transition in a way that she didn't nearly two decades earlier.

"I don't want you dressing at home, I don't want the kids to see it," she told me one day.

"What do you suggest?"

"I don't know, I just don't want it here."

"Do you want me to move out?" It certainly wasn't what I wanted but I still had to do everything that I could to protect my family, even if it meant leaving them.

"Maybe, for a bit, just to give everyone time to get used to it."

Tears started to roll down my face. "I love you."

"I know, and I love you too but I can't do this at the moment, it won't be forever, this will always be your home."

At that moment I really believed that, at that moment I saw a future where we would be together forever, our family, together just a little different.

I saw a future.

. . . . .

I began searching for somewhere to go, away from Bournemouth, where I could learn who I was and finally allow Sophie to inhabit this body. On a transgender website I found a house share in Birmingham, a double room in a three bedroom house in a nice area of the city, £350 per month, all bills included, I showed Dawn the pics and got in touch with the landlady.

Barely a month after my epiphany in Bradford, and a week after telling the kids that I was going to be working away for a bit, I arrived at my new, supposedly temporary, home. It sat at the end of a cul-de-sac near Bournville on the outskirts of the city. An area famous for the Cadbury's chocolate factory that had made its home in the village since the late 19th century and where George Cadbury, a Quaker who believed in treating his employees with dignity and respect, had built a model village designed to 'alleviate the evils of modern, cramped living conditions'.

My new home was of later construction, it was spacious and clean but there was a surprise in store for me. I had been expecting to be lodging with a family, my landlady was married and she'd told me about her son and the fact that she was pregnant expecting their second child. However when I arrived at the house it was deserted, entirely vacant, with no signs of life save for a few pieces of furniture. It definitely wasn't the bustling family home that I had been expecting.

"Oh, I don't live here," my landlady explained to me, "I live a couple of miles away, this is where I work".

"What do you do?"

"I'm a dominatrix and occasionally I'll see my clients here, in the spare bedroom but I'm not working much at the moment", she said, stroking her pregnant belly.

"OK", I replied, a little stuck for words, well what do you say when your landlady tells you that you've just rented a room in a house that's used as a BDSM dungeon, "cool".

As it turned out she really wasn't working much at all and over the coming weeks I never saw her, effectively giving me full run of a three bedroom house for a knock down price. I set up my laptop on the kitchen table and began to build a new website, for Sophie Cook, photographer.

· · · · ·

AFC Bournemouth were still pushing for promotion to the Premier League and whilst I was Sophie during the week in Birmingham at weekends I would travel to shoot the club's matches around the country as Steve. Home matches were particularly welcome as it meant a trip home to see Dawn and the kids. Each time I would feel the need to drive closer and closer to my destination before shedding Sophie and transforming back into Steve. At first I would stop in a layby in the New Forest, 20 or so miles from Bournemouth, climb into the back of my VW van and get changed, taking off my wig and makeup, dress and sandals, and donning the jeans and t-shirt that I felt so uncomfortable in. Within a few weeks I was stopping around the corner, barely a few hundred yards from the house, it pained me so much to revert to being Steve that I did everything that I could to minimise the time that I had to endure.

I was always very careful to ensure that all traces of makeup were removed and that there was nothing to give me away but people began to realise that something was different.

The first change that people noticed was my weight loss. Having spent a lifetime hating everything about my body and finally resorting to abusing food, both as a mood modifier and as a form of self harm, my weight had ballooned up to 23 stone. The further that Sophie retreated into my being, the more walls of fat I added to the prison of flesh around her.

For the first time I was beginning to care about myself and this led me to start eating healthily. Cutting out the carbohydrates that had formed the majority of my pre-Sophie diet, the bread and pasta were joined on my banned list by rice and potatoes, and soon the weight began to fall off me.

As the weight fell, I also found that the joint pain that had restricted my exercise reduced, enabling me to start running again, further adding to my motivation to look after myself.

By May when we achieved promotion, just four months after my epiphany in the hotel in Bradford, I had shed five stone. When the end of season awards at the football club came around none of my tailor made suits fitted me any more and I don't think that the club was ready for me to turn up wearing an evening dress so I had to go shopping for a new suit, scouring the charity shops in the knowledge that this would be my one and only time wearing it before I came out.

I also got both of my ears pierced, an act that got noticed, even in the blingy world of professional football, and I began to smile.

I honestly wonder if anyone had ever truly seen me smile for years, there was always a pain underlying it before, but now my joy of self discovery was beginning to shine through, even on the days when I was in man drag as Steve.

· · · · ·

Back in Birmingham I was eager to prepare myself for a life after coming out.

I began to visit the gay village, finally free to be myself, and I found a home in The Village Inn on Hurst Street. During the day I would sit at the bar drinking coffee and responding to emails, chatting to the staff and customers alike, building my confidence in being me. On the nights that I went out I met some amazing characters that soon became friends, including the resident drag queen, Charlotte the Harlot.

Following a lifetime in the closet it felt amazing to be me, out in the world, free to express myself, to dance and laugh. I was like a prisoner finally set free after a life sentence was unexpectedly commuted, pardoned and released.

From being a depressed, self harming introvert I was suddenly the most ebullient of extroverts, vivacious and open, ready to speak to anyone and everyone, ready to begin living.

· · · · ·

Sophie: Felt great last night, feel depressed now. Probably going to delete my profiles from all the various transgender websites as I've decided that I don't want what's being offered to me on them. Is this what cis women have to put up with? The only way that I'm going to be able to make my transition worthwhile is by being proud of who I am, not by being degraded.

Lexus: Women get offered cock so many times a day it's untrue. Here let me hold that door for you (want some cock), oh Sophie I really like that name (want some cock), I'm not like the others, I'm interested in you as a person (as long as I can give you some cock). It's so boring, there's been times I've actually thought a guy was doing alright, he's not mentioned it once. Then they've got pissed and plucked up the courage to send me a nasty cock picture, and that was the last time they ever spoke to Lexy haha.

Jet: Good for you honey! There's far too many people that seem to think that Transgender Girls are easy targets, they don't seem to realise that we have enough to worry about. These idiots are not worth getting upset over.

Sophie Cook, Facebook, March 5, 2015

. . . . .

The first time that I received an unsolicited dick pic I was more bemused than outraged and certainly not feeling the arousal that the sender hoped to illicit.

Is this what men thought women wanted to see? Or did they just do this to trans women who were neither seen as women nor deserving of real human interaction. I was to discover as my transition progressed there was no shortage of men that were attracted to transgender women, that fetishised us and treated us like their sexual fantasies built around the falsities of the pornography industry, but there were very few that would acknowledge that attraction openly and engage in a real, caring relationship with them for fear of being labelled as… well, who knows.

I was continually being surprised and shocked by some of the behaviour and attitudes that I saw exhibited by men, not just to trans women but to all women and I began to understand a little about why women were often inclined to stay in relationships despite appalling treatment from their supposed loved ones.

"Well he doesn't hit me", I was horrified that the absence of domestic abuse was seen as the standard required for a relationship in many cases, that some women saw it as being so difficult to find a 'good man' that they were happy to accept one that was prepared to emotionally control them simply because he didn't resort to physical violence.

Men and women can be very different creatures and they often have differing needs in a relationship, obviously I can't generalise too much but it's worth remembering that most stereotypes start from either a basis of fact or a basis of bigotry.

Brain chemistry affects so much of our personality and behaviour, I know for a fact that my wants and needs in a relationship are very different now that my brain is full of estrogen than when it was full of testosterone, my sexual appetite has changed, so too has my emotional connection to the world around me. Another big problem when it comes to behaviour around relationships is societal and cultural references. The patriarchy fails both our daughters and our sons.

Our daughters are told that they are worth less than their male siblings, that they are weaker, less intelligent, less capable and that their life opportunities will be limited by their position in society.

Our sons are given unrealistic and unattainable standards of masculine perfection that they struggle to achieve. They are told that they must not show weakness, physical or emotional, that they must be brave and strong and this is a direct contributor to poor mental health and high levels of suicide within young men.

It also instills in our son's a sense of entitlement and superiority that makes it difficult for them to build meaningful relationships in their lives. When you couple this sense of entitlement with popular culture that over sexualises women and celebrates rape culture then you begin to see why some men find it difficult to see why a dick pic might be offensive.

In these days of constant 24/7 internet connection, social media, instant messaging, free high definition porn streaming anything that your heart, and other body parts, might desire straight to your mobile device it's worth remembering that if a certain behaviour is unacceptable in the real world then it surely must be online.

If it's wrong to abuse someone because of their race, religion, sexuality or gender identity on the street, then how can it be OK online?

If it's wrong to spread lies and slander on the street, then how can it be OK online?

If it's wrong to expose yourself to a stranger on the street, then how can it be OK online?

It is this separation between the real and the virtual world that has allowed the proliferation of internet trolls, feeling totally above the law and able to preach hate at will. When people feel that their actions take place in isolation, with no physical connection to the victim, and no fear of the consequences then the behaviour will continue unabated, continually escalating until something blows. We saw that with the way divisive, hateful rhetoric around the Brexit referendum led to the murder of Labour MP Jo Cox and we will see it again. Hate has consequences, and the virtual world has an impact on actions in the physical world.

. . . . .

Being self employed the temptation was to stay locked inside my new home in Birmingham, working away on my laptop at the kitchen table, only ever interacting with the outside world via email or phone. I soon realised that if I was going to do that then I would never build the confidence required to lead a full and rewarding life as Sophie.

To this end I set myself a series of rules:

- Put face on every day. It was essential that I find my own identity, I know that a lot of women don't wear makeup every day and some never wear it but I needed it to reinforce my identity to anyone that I met. I was misgendered, called 'sir' or 'he', enough even with makeup and I didn't want to increase the chances of that happening by appearing as anything less than my glamorous best. It's also a steep learning curve suddenly having to acquire all of the makeup and fashion skills that cisgender women spend a lifetime learning and I needed all of the practice that I could get.

- Go out every day, and not just to the gay village. If I was to ever find my place in the world then I would have to become comfortable in all situations and locations. I knew that I would always get a warm welcome in the LGBT bars and clubs around Hurst Street but I couldn't allow myself to begin my new life restricted to a ghetto of my own making. To live, to work, to succeed I had to be strong and venture outside of my rainbow tinted comfort zone.

- Talk to strangers every day. Transgender people are at their most vulnerable early in their transitions, they still retain a lot of their old looks, and they are liable to receive strange looks and unkind words at a time when they may be emotionally vulnerable. after the strain of coming out. The only way that I was going to build the strength and resilience to be out in the world was by interacting with people, chatting to the woman serving me in the supermarket, speaking to the guy behind the counter in the petrol station or ordering my coffee in a cafe. They all presented difficulties, fear of humiliation and abuse, but they all helped to build my confidence in my identity.

Transgender people have a concept called 'passing', the ability to go about your daily life without anyone realising that you are transgender, or 'reading' you. For decades this had been the panacea for trans people hoping to live a life free from prejudice, bigotry, abuse and violence. Some may achieve this, being blessed with the right bone structure, facial features or body proportions, for others, like me, it was always going to be a challenge.

Five decades of testosterone taking its toll on my body meant that my features had developed in a certain direction meaning that, no matter how hard I tried, I would always be 'read' as transgender.

The world can be a cruel place for a trans person, especially a transgender woman, seen as an aberration, a freak or a pervert, always the outsider, always the punchline of the joke.

During my time in Birmingham there were many occasions when I was attacked purely for being different. One such incident occurred when I found myself at a local parade of shops just as the neighbouring secondary school finished for the day. Walking past a group of around a dozen teenage boys one of them suddenly shouted, "It's a man", pointing at me and laughing.

His friends soon joined in, circling around me, laughing, jeering and shouting. One of them shouted "paedo" and spat at me.

The word hit me like a bullet, there are few words in the English language that can hurt as much, different races and religious groups have their own particular words that hurt more than others, for me "paedo", "rapist" or anything to do with racism are the ones that really hurt.

I kept my head down, walking briskly back to my car, locking the doors and driving straight home where I collapsed in tears. The pain of isolation hurting more than the words, only a few months earlier I had been married, living with my children, the photographer for a Championship football club, with friends and respect. Now I was an outcast, abused on the street with questionable prospects for any future happiness or even income, I'd applied for jobs at local supermarkets, stacking shelves and hadn't even been invited for interview.

As I said in my Facebook post: "The only way that I'm going to be able to make my transition worthwhile is by being proud of who I am."

. . . . .

The more abuse I got the more I questioned my self confidence, and the more I wondered what I'd thrown my whole life away for.

I'd been through hell to finally be me and I wasn't going to let anyone else's bigotry destroy me. I knew what I had been forced to endure, I knew how much pain and sacrifice. Rather than being ashamed of that journey I was determined to be proud that I had survived this far.Every single person that I was ever going to meet was always going to know that I was transgender, no matter how much weight I lost, no matter how my body responded to hormones, The younger that people are able to transition the better the physical results of their transition. I'd simply transitioned too late to undo the 50 years of male body development.

If I had any hope of ever returning to my life in Bournemouth as Sophie then I would need strength and conviction in my new identity. I would need to reject the shame and guilt at being transgender and fully embrace my journey, proud of myself and my struggle, and so I rejected the concept of 'passing'.

Sure I was going to do everything that I could to be the most attractive and amazing version of me that I could possibly be but it wasn't so that others could judge my identity as passing or not, it was for me, it was so that I could learn to love myself.

I didn't choose to be transgender but I could choose not to be a victim.

· · · · ·

International Transgender Day of Visibility (TDoV) is an annual event dedicated to celebrating the accomplishments of transgender and gender non-conforming people around the world and for raising awareness of the continuing fight for transgender rights. Founded in 2009 it sought to redress the lack of LGBT holidays celebrating transgender people.

March 31, 2015 was to be my first TDoV as my true self and I was determined to be visible.

In the front bedroom of the house in Bournville I applied my makeup, did my hair and dressed. I had no plans for the day, no events to go to, I was just going into town and interact with people, being visible, before heading to the Village Inn to celebrate my act of subversive pride.

Looking out of the window I was horrified to see a group of workmen tarmacing the pavement in front of my neighbours house. In all of the time that I'd been in the house I had never met my neighbours and certainly didn't feel ready to meet them and a gang of burly builders all at the same time.

My strength and confidence drained out of me and I slumped to the bed. I was proud of who I was but I didn't yet have the strength to face whatever may await me outside of that front door.

· · · · ·

"No, no, no!"

My sobbing wakes me, I'm shaking, I'm terrified.

"What have I done? I can't do this, I can't, I can't lose them."

I've made a terrible mistake, I love my family with all of my heart. My beautiful wife that I always thought I'd spend the rest of my life with, my amazing kids who I loved more than life itself. I was going to lose them and I couldn't bare the pain.

I know that I'm Sophie but the cost of transitioning is too high, I could go back, I could try again. Maybe I could be Sophie with them, this was my hope and my dream. The original plan had always been that I would go away to find my identity and then go home, to be with them. That could happen, Dawn had always told me that my exile "wasn't forever" and that the house in Poole would always be my home. I knew now that I needed that more than anything in the world, I needed my home, I needed my wife, I needed my children.

Climbing out of bed in a blind panic I begin pacing the house, "no, no, no".

Pulling some clothes on I immediately start grabbing my belongings and throwing them haphazardly into the back of my van, packing nothing, clothes thrown on the bed and carried to the waiting vehicle wrapped in the bedding.

Within thirty minutes every trace of Sophie is gone from the house. I place my keys and the final months rent on the kitchen counter together with an apologetic note to my landlady and, without looking back, lock the front door behind me.

Dialling Dawn the relief floods through me when she picks up.

"I can't do this, I can't live without you all, I'm coming home."

Fifteen years after I originally tried to transition my new life as Sophie had lasted two months.

· · · · ·

Back in Poole I immediately regress, it was wonderful being with my wife and children again, to hold my wife, to tuck my children in at night, to be with my family, but inside something was dying.

I'd never felt more alive than during my time in Birmingham, the world was big and scary but, for the first time in my life, I felt right, I felt whole. If only I could combine being Sophie with being with my family, that could happen, I was sure it could. Love would, after all, prevail.

Dawn, however, had other thoughts.

"The new, happy Steve can come back but I can't live with Sophie."

I was destroyed, yes I was happy now, my black moods had lifted and I was beginning to recover from a lifetime of mental anguish but the change had come because I was Sophie, Steve hadn't made that recovery, she had.

I loved my family, I couldn't live without them. What value was there in finding myself only to lose them? I could do this. I had done it before, for fifteen years I had suppressed Sophie, I had buried her for the sake of my family and I could do it again.

I packed my female clothes up, my dresses, tops and skirts, my underwear, my wigs, and stuffed them under the bed. My makeup and toiletries went into the bin.

For the second time in my life I erased Sophie, she had been my salvation but the price was too high for me to pay.

. . . . .

I threw myself into family life, decorating my office, making big plans, trying to find a direction.

The time apart had been hard but now I was back and I was going to make this work.

Our tenth wedding anniversary was approaching and I saw this as an apt time for renewal, a time to put the difficulties behind us and find the way forward for the next decade.

Dawn was distant, I'd hurt her, I knew that. She didn't know who I was and was confused about her feelings towards me. In some way she saw my gender identity as an invalidation of her as a woman. There was still a mutual love but something had changed, I had to try to fix it but I didn't know how.

She had been alone, she had been in just as much pain as I had, and in her search for solace she got in touch with an ex-boyfriend. Nothing happened but the discovery was like a knife through my heart.

My relationship with the woman that I loved, that I thought was my soulmate, that I believed I'd grow old with, was floundering and the guilt of knowing that this was all my fault was more than I could bare.

. . . . .

The house is dark and silent.

Climbing out of bed I feel for my clothes, pulling them on and quietly making my way out of the bedroom.

Downstairs the dog raises his head to look at me as I don my coat and shoes, I pat him on the head and give him a quick stroke along his back.

I pick up my keys and silently open the front door, step outside and close it behind me.

The night is cold and I can see my breath, shining orange in the light from the sodium bulbs that illuminate the street. Pulling my coat tight around me, I press play on my iPod and bury my hands deep into my pockets. Without direction I begin to walk.

Through empty streets, I march on, driven by pain and fear. The pain of loss, both of my marriage and of Sophie, and the fear that I caused all of this and the sure knowledge that there is no way in which I can fix it.

With no plan, no intention, I find myself walking along the promenade that borders the beach of the Sandbanks peninsula and my gaze falls to the dark, cold waters of North Haven Lake, extending out into Poole Harbour and the distant Brownsea Island flanked by the Purbeck Hills that rise, unseen, in the darkness.

I walk until I run out of land, pausing briefly at the slipway to the chain ferry that carries vehicles across the 400 yard stretch of water to the untouched beaches of Studland and on to Swanage. At this hour the ferry sits, deserted, moored on the far shore.

Turning south I follow the road back to the car park and the colonnaded beach huts that face the sea, unseen and hidden by a veil of fog that has descended, mirroring the fog that pervades my thoughts obscuring the way ahead in my life as surely as it obscures the breaking waves, heard but unseen, in front of me.

I'm tired, not just by the lack of sleep that has eluded me since my return from Birmingham, but tired of life.

I could walk into the dark embrace of the sea, never to return. To simply cease to be, lost forever under the waves that whisper to me as they gently caress the shoreline. Seeming to call me, inviting me to join them.

A black shape moves through the fog, four legged and low, a fox? A black dog?

It passes by me, close enough to see its form but impossible to identify in the half light of the smothering miasma.

"You know that it would be so easy."

The temperature seems to drop further as the dark void beside me begins to recite his litany of despair.

"They would be so much better off without you. You've destroyed everything, your marriage, your family. Everything that you've ever touched has withered and died."

The words make a valid point, the insidious message of failure.

"Neither man nor woman, what are you? What are you worth? Who could ever love you?"

I feel his presence growing and my heart turns to ice as his dark, misty tendrils reach for it, holding it, caressing it, filling it with anguish and pain.

"You can do it, now, one foot in front of another. Into the fog, into the sea. Like you were never here. It's for the best, you know it is. Don't worry, you won't be alone, I'll be there with you, like I always have. Together, finally, for eternity, no pain, just you and me and peace."

I stand without thinking, his words directing my muscles, my limbs.

The sea whispers its welcome a few feet ahead of me through the fog, the only sound in the world at that moment.

I take a step, then another, the sound of the waves gets louder with every step. The white tips of the breakers are now visible to me, they rise to say hello before falling, no longer single waves but a frothing mass of icy water.

"You can't be Steve and you can't be Sophie, you're lost, between two realities. Heart and mind, body and soul, forever mismatched, forever at war with each other. There is only one path, there is only one salvation, there is only one escape from the pain."

The sibilant voice caresses me, holds me in its thrall, directs my thoughts and movements.

"Come, be with me, now and always, free from pain, at peace."

I close my eyes, steadying my breath as I take a step.

My next step takes me further from the water as I turn and walk up the beach, away from the roiling surf, away from his black, despairing void, away from the darkness.

· · · · ·

Two hours later, as the day's first light breaks through the trees, I climb back into bed beside my sleeping wife. I know what I must do and I know that it's going to hurt.

12

TOGETHER ANYTHING IS POSSIBLE

While my personal life was imploding, back at AFC Bournemouth things couldn't be going any better. After a run of good results the final home match of the season against Bolton Wanderers gave us the opportunity to secure a Premier League future with one game remaining.

Ever the professional I stuck to the task in hand capturing all of the action as Marc Pugh, Matt Ritchie and Calum Wilson banged in the goals that would ensure promotion. Inside I was jumping around and celebrating as much as any other Cherries fan but on the outside I was restraint personified.

As the final whistle approached I packed up what kit I could and moved all of my equipment into the tunnel. I'd been part of a promotion only two years earlier and I knew that if I wasn't in position before the end of the match then I would be swamped by fans, all eagerly invading the pitch to celebrate with the triumphant team.

Nerves were running high in the dugout, every second stretched into minutes, waiting for the referee to blow time. Players and coaching staff were hugging each other, exchanging excited smiles and sharing the disbelief of the fans that this day had finally arrived for lowly Bournemouth.

I don't know which came first the whistle or the roar from the crowd which seemed to erupt as the referee raised it to his lips, within seconds the first fans were on the pitch, jumping on players, swamping them, hiding them from sight. Eddie Howe and the rest of the coaching staff headed straight into the changing room and a cordon of stewards formed around the entrance to the tunnel.

I waded into the crowd, capturing images as players emerged from the thronging mass, red faced and grinning. Tommy Elphick, our captain, appeared, head thrown back, screaming in joy as the tendons in his neck stood out with the exertion.

Back in the dressing room Sky Sports were setting up to interview the players, warning everyone that we were about to go live and therefore everyone should be careful not to swear. Matt Ritchie and Tommy were ushered forward and into position as the feed went live, players and coaching staff celebrating wildly behind them. The interview came to an end and the reporter was about to sign off.

"We'll let you go and enjoy it", he said looking at the jubilation behind him, as club chairman Jeff Mostyn bounced into shot, grinning wildly and throwing his arms around the players.

"We are going up," he shouted, ecstatic at the promotion.

"Oh my God, I love these fucking boys!"

Falling backwards into the throng of players Marc Pugh and Harry Arter lifted the chairman by his arms and legs and Calum Wilson appeared to smack his bottom as the camera cut back to the studio nestled between the North and West stands of the compact stadium where presenter Simon Thomas sat with a laughing Harry Redknapp.

"Apologies for that language but we quite understand, emotions understandably high here and why not on a famous night for Bournemouth football club."

The night may have been famous but the hangover the following day was legendary.

. . . . .

When we arrived at Charlton Athletic four days later we were still suffering from the promotion party, especially Yann Kermorgant, our French striker, whom I'd found stalking the Dean Court pitch following the Bolton match carrying the last remaining bottle of champagne.

"I'll have to get a photo of you spraying it", I told him.

"No, I will drink it", came the reply in his thick accent.

Watford were in pole position to win the Championship, they'd topped the table for weeks, and we would finish second, promotion already secure. All Watford required was a home win over Sheffield Wednesday and the title was theirs, but when the Yorkshire side equalised in the closing minutes of the game everything changed and Bournemouth finished the season as Football League Champions.

At the centre of the celebrations my mood was mixed. My marriage was falling apart, I was in danger of losing my family and with the realisation that I had to transition in order to save my life I feared that this would be my final match in the sport that I loved so much.

Walking off the Valley pitch that day, on the greatest day in the history of my club, a sense of impending doom overwhelmed me. I knew what had to happen but, as yet, I had no idea what the consequences would be.

· · · · ·

I'd already told Dawn that I was going to have to transition, that I had no choice if I ever wanted to end the pain that I had endured for as long as I could remember. Without this I was going to fall further and further into the abyss, the suicidal feelings would become more frequent and eventually it would finally destroy me. She had not been happy but she could see what damage it had been doing to me.

Now that it was decided it was time to tell the two most important people that were to be affected by my transition, Noel and Sadie.

Sadie was 11 years old going on 17 and, as such, was as obsessed by reality TV as any other teenager of her generation. She'd been watching the American show 'Keeping Up With The Kardashians' and as the story of Bruce Jenner's transition into Caitlyn began to make headlines Sadie's natural inquisitiveness led her to begin questioning the subject.

"Sadie's been asking all sorts of questions about it", Dawn told me one day, "do you think it's time to tell her?"

Never one to let an opportunity slip through my fingers, I knew only too well that it may not present itself again for a long time, if at all, I decided that we would tell the children that afternoon after school.

"You know the way that you've always known that you're a boy, Noel. And Sadie, you've always known that you're a girl."

They sat on the sofa, unsure of what to expect next.

"Well it was never like that for me. When I was growing up, I always felt that I should have been a girl and that caused me a lot of pain."

I explained to them how my mental health had been affected over the years and how much happier I was now that I had decided to live as Sophie. I told them that I would always be their parent and that I would always, always love them.

I had dropped a hand grenade into the heart of my family and now all that I could do was to wait and see what happened.

Noel was his usual laconic self and expressed no opinions until asked directly, "is that OK?" to which he just smiled, looked sheepish and replied "yes".

Sadie on the other hand began screaming, "No! No!" All the while sobbing and staring at me in disbelief.

Over the next ten minutes or so she cycled through all five stages of the Kübler-Ross model of grief. First introduced by psychiatrist Elisabeth Kübler-Ross in her 1969 book 'On Death and Dying', the model was inspired by her work with terminally ill patients and as far as Sadie was concerned she had just faced the loss of her Father..

The five stages, and Sadie's reactions were, chronologically:

- Denial - "No! This isn't happening."
- Anger - "You can't do this!"
- Bargaining - "Please no! Please take it back, please make it right."
- Depression - "No…" as the screams subsided, she began sobbing, burying her face in a pillow.
- Acceptance - "What's in your makeup bag?"

This final question became her standard opener every time we saw each other for the next couple of years before she finally realised that it was always the same answer, "I'm 50 so it hasn't changed since the last time you asked". When you're older you find the products you like and then you stick with them, unlike Sadie who had drawers of the stuff, all categorised and sorted. I guess it's the teenage girl equivalent of my alphabetically arranged record collection so who am I to judge?

But what were they to call me, Sadie wasn't keen on Sophie, it was her best friends Mum's name, but I pointed out that I'd been Sophie for longer than she'd been alive.

'Dad' felt like it might be inappropriate in certain social situations and I felt uncomfortable asking them to call me 'Mum' since they already had a perfectly good one of them. I suggested a hybrid contraction of 'Mummy' and 'Daddy', coming up with 'Maddy' or 'Dummy', both suitably disrespectful and highly appropriate for me.

Finally we settled on 'Cooky', the nickname that I'd had since childhood and which Dawn had always used for me. It took a while to settle in though and one afternoon as I enjoyed the sun in the back garden Noel leant over the garden fence to inform the neighbours that "My Daddy's a lady".

Luckily I'd already told them and Noel wasn't inadvertently outing me to all and sundry.

That night I posted an update on my 'Sophie' Facebook profile telling all of my new friends about my coming out.

· · · · ·

Well, it's done, came out this afternoon to my 14 year old son and 11 year old daughter. After a few tears my daughter has now pinched half my makeup and bags, tried to rename me and my son still wants me to play cars with him. I've just given the kids their first goodnight kiss as their second Mum, in my shorty PJs with nail polish selected by my daughter - happiest day of my life xx

Sophie Cook, Facebook, April 25, 2015

. . . . .

As the season drew to a close I once again moved out of the family home and rented a bedroom in a shared flat above a cafe in Brighton. Dawn and I had tried to find a way to keep the family together and I even suggested, more out of desperation than any sense of practicality, that we convert my garden office into a self-contained flat for me to live in. The idea being that I'd still be close to home but have the space to continue my transition.

It looked good on paper but I quickly realised that it could have a devastating effect on my mental health, exiled to the bottom of the garden, spectating on my family's lives from afar, there but absent.

As soon as I arrived in Brighton I felt at home. I had loved the city since childhood, the scene of The Who's Quadrophenia, it was the spiritual home of the Mods and was famous for its diversity and vibrant LGBT community.

After years of isolation I finally found myself amongst people like me, I had found my tribe. I was overwhelmed by the richness of life within the LGBT community and my diary was soon full of events, social, educational and cultural. Within days I was attending a 'Trans Poetry Evening', something that I could never have imagined a few weeks earlier, and later that evening visited Brighton's famed queer venue The Marlborough for the first of many times.

Chatting away to the customers and staff I met a young Spanish woman who introduced herself as Laura. She had been at the poetry event and was feeling a bit isolated and alone in the pub as she didn't know anyone there, I told her that I felt the same and asked her if she wanted to play pool. It transpired that we were both as bad at pool as each other and the game lasted long enough for us to get to know each other.

Laura explained to me that she was gender fluid, a term that was new to me. She explained that she felt like a mix of male and female, some days feeling more masculine and others more feminine. She was a photographer as well and we began chatting about art and made plans to meet up for a day out taking photos, using each other as models.

When the day arrived I drove us along the coast to Worthing and over a couple of hours we became firm friends discussing everything from our gender identities to love, politics, art, history, music, films, oh and we also did some photography.

I told her how I felt like I was finally at home in Brighton, free to be myself after being so exposed in Birmingham.

"Yeah, you've got to work really hard to stand out in Brighton."

Over that summer we became firm friends, bonding during long summer evenings sat on the beach talking about anything and everything. We were both financially limited and the cheaper we could make our evenings the better. She became the person that I confided everything to, my life, my marriage, my mental health, my fears and dreams.

Together we helped each other to become more secure and confident in our identities, sharing ideas about what it felt like to be transgender or gender fluid, questioning each other, building our strength and self esteem. For the first time in years I didn't feel alone, isolated by my secret, she was the first person that learnt who the real Sophie was and we became like family.

I finally felt good about myself, my weight was continuing to fall and I began running regularly. The early morning jogs along the seafront, past brightly painted beach huts and the glorious decay of the crumbling West Pier did as much to improve my mental health as my fitness. My heart felt free, here in the city that had become my sanctuary, my home, I began to fix myself.

· · · · ·

There are many things that can be uncomfortable for a transgender woman transitioning later in life. Things that you haven't had years to get used to like the underwiring from a bra stabbing you in the armpit or the discomfort of twisted tights but the one that was causing me most distress was the need to wear a wig.

Prior to my transition I'd always kept my hair short, attacking my head with clippers at the first sign of summer, shearing off all but a few millimeters of hair in an effort to keep my head cool. Additionally five decades of testosterone had given me male pattern baldness and my forehead had expanded as my hair started to slide off the back of my head.

Wearing a wig, day in and day out, can be uncomfortable and itchy and, as summer approaches, increasingly hot and sweaty. The matter was exacerbated by my new found interest in exercising and I was desperate to find an alternative.

One Friday afternoon in July I visited my local hairdresser to discuss the possibility of having hair extensions fitted, my own hair had started to grow and was deemed long enough to be suitable for bonding to the hair of a very nice Russian lady, I'm assuming that she's very nice, I've never met her but she did sell me her hair so that's good enough for me.

"I can fit them now if you want," she, the hairdresser, not the Russian lady, said.

Well, as we've previously established, I'm not one to let an opportunity slip through my fingers. This was my chance to ditch the wigs and have a full head of hair. It would look better and it would certainly feel better and help my confidence.

"God yes," I replied, excited, "let's do it!"

The hairdresser carefully began colour matching swatches of the extensions to my hair, selecting the required length and preparing the equipment required. My hair was washed and separated strand by strand in order for the extensions to be bonded onto my own hair by way of a crimp, not at all dissimilar to the ones that we had used on aircraft years before. As she worked her way around my head, row by row of hair slowly transformed with the addition of the new extensions, this was going to look amazing… but.

But I was due to be back at AFC Bournemouth on Monday morning, photographing the team's return for pre-season training. It suddenly dawned on me that there was no going back now, it was impossible for me to continue pretending to be Steve now that I couldn't simply remove a wig.

I had to tell the football club, I had to come out.

Frantically I tried to contact my boss at the club, commercial director Rob Mitchell. No response to email, out of office, not answering his phone, voicemail, Facebook messenger, all no answer.

. . . . .

As I pulled my car onto Dawn's drive having just driven from Brighton to see the kids the phone rang. I applied the brake and killed the engine as I hit the answer button on the steering wheel.

"Hi Steve, it's Rob Mitchell, just got your message. Sorry I couldn't get back to you sooner, I'm at a family barbecue and I've just popped out to call. Is anything the matter?"

Is anything the matter? Well there might be in about sixty seconds time I thought. This was it, this was the moment of truth, the next few minutes would probably mean the end of my career in football. Say goodbye to the Premier League because you're not invited. There'd never been an openly transgender woman working in professional football before and I really didn't expect that to change with me.

"Thanks for calling Rob, I'm really sorry to do this to you at a family barbie but I've got to tell you something before Monday."

Dawn was banging on the living room window and waving at me. I gestured back with the universal hand signal for phone, holding my fist by my right ear and extending the thumb and little finger to imitate a handset, mouthing the words, "I'm on the phone".

I was later to discover that she already knew that, I was on handsfree and not only could she hear my conversation but so could half of the street meaning that I came out to the whole neighbourhood at the same time as coming out to the football club, very efficient.

"What's up?", he asked, sounding concerned.

I took a deep breath, steeled myself and just said it.

"I'm transgender."

At this point perceptions and memories vary depending on which end of that phone call you were on. For my part I felt like I'd stepped off a cliff but rather than falling I floated in a dark void, all time stopped. My past, present and future all colliding, twisting and tangling together. The great times that I'd had with the club, the triumphs, the pain, the goals and the fans, the dream of the Premier League. They bombarded me as a sense of loss overwhelmed me, this was it, I'd lost everything.

On the other end of the line, separated by a dozen miles and a lifetime of pain, Rob was trying to process what he'd heard. Trying to work out what this meant for me, for the club, and what it meant for the future.

A year or so later Rob would be in the audience at a conference as I was retelling the story of this phone call and afterwards he approached me and asked: "Do you remember what I said next?"

"No", I replied, "I was sort of freaking out at that point."

"Because you'd lost so much weight so quickly and because you needed to talk to me so urgently we all thought that you were dying. So when you told me I replied 'is that all?'"

So there you have it, Premier League football club says that it's better to be transgender than dying, and you know what? I'm inclined to agree, even if that wasn't always the case.

· · · · ·

Sitting in my car, parked in my usual parking space, I looked across at the football stadium. Dean Court had been a second home to me and I was going to miss it if things didn't go my way.

I lowered the sun visor and checked my makeup in the vanity mirror, looking good, well here we go.

Walking into the main reception wearing a pencil skirt and heels was something that I had never imagined yet here I was. I'm not sure which was more of a fantasy, me, a transgender woman arriving for a meeting about her future at the club or the fact that AFC Bournemouth were now a Premier League club.

"Hi there, Sophie," beamed the receptionist. "The meeting's upstairs, in the owner's box. You're the first here, so feel free to grab yourself a drink."

Upstairs I poured myself a coffee and walked across to the glass sliding doors that opened onto the seating area outside the owner's box. The sun cast the long shadow of the West Stand almost to the edge of the penalty area along the length of the pitch, green and lush, freshly laid and ready for Premiership football.

"Sophie, how are you?"

Club chairman, Jeff Mostyn, burst into the room, ebullient as ever. Jeff's one of those men that if they're not the life and soul of the party then you know that something serious is going down.

"I'm good thanks Jeff, great to see you."

He leant in, put his arms around me in a big hug and gave me a peck on the cheek.

"Thank you so much for coming in to see us."

"No, thank you", I replied, genuinely moved to be back at the club and having this conversation.

Rob had arrived with Jeff and we were soon joined by my immediate boss, the head of media Max Fitzgerald, and general manager Liz Finney.

"Apologies, Sophie, but we'll have to wait a few minutes before we begin the meeting," said Liz. "Eddie and Jason have asked to join us, and they've not quite finished training."

I wasn't expecting our manager Eddie Howe and his assistant, Jason Tindall, to be at the meeting, still hopefully it was a good sign.

"Looking great, by the way", Liz added.

A few minutes later there was a knock on the door and the two track-suited coaches arrived.

"Hello Sophie", Eddie Howe said as he shook my hand and took a seat.

Increasingly in society many people know someone who's gay, a friend or relative, but the majority of people still don't have personal experience or knowledge of a transgender person. We never had the conversation but I'm pretty sure that I was the first trans person that most, if not all, of the people in that room had ever knowingly met. I have no idea if they were expecting David Walliams to walk in and declare "I'm a lady", but I hope that I presented a classier persona than that.

Rob began the meeting and explained our recent phone call, going on to explain that the club would be supportive of my transition and that they were happy for me to continue working as club photographer if that was what I wanted.

My contract was to change and I would only be shooting home games from now on. While I had always loved visiting other grounds, and had been looking forward to Premier League away days, I'd already realised that away matches represented the greatest danger for me. The club could try to protect me at home, hopefully the Cherries fans would get used to me but there was no guarantees at away grounds where I could be open to all sorts of abuse and hate. It was a compromise on my contract but one that I felt I could live with, after all I was more than pleasantly surprised that I still had a job at all.

Rounding off the meeting the chairman addressed us all, praising me for my honesty and courage, before asking Eddie if he had anything to add. Our manager looked me straight in the eye and asked: "What can I do to make things easier for you?"

When people come out they can't expect everyone to understand immediately but if your boss asks you what he can do, personally, to make things easier for you then you couldn't ask for more.

With that question he showed me that, no matter how high the club climbed, I was still a valued member of the team, respected and appreciated. A sign of solidarity that mirrored our club motto of 'Together anything is possible'. Words that encapsulated our rise from the bottom of League 1 to the Premier League and that I hoped would apply to the impossible dream that a transgender woman could have a place in football.

"I need to meet the players", I told Eddie, "the first time that they see me shouldn't be as they run down the tunnel".

The business of the meeting over we chatted for a while and I told the club's leadership a little about my journey, the mental anguish, the self harming and suicidal feelings.

Each revelation was met with genuine care and empathy and I began to believe.

Together, anything is possible.

. . . . .

I can feel the eyes on me as they run past.

Keeping my head down, I focus on what I'm doing, trying not to make eye contact.

Assembling camera bodies and lenses, inserting memory cards and attaching straps, checking settings and adjusting film speeds. These had become automatic movements for me, processes that I could carry out in my sleep. Muscle memory guiding my hands across familiar equipment in actions that I had performed so many thousands of times in a different life, different hands. These hands, these fingers had changed since they last performed these functions, the nails had grown and now sported bright nail varnish, the colour of Bournemouth's shirts. Cherry red.

The players begin warming up at the far end of the training pitch that lies to the south of AFC Bournemouth's home, Dean Court. I remember the days when this was home to a miniature railway complete with a stone railway station and steam trains that I would be allowed to ride, as a treat, in my childhood. The land had stood empty and derelict for almost a decade before the club's rise finally made it viable to construct new training facilities on the site.

Picking up my camera I walk across the pitch to a lone figure stood watching the squad from the centre of the training ground. Dressed in black jeans and trainers, the only change to my matchday attire is the figure hugging long sleeve t-shirt that shows off my developing curves and new svelte figure.

As I approach Eddie Howe turns to me and smiles.

"Sophie, great to see you. How are you today?"

"I'm good thanks Eddie."

"Scared?"

"A few butterflies maybe", I reply, "but not scared. If anything, I feel excited. For the first time in my life I'm totally at ease with who I am. I don't have to hide anymore."

"Great to hear that", he smiles. "Come on, let's get this done."

The assistant manager Jason Tindall blew a whistle, calling the squad together as Eddie and I approach. A few of the players smiling and chatting away to each other as they look in my direction.

Stood beside Eddie and I, Jason addresses the circle.

"I suppose you've noticed that our photographer has changed a bit since last season", Jason grins, gesturing towards me. "She's lost loads of weight and grown her hair, I'd like you all to meet Sophie."

My heart stops.

What would happen next? This was uncharted territory.

Ever the leader and, equally, the gentleman our club captain Tommy

Elphick steps forward, flashes me a smile and begins to clap. Within moments the rest of the players follow suit, applauding me and expressing their best wishes, respect and support.

I look at Tommy who is still smiling broadly and mouth "thank you".

"Right, boys", yells Tommy, "let's go train. Lots of work to do".

"Is that it?" I ask myself as Eddie, Jason and the players return to running drills and testing fitness levels.

I'd built this moment up so much in my head, I'd worried about it and now it was done. The least I expected was rainbows and unicorns, a marching band and maybe a Red Arrows flypast.

But the club had handled it perfectly. It shouldn't be a big thing, in fact, the less attention and drama the better. Keep calm and carry on. The reality was that the players had been given a new piece of information, that's all it was. It didn't directly affect them so why did it need to be a big thing.

In fact when anyone comes out, about their gender identity or sexuality, that's all that it is, a new piece of information. No drama, no hysterics, ok we've got it, now let's move on. Too many people feel entitled to express an opinion about someone else coming out, despite it not affecting them personally in any way.

Picking up my camera I wander across to the edge of the pitch, close my eyes and breath in the fresh summer air as the sun shines, bright and warm, on my face.

"Soph, make sure you get some decent shots of me", jokes Jason Tindall as he jogs past. "I've spent weeks working on this suntan."

"'I'll try my best", I laugh, aiming my camera at his laughing face, adjust the focus, and press the shutter, just as I'd done countless times before.

Nothing, and everything, had changed.

13

OUT IN ALBION

My finger hovers over the button, a sense of impending catastrophe severing the connection between my brain and the muscles that should be making my finger descend on the enter key.

I check the screen for what seems like the hundredth time. Is that paragraph clear? Do I make my point there? How will people react to that sentence?

Taking a deep breath I post the status and walk away from the computer.

In a server room, thousands of miles away, my keystrokes are converted into binary, translated into letters, words, sentences and posted as a status update on Steve's Facebook account.

. . . . .

This will be my last ever Facebook post for reasons that will become apparent below.

Since January this year I have lost 5 stone and 12" off my waist, I have done this through cutting out carbs and exercising.

But the greatest contributing factor to sorting my health out was getting my head right.

Over the past 15 years I have suffered from depression, every single day a little voice in my head would suggest how easy it would be to end it all, even on good days, totally out of the blue. I hated myself and I self harmed with food, eating crap because I hated my body and then hating my body even more because of the crap I'd eaten.

In January I realised that the negative thoughts all stemmed from a condition that I'd lived with all of my life but had never been able to seek assistance for.

I am transgender, all of my life I have felt like a woman, I know that I've hidden it well but that's what you do when you have to repress your true nature.

I tried getting help with it 15 years ago but stopped after our son, Noel, was born with a disability as I didn't feel that I could put my family through this at the same time as dealing with his issues.

Since coming to this realisation and accepting it my mental state has been transformed, I like myself, I'm happy and I even smile - my family said that I'd been a miserable sod for the past 15 years (at least!).

I'm currently being treated for my dysphoria, and I'm now living full time as a woman.

Gender Dysphoria is a chromosomal condition, caused in the womb, it's not a mental condition and as such it should be treated like any genetic condition and not be stigmatised.

I have the full support, acceptance and love of my family and could not have wished for a better reaction from them.

I hope that my friends are open enough to support my change even if it isn't entirely understandable for them.

If you have any questions please don't hesitate to ask, I've spent too long keeping secrets and will be as candid with you as I can.

I sincerely hope, and believe, that this won't affect our relationship but if you do have an issue just unfriend me and you will never hear from me again.

If you do want to continue with me on this amazing journey called life please pop over to my new profile, Sophie Cook, and send me a friend request.

Thank you, in advance, for your understanding.

Steve Cook, Facebook, July 18, 2015

. . . . .

Once it was confirmed that I would continue to work for AFC Bournemouth I came to the realisation that I had to tell the world. I figured that there was nowhere to hide when you're sat on the touchline at a Premier League football match, it would soon be public knowledge and I should be the one to announce it.

There are very few things that I could possibly have announced on that Saturday morning in July that would have been more unlikely for my friends. No one had the slightest idea of my true gender identity. I was not seen as effeminate or flamboyant, all signs that are falsely attributed to transgender women. Women are not effeminate, women are feminine, to a greater or lesser degree, and I had always been forced to totally suppress any femininity in my personality.

I'd spent a few months surreptitiously testing my friendship group, posting updates about LGBT rights and then unfriending anyone that posted anything remotely homophobic. I also used these posts as bait to find potential allies and would send my 'coming out' status to them as a confidential private message. The overwhelming love and support that I received in response to these messages helped to build my strength in the days and weeks leading up to the full public announcement.

But the fear as I made that announcement was very palpable, the possibility of hate, humiliation and rejection high. As it transpired I needn't have worried and over the coming hours I received hundreds of friend requests on my new 'Sophie' Facebook profile and an avalanche of supportive messages.

$$\cdots\cdots$$

Richard: Dude! Your a dudette! Still awesome! Beer sometime, or do we have to have wine now?

Sophie: Richard, it's a glass of wine or fruit based drink for the lady, everyone knows that x

James: Doesn't change who you are and what you stand for. Good for you.

Tamara: Good post. Well done Sophie :-). And remember, the very few plonkers that disappear were, after all, just plonkers xxx

Paul: Total love and respect. Simple as that.

Ian: I admire your courage and no more being a miserable sod!

Maria: It takes guts and courage to do what you've done & be so honest about it. Wishing you and all your family every happiness for the future xx

Neil: Total respect for you... I can only imagine how difficult the last 15 years have been for you.

Sophie: Thank you Neil, it's not just the last 15 years it was my whole life, out the other side now and loving life.

Vicky: Inspiring x

Steve Cook, Facebook, July 18, 2015

$$\cdots\cdots$$

Now that I had crossed the Rubicon there was nothing left but to go for it and forge ahead with my new life.

The first, and for many transgender people, most important, step is to formally change your name.

But what name?

As a child I'd assumed the identity of Jenny but for whatever reason when I attempted to transition in 2000 I'd settled on Sophie. Many people have asked me where that name came from and to be honest I really couldn't tell you other than a wish to retain the same initials.

My mother had previously told me that both she and my eldest daughter didn't like the name Sophie to which I'd replied that I hadn't changed it legally yet and so it wasn't fixed in stone.

"We like Rhea," she informed me.

Rhea? The Titaness goddess of Greek mythology, daughter of the earth goddess Gaia and the sky god Uranus, sister and wife to Cronus, Greek mythology was quite incestuous. The mother of gods, goddess of female fertility, motherhood and generation.

Somehow it didn't seem to be entirely appropriate and besides, Rhea Cook sounded rubbish.

"Or Roxy," she added.

"Bloody hell Mum, I'm not a stripper!" I replied.

The year that I came out and changed my name, 2015, a record 85,000 people changed their name by deed poll in Britain. Unlike my fellow name changers Bacon Double Cheeseburger and Sarge Metal Fatigue I wanted something a little more traditional.

It was important to me that my new name was historically accurate, after all how many 50 year olds do you know called Beyonce?

So I turned, as always, to the internet for some help.

Most popular girls names 1967 (and their popularity in 2018)

1. Susan (Currently 1,525)
2. Julie (1,241)
3. Karen (1,689)
4. Jacqueline (1,834)
5. Deborah (544)
6. Tracey (3,609)
7. Jane (1,370)
8. Helen (622)
9. Diane (3,609)
10. Sharon (1,142)

I recognised so many of those names from my contemporaries at school, girls who rejected me, looked straight through me and called me names.

Incidentally Roxy, short for Roxanne, appears at number 29 in the list of most popular strippers names. The top five of which are Crystal, Tiffany, Amber, Brandy and Lola. Perhaps Lola might have been more appropriate thanks to The Kinks 1970 hit.

"Well, I'm not dumb but I can't understand
Why she walk like a woman and talk like a man
Oh my Lola, lo lo lo lo Lola, lo lo lo lo Lola
Well I'm not the world's most masculine man
But I know what I am and I'm glad I'm a man
And so is Lola
Lo lo lo lo Lola, lo lo lo lo Lola."

Lola, The Kinks, 1970

Not only that but Roxanne means 'dawn' and I didn't think selecting a new name that meant the same as my wives would have been appropriate.

There are no legal restrictions on the names available to you in the UK but authorities have been known to step in to block names that include numbers, punctuation marks, and symbols.

Likewise company or organisation names, blasphemous words and anything that infers a title or rank are out so a deed poll isn't the way to become a Doctor, Sir, or Admiral, they still need to be achieved the old fashioned way through years of work or perhaps a donation to the Conservative Party.

The name change can be done with a statutory declaration witnessed by a magistrate or solicitor but that all costs money and I decided to change mine by downloading the deed poll forms from the internet and then putting a call out on Facebook for anyone who was free to come and witness the forms.

And so Sophie Rose Cook was officially born on the kitchen table on July 21, 2015.

· · · · ·

A month earlier I had secretly come out to the other people that I regularly pointed my camera at, The Libertines. It had been seven years since I first started shooting Peter Doherty, and 11 months since the triumphal gig at Hyde Park, and I was keen to continue working with the band.

I sent my, by now, standard coming out message to Peter's manager, Adrian Hunter, a no nonsense Scot, and held my breath. Once again the news was greeted with a show of love and support that would become familiar to me over coming months and that led to what could almost be described as an addiction to 'coming out', the positivity that I received in response was that intoxicating.

· · · · ·

Hi all,

You may remember Steve Cook who has photographed Peter for years and more recently photographed The Libertines with Roger at Hyde Park and Ally Pally. Well Steve has messaged me this morning to very bravely tell me of a condition he has been living with for many, many years. The condition is gender dysphoria which led to Steve telling me that he is now living as a woman called Sophie.

Adrian Hunter, Email, 2/6/15

Hey Sophie!

How you doing! Adrian sent me an email telling me about your life change and I for one think that what you're doing takes a lot of courage and you should be extremely proud of yourself!!! Wish you all the very best in this new and exciting journey and let me know which Libertines shows you wanna come to and I'll make sure there's a AAA pass with your name on it! Look forward to seeing you. All the best!

Mario Galvan, Libertines tour manager

I for one fully support and salute her x
David Bianchi, Various Artists Management

Goes without saying. Full support here! x
Iain Slater, Libertines sound engineer

That's awesome! Total support here.
Gary Powell, drummer, The Libertines

· · · · ·

"You look like the Lara Croft of photography!"

This was Laura's first time backstage at a Libertines concert and I must admit that she had a point. With my standard all black stage wear, similar to what I would have worn as Steve but now fitted and showing off my curves, black scarf, hair tied up in a pony tail and a camera on each hip I did look like I was ready to raid any tomb in search of a great shot.

The Libertines compound behind the mainstage at the Reading Festival consisted of a group of portacabins containing production offices, dressing, crew and reception rooms. This was my first time back with the band following my transition and public announcement a month before.

As each member of the band and crew met me I was greeted with big hugs, congratulations and words of support. The only person that I hadn't managed to have a proper chat with was Peter who usually likes to spend a little time alone before he goes on stage. Stage time approached and the nervous energy of all involved began to climb, all except bass player John Hassall who, like many other bassists, was the calm centre of the universe allowing the madness to carry on without seemingly touching him.Mario stuck his head around the door announcing that the pre-set warm up film created by Roger Sargent was on the screens and that we would be on in a couple of minutes. En masse band, management and guests headed out of the compound and up the ramps that led to the stage where the crew were already in place, guitars in hand ready to hand off to the band. I captured a few images as the guys had their final huddle and headed over to the right wing, Peter's side, of the stage.

The final strains of Vera Lynn's 'We'll meet again' rang out as the band plugged in, Gary Powell settling in behind his drums and Peter and Carl laughing and joking.

"We'll meet again, don't know where, don't know when
But I know we'll meet again some sunny day."

We'll meet again, Vera Lynn

Gathered together in front of Gary's drums, Peter, Carl and John readied themselves as Gary marked out the time for the opening song.

"I've been following
Your minds instructions
Oh how just to slowly, sharply screw myself to death."

Horrorshow, The Libertines

An hour and a half of intense energy and 23 frenetic songs later, Carl was singing the lyrics of the final song as Peter fell backwards into Gary's drums, still playing, as the set came to an end.

"I get along just singing my song
People tell me I'm wrong
Fuck 'em!"

I get along, The Libertines

"And don't forget that you are all Libertines!" Gary shouted to the 90,000 strong crowd before bounding up to me and giving me a big, sweaty hug.

Knowing how difficult, almost impossible, it was to shepherd the guys together for a full band photo once they started relaxing after the show I jumped in and grabbed a few shots as they headed back to our compound and as Peter looked up at me he asked:

"And who's this beautiful young woman?"

Five years after they'd been forced off stage at the festival mid-song due to a crush in the crowd The Libertines had conquered Reading and I had survived my first gig back as Sophie.

. . . . .

Relaxing in a wooden summerhouse in the garden of The Boogaloo pub in Highgate, London following an intimate set at HMV's Oxford Street store, I shared a beer with Carl, John and Gary and told them my story. How I'd known that I was transgender since I was a kid, my mental health issues, the self harming and suicidal feelings. How I was now, for the first time in my life, comfortable with who I was.

I also told them how some of the songs on the new album, 'Anthems for doomed youth', which had grown out of the bands personal battles with self destructive behaviour applied to my own struggles.

"Woke up again
To my evil twin
The mirror's fucking ugly and I'm
Sick and tired of looking at him.

Oh, the road is long
If you stay strong

159

You're a better man than I
You've been beat and afraid
Probably betrayed
You're a better man than I."

Gunga Din, The Libertines, 2015

"No one can hold a light to your misery
You're the number one
At being hard done
Hard done by.

With all the battering it's taken
I'm surprised that it's still ticking
Yeah with all the battering it's taken
I'm surprised that it's still ticking

Let's get straight to the heart of the matter
Why so glum, it's all on a platter
So what's the matter, what's the matter today?"

Heart of the matter, The Libertines, 2015

John told me how Buddhism had helped him and I replied that I'd always felt drawn to the philosophy of the religion. How Buddha was in all of us and the path to enlightenment and peace was through self awareness and finding the Buddha within. This concept mirrored my own beliefs that 'all I need is within me now', and the focus on compassion both for those around you and yourself resonated with me.

The band and crew truly felt like family and I knew that they would always have my back.

· · · · ·

Some of the warmest responses that I received on announcing my transition came from women. They opened their arms and welcomed me to womanhood and this was equally true with the band where my friendships with the partners of the 'boys in the band' provided me with much needed support. Not once was I met with wariness or distrust and an online conversation that I had with Peter's girlfriend Katia was particularly warm.

Katia: Hello Sophie! I hope this is not going to sound rude, it is incredible how I don't remember you as a bloke, but you are such a radiating person that I know exactly who you are now. And it's not because of any transformation, it is clearly because now you radiate.

Well done, love Katia

Sophie: Thanks love, I look at pictures of me as a guy and I always looked like a zombie, I tried to hide, I had no confidence or power despite having done some amazing things. As a woman my whole life is about joy, except for the odd breakdown but hey we all have them x

Katia: When you aren't confident and don't feel that you're where you should be, you get to be invisible. It's not you hiding, or maybe you were, but I think it's more about vibration, presence. You are fully there now, you will never hear "who is Sophie?"

Sophie: Funnily enough the words of Gunga Din are really relevant to me and the feelings I've struggled with all my life, feeling sick and tired, my evil twin, beaten, flayed, betrayed and escaping into drinking.

Katia: I'm glad that Sophie came to life then, and I think about all those that don't let their true selves out.

Facebook, 14/9/15

· · · · ·

The pub is already full but that's hardly surprising. Life with the Libertines is never boring and never follows a formula. Six days after headlining Reading Festival in front of 90,000 people we're squeezed into the back room of the infamous Dublin Castle public house in Camden, where Madness had built their reputation, capacity 150.

The boys are due on stage around 9 with a curfew of 11.30, all of which works nicely as I'm supposed to be in Derby for an RAF reunion, my first since my transition, and I've got a three hour drive ahead of me following the gig.

Everything is in place, amps and drums fill the tiny stage leaving very little room for the band, let alone the photographer. I finally decide that the only possible spot for me to shoot from is on John's side of the stage, mere inches from the head of his bass guitar. There's no barrier and it's clear that a good percentage of the audience will be joining us on stage as soon as the band arrive.

Carl, Gary and John are holed up in a flat around the corner but there's still no sign of Peter.

"He's just left Paris," someone says, even with the Eurostar shrinking the journey to a couple of hours we're going to be pushing it to be onstage at 9. It'll be fine I tell myself, no worries. At 10.30pm there's good news for the waiting fans as the band tweets, "We'll be on in the next few hours X".

With no dressing room to wait out the hours I wander the bar and pavement outside, chatting to fans and enjoying the warm September evening. At midnight I get a nod and take up my position, waiting for the bands arrival which is heralded by a raucous cheer from the throbbing, flowing mass of people through which they are struggling to reach the stage.

As the gig unfolds it's obvious that there's no set list, Peter and Carl just start playing whatever they want next and everyone else has to work it out quicktime and catch up. There's a constant stream of drinks being ordered from the stage and the band seem to be playing rush goalie with frequent crowd surfing trips to the toilets at the back of the room. Gary jumps into the crowd and Carl takes over on drums only to dive full length off the stage upon Gary's return. Peter jumps on to bass and John takes the microphone, pork pie hat and Ray Bans, cigarette hanging from his lips.

The crowd is so close that every time I switch cameras, the one hanging on my left hip hits a blond woman on the head, every time it happens I apologise profusely and every time she replies that it's ok. It may seem like an unlikely start to a friendship but Helen, as I later discovered her name was, went on be one of my best friends, always ready to help out with support whenever life chose to give me a beating.

Fans are invited on stage to play Libertine karaoke as the crowd swirls around the bands feet, like waves washed up on the low shore, before Peter and Carl finally collapse on each other, rolling around on the floor submerged in the human surf like Burt Lancaster and Deborah Kerr in 'From here to eternity'.

It's gone 2am but the atmosphere is electric as the band struggle off the stage and out of the doors, I'm exhausted and I've still got to drive to Derby.

· · · · ·

In the 27 years since I'd left Germany I'd only seen my former RAF colleagues once during a reunion a couple of months before my epiphany in the hotel in Bradford. I'd been fat, bald and depressed, now I was going to see the same guys less than a year later five stone lighter, long, dark hair, happy, and as a woman.

When we'd returned to the former West German airbase that had been our home during the 1980s I'd been at breaking point. Sitting in the bar sharing beers with old friends, separated by decades from the damaged teenager that I'd been last time I was there.Still damaged, the years having added to the pain rather than reducing it, feet away from the toilet where I had self harmed so many years before.

Arriving at the hotel in Derby barely hours after leaving the sweaty, heaving mass of the gig at the Dublin Castle I was exhausted but at least I was sober, unlike the hungover wretches that I met in the breakfast room. They'd all been pre-warned about my transition when I came out in the squadron Facebook group but this was the first time that they'd seen me in the flesh.

Many of my LGBT friends feared the reaction that I would receive in the supposedly hyper-masculine worlds of professional football and the military and I'm not going to kid myself that I'd have got the same reaction at a different football club or with a different group of veterans but I was lucky.

As had happened in football and the music industry I was welcomed with open arms at this reunion of 20 Squadron, Royal Air Force, engineers.

I told them my story, including the self harming and suicidal feelings that I had endured almost three decades earlier when we had been stationed in Germany together. They expressed shock at what I had been through and told me that they wished I'd been able to tell them. I explained to them that I wasn't ready to say anything, they probably weren't ready to listen and that the RAF had definitely not been ready to welcome a suicidal, self harming, transgender woman into the service. Indeed until 2000 it was still illegal to be lesbian, gay or bisexual in the UK's armed forces and transgender people were barred from serving until as recently as 2014.

The guys had planned to spend the day in a sports bar watching rugby, followed by a visit to an Indian restaurant in the evening. The idea of a room full of drunken guys watching rugby filled me with dread, and so I arranged to spend the day with some of the wives.

We checked out the shops, had a nice meal, cocktails and I got a piercing, I won't tell you where, before we joined the guys in the sports bar.

They were going to head straight from the pub to the restaurant, ah the simple life of a man, but we were going to get changed. Back at the hotel I rendezvoused with the girls in the bar where it transpired that the guys were still in the pub, we could either head over to the Indian restaurant or have a drink first.

"I didn't make myself look stunning and squeeze into this dress just to be sat down when they arrive," I said, "I want to make an entrance".

. . . . .

The overwhelming response to my revelations about my gender identity when I came out was praise me for my bravery, but the funny thing was that I didn't feel brave. I just felt like me.

A great many transgender people delete their previous identity on transitioning, to protect themselves from bigotry, to insulate their feelings against the trauma of living a life in the wrong body, to get a fresh start.

I knew that this wasn't the right path for me, I had children, I had a public profile which meant that there would always be people that knew. I also felt that it would be doing Steve a disservice, he had done amazing things in his life, all while wishing that he was dead. Indeed he'd held on long enough, against the daily struggle of suicidal feelings, to allow me to be here.

This revelation transformed my relationship with him. I saw his strength, I saw his struggle, and I loved him in a way that he'd never been able to love himself.

I wanted to thank him for his strength and bravery, for he truly was the braver of we two, and so I wrote him a poem which I shared on social media.

. . . . .

This is the hug that I'd like to give,
To the brave man who went before me,
Who suffered for years.
Filled with self loathing and pain.

Whose bravery and strength,
Meant that I could one day emerge,
To dance in the rain.

He was the brave one,
He took the pain,
He suffered in silence,
So I could dance in the rain.

He kept me safe,
Hidden inside,
He paid the price,
Now I feel the pride.

He had the strength,
To fight to the end,
He was my hero,
Thank you,
My friend.

Sophie Cook, June 17, 2015

· · · · ·

The poem received a flood of supportive messages but one in particular would reduce me to tears, and, in its way, change my life as my 11-year-old daughter perfectly encapsulated the power of living authentically, true to yourself.

"You're my hero. Steve was amazing but Sophie is better x"

Sadie Cook, Facebook, September 23, 2015

14

THE STARFISH

A dame of two halves

A football photographer has broken new ground by becoming the first transgender person to work for a Premier League club.

Over the summer, married dad Steve Cook, 48, finally took the plunge to become Sophie by taking female hormones.

She also lost 5st.

AFC Bournemouth's snapper said life as a man had been "mental torment". But the support of players and fans has helped Sophie find happiness.

Sophie, who was nervous when the team were told, said: "The assistant manager called the players together and said, 'You'll probably notice our photographer has changed a little from last season, lost a bit of weight, and grown her hair. I'd like you all to meet Sophie".

"Suddenly the team captain started clapping and the rest of the boys joined in. I haven't looked back. It feels amazing. I've been totally accepted by the players and fans."

Sophie began questioning her gender as a child.

The snapper, who has three children and has worked for the Dorset club since 2012, has now split from her wife but said they remained pals.

Sophie added her daughter, 12, declared: "Steve was great but Sophie is better."

Daily Mirror, January 4, 2016

· · · · ·

The present that I received for my 49th birthday was full page stories about my transition in the tabloid press. The Daily Mirror, Sun and Star all featured me prominently in their print editions with most other publications covering me online.

The story went global and within 24 hours I was making news as far afield as Brazil, Poland, China, Ireland and Italy. I was interviewed on TV and radio and the coverage was universally positive, although the same couldn't be said for the comments.

Throughout the previous summer I had been pursued by a Sun journalist, eager for me to tell my tale. There was no way that I would ever talk to the tabloid universally reviled for its coverage of the 1989 Hillsborough disaster in which 96 people lost their lives.

The front page of their April 9, 1989 edition carried a story headlined 'The Truth' which quoted unnamed police sources and a Tory MP who claimed that drunken Liverpool fans urinated on and picked the pockets of the dead, hampered rescue efforts and attacked policemen.

The Taylor Report into the tragedy totally exonerated fans and laid the blame squarely at the feet of the police for their decision to open a gate in an effort to ease a crush outside the ground.

Three decades later the people of Liverpool and throughout football have still neither forgiven nor forgotten the slanderous lies of that day and the 'Don't buy the Sun' boycott has now grown to include fans from more than 70 football clubs.

I knew that the tabloids would try to sensationalise my story and so I sat down with a freelance journalist that I knew from my time as editor of Seeker News and together we wrote the piece.

We made no mention of the aspects of the story that tabloid newspapers would normally fixate on, the surgical status of my genitals, my sexuality and my children. The story was full of positivity including the support that I'd received from players and fans and the content left no openings for them to edit it in a way that would eradicate that positive message. If they dumped those aspects then there was nothing left for them to use.

· · · · ·

When I transitioned I was presented with a choice.

To either keep my head down, hide and try to get on with life with as little attention as possible or to use my position within football to try to raise awareness of issues that most people would rather forget.

I looked back at the abuse and alienation that I'd suffered at my first attempt to transition fifteen years earlier and how much fear I had felt before coming out to the football club and I realised that these experiences were more difficult because of a lack of awareness and familiarity with transgender people. There were no trans role models in 2000 and by 2015 this hadn't changed much.

If I could speak out about my journey then I hoped that I could make it easier for the next person to tread that path.

But it wasn't just openness about being transgender that I felt was needed, I felt very strongly that I should also speak up about my sexuality and my mental health.

· · · · ·

Being bisexual is not, as many would suggest, being greedy.

It's also nothing to do with being indecisive and unable to 'pick a team'.

When people asked me "how can you be attracted to both genders?", my response was always, "how can you not be?"

People came in all shapes and sizes, of all gender identities and sexualities and it was impossible for me to say that I couldn't be attracted to any of them.

Sexuality and sexual attraction are made up of two elements:

- Romantic orientation - who you are romantically attracted to, this is unrelated to sexual attraction.
- Sexual orientation - who you are sexually attracted, turned on by or who you would want to have sex with.

Many people would claim that the two are the same but they clearly are not, you only have to look at the number of straight guys that like to have sex with other men, they're sexually attracted to them but are not remotely interested in them romantically.

Sex and love are two very different things and a lot of the problems in relationships are caused by confusion over this and the dishonesty that people employ to navigate these treacherous waters.

Sexual attraction isn't the clear cut, straight/gay binary that many would have you believe, it's nuanced, a spectrum, not mutually exclusive and it can change.

- Heterosexual - the attraction to a gender different from your own, straight.
- Homosexual - the attraction to a gender the same as your own, gay.

- Lesbian - women who are attracted only to other women.
- Bisexual - when you are attracted to two or more genders, please note that you don't have to be equally attracted to each gender.
- Pansexual - when you're attracted to all genders and their gender is not a consideration when you're attracted towards someone.
- Bi Curious - people who are open to experiences with all genders, often a heterosexual person interested in having a sexual experience with a person of the same sex.
- Asexual - not experiencing sexual attraction.
- Demisexual - when you need to form a strong emotional or romantic bond with someone before you can experience sexual attraction.
- Sapiosexual - a person who finds intelligence sexually attractive.

So no, definitely not just gay and straight.

. . . . .

Whilst I believed that we needed to raise awareness of gender identity and sexuality the most important conversation that I wanted to start was around mental health.

Yes, I was transgender and bisexual, but these were only part of my journey, they did not define me. The most important battle in my life hadn't been with either of these issues, although they had both contributed to it, my battle had been with my mental health and this was where I desperately wanted to make a difference.

The very first time that I spoke publicly about my mental health was at a business breakfast meeting at a hotel in Haywards Heath. Over the full English breakfast I told an audience of fifteen business people, accustomed to hearing from accountants and network marketers, about my history of self harming, PTSD and suicide.

They were shocked out of their early morning stupor by the frank story of issues that most people kept hidden and following the meeting a woman approached me to say that she had suffered with her mental health but had never told anyone, the discussion had started.

I posted a video of the talk online and within 24 hours hundreds of people had watched it prompting a flurry of messages from viewers.

"Hi Sophie, hope you don't mind me contacting you. I've been thinking about the video you posted earlier, while I am a cis gay man, so can't directly draw any comparison with your and thousands of others journey, I can relate to the issues surrounding acceptance and feelings of social isolation and ultimately suicide.

"After over 2 decades of struggling with a roller coaster of a life I was diagnosed with bipolar 7 years ago, following my 3rd serious attempt on my life. Now although my meds have stabilised me, and my life is back on track, I feel that the issues surrounding my suicide attempts still need to be addressed.

"I do have a wonderful supportive family and a close group of friends who look out for me, but it's still something that is never discussed. I guess I really just wanted to say thanks for starting the discussion, which needs to be had, by so many families in the country.

"I am no shrinking Violet, but, I know it takes a very special individual to stand in front of others and bare their sole so eloquently. Thank you for being that person!"

I now had no choice, this was the path that I had to take, this was how I could really help people. If the only thing that I achieved with my transition was to be me, then I wasn't convinced that it had been worth the price.

This would bring meaning to everything that I had lost when I transitioned.

Over the next twelve months I spoke to thousands of people. I spoke at Wembley Stadium, Anfield, Old Trafford. My client list included companies like Google, JPMorgan, Virgin Media, and Nationwide and I received standing ovations at the TUC and Stonewall.

Three years later I would take to the stage in Brighton's historic Dome Theatre to deliver a TEDx Talk to 1500 people, sharing the story of my mental health with a highly appreciative audience.

Just before I went on the compere asked me how I would like to be introduced to which I joked "the Queen of the fucking world".

Standing, barefoot in the wings, I mentally prepared myself as the host stepped onto the stage and announced "I'd like you all to give a massive TEDx welcome to the Queen of the fucking world, Sophie Cook!"

The spotlights made it impossible to see the audience but as I stood on that red circular carpet in the middle of the stage I could hear every laugh, gasp and tear as I took them on my journey with me.

Social media can be a force both for good and bad, I've experienced horrific trolling and death threats on Twitter but it's always a positive experience checking the notifications after speaking at a major event and TEDxBrighton did not disappoint.

"All the speakers were brilliant today but Sophie Cook really lived up to her Queen of the F***ing World title. I laughed, I cried, I had snot pouring down my face. Such a moving and honest account of coming out as transgender."

@LauraMitchell15 on Twitter

You can't really ask for more as a speaker, to evoke such an emotional response that your audience is covered in snot, you know that your message really got through.

· · · · ·

My position in football also presented possibilities to raise awareness of the issues that mattered to me through TV interviews and both Premier League Productions and the BBC produced films about my story, following me for entire match days together with supplemental filming at my home in Brighton.

When the BBC film was screened on Match of the Day: The Premier League Show Gabby Logan introduced it saying that she had presented sports programmes for more than a decade and that she never thought she would be introducing a film like this.

When I first saw the film, shortly before it was broadcast, I thought "wow, they managed to make me look cool!" Mods and rockers, The Who, the RAF, mental health and football, they were all there and I was excited at the positive message about diversity and inclusion that we were sending.

Unfortunately not everyone agreed.

Gabby tweeted after the show that it was amazing that in a show that featured the first in-depth interview with Jose Mourinho as Manchester United manager all of the social media comments were about my film.

In a pattern that would become familiar to me the abuse began during the transmission.

"Man in a dress", "geezer bird", "pervert", "ugly", "sickening" and more. "I'm not a bigot but why do these freaks have to force this down our throats on a football show, it's disgusting."

Whenever someone starts a statement with "I'm not a bigot / racist / transphobe / homophobe / etc but..." you know full well that they will then proceed to prove that they are precisely that with the rest of the sentence.

Hundreds of messages of abuse came in, predominantly through Twitter where the ability to post hate anonymously made it easy for the faceless keyboard warriors to spread their hate.

I did, however, also receive a number of supportive messages, both from people that knew me and total strangers, trans people and cisgender, gay and straight.

Obviously not everyone on social media was a hate filled troll and these messages of support have always meant a lot to me when I'm under attack online.

The fight against discrimination within football had been ongoing for decades and I was honoured to be approached by several of these organisations with requests for my help.

Lindsay England at Just A Ball Game? the campaign organisation set up to encourage LGBT+ inclusion in football and to combat discrimination and abuse, invited me to become a patron alongside others including Beth Ditto of pop group The Gossip, paralympian Claire Harvey and former footballer Clarke Carlisle.

Kick It Out had been established as 'Let's Kick Racism Out of Football' in 1993 and worked within football to challenge all discrimination, including that directed at LGBT people as well as racism and religious discrimination.

The team at Kick It Out became close friends and I was surprised to be asked to become an ambassador alongside many famous footballers.

It was an honour to be asked to speak alongside their Director Roisin Wood and Education and Development Manager Troy Townsend at venues like Arsenal's Emirates Stadium and Sky Sports TV but it was on one campaign launch press trip to BBC MediaCity in Salford that I felt the full force of opposition to the causes for which we campaigned.

It was just a Facebook Live interview, filmed by one reporter on an iPhone and shared instantly on the BBC Sport Facebook page. I was used to doing TV interviews including a live appearance on BBC2's daytime current affairs show 'Victoria Derbyshire', this was going to be a nothing event I told myself.

There is a very distinct difference between broadcast TV and live social media interviews and that is instant feedback. Over the following 24 hours it felt like the majority of the 100,000 people that viewed the interview had an opinion about me.

Oscar Wilde wrote in 'The Picture of Dorian Gray' that "there is only one thing in the world worse than being talked about, and that is not being talked about".

Oscar Wilde lived in a time before social media, perhaps today his views might be different.

. . . . .

Back in Brighton I had been invited onto the local TV channel, Latest TV, to be interviewed about my story and impressed with my performance on air they approached me about becoming a newscaster for them, the first transgender person to act as news anchor anywhere in Europe.

. . . . .

Premier League photographer becomes first transgender news anchor in Europe

A woman has spoken of her pride at becoming the first transgender news anchor in Europe. Sophie Cook, 48, has joined Brighton's Latest TV as an on air personality and head of diversity. 'It's a great honour for me to be given this opportunity by Latest TV and is a real step forward for transgender visibility and awareness,' she said. 'Brighton & Hove is a unique city, full of amazing diversity and I'm proud to be able to reflect this by bringing the news to everyone in the city on Freeview channel 7 and Virgin Media 159 and across the world online.'

It's not the first time Ms Cook has been a pioneer for the LGBTQ community.

Earlier this year she became the first transgender woman to be employed by a Premier League club after she transitioned while working as a photographer at AFC Bournemouth last summer.

Bill Smith, CEO of Latest TV, added: 'Brighton is an island of sanity in what can often be seen as an ocean of intolerance. 'Latest TV brought the first exclusively LGBT show to terrestrial television, Q Tube, and now we are appointing Sophie Cook to lead the LGBT TV news revolution!'

Metro, Jun 10, 2016

Strangely Metro also ran virtually the same story four months later...

Meet Britain's first transgender newsreader

This is India Willoughby – Britain's first transgender newsreader. She worked for ITV regional news for 10 years before quitting to undergo gender reassignment five years ago, and now she's back working for the broadcaster.

Metro, Oct 3, 2016

Like they say, don't believe everything that you read in the papers.

. . . . .

Run out of a music bar in Brighton's Kemptown, Latest TV was a shoestring affair that tried its best on very limited funds to provide local programming for the people of the city. I was brought in to co-host the news alongside veteran broadcaster Mike Mendoza and while he was considered the experienced hands I was there to give visibility to the thriving LGBT community.

The first day that I presented the news we were filming links between the news packages on the promenade outside the Palace Pier when a group of lads, down for the day from London, allowed their inquisitiveness to interrupt the filming.

"Are you a geezer?"

I continued to film the link, the cameras were rolling and I was determined to remain professional on my first day in the job.

"Oi! Are you a man?"

As the link ended and the red light blinked out on the camera I turned to my antagonist and calmly asked him if he was. Even on the streets of the LGBT haven that is Brighton and Hove there is still abuse and even danger for those that don't fit with the prescribed norm.

As well as presenting the news I was also filming news packages, two minute stories that shed light on the lives of local LGBT people. It was always important to me that these stories depicted the reality of our existence, after all gay and trans people's lives weren't just one big camp, rainbow coloured, Pride party. We were affected by bigotry, prejudice, hate crimes, mental health issues, the battle against HIV and all manner of issues that didn't involve mirror balls and face paint.

This was reflected in the title of my news and chat show 'Beyond The Rainbow', the first series of which was simply a weekly omnibus of my news reports but by series two had developed into a proper, and I say that very loosely, chat and magazine show.

Set in the cellar bar of Latest TV's home it allowed me to have informal, pub style chats with guests, introduce live acts, the wonderful Hannah Brackenbury becoming our resident troubadour and exchange banter with our glamorous drag queen bar maid, Britney Fierce. I don't think that I'd ever had so much fun masquerading as work.

· · · · ·

How do you learn how to be sexy?

No, it's not a rhetorical question, I'm really asking you.

I guess that as we grow up we take in all manner of cultural references and try to square them away with the vagaries of our own bodies.

Young men watch James Bond and learn a certain type of bravado, stylish dressing and misogyny.

Young women watch pop stars and mimic their gyrating dance routines and revealing clothing.

Of course there are also a million other influences but you get my drift, our idea of what is attractive and desirable to others is built up over years. I was now in my 50s and I had to learn how my body could express my female sensuality after decades of suppression, but how?

My saviour came in the shape of a perfect 5' something blonde bombshell by the name of Veronica Blacklace. The sexiest woman alive. Not due to her body or looks, although she is very attractive, but down to her knowledge of and skill at just 'being sexy'.

Veronica taught me burlesque.

Burlesque isn't about showing flesh, although you do, it isn't about stripping, although you do, burlesque is about the body confidence that allows any woman to tease, to flirt and unleash her personal sensuality. This is what's sexy.

Over the course of a few months I was taught not only how to dance with boas and take off stockings with my teeth, I was taught to be comfortable about my own body. I'd spent a lifetime hating everything about myself, I was overweight, my body was too manly, no one could ever find me attractive, but Veronica and burlesque taught me that we are all sexy, we just need to believe.

Burlesque also introduced me to some amazing friends, non-judgemental, supportive and totally inclusive and welcoming of this 50 something trans woman trying to find her place in the world.

Most of all burlesque taught me to love my own body, whatever shape it is or as I declared to a friend one day whilst naked sunbathing on the beach near Hove, "you don't have to have a bikini body if you're not wearing a bikini".

. . . . .

The validation for my new identity was beginning to have a positive effect on my mental health, I was learning to love my body, I had a new career in TV and my speaking was making a real difference to people's lives.

The price that I had paid to be me was much higher than I had ever imagined, I had lost my marriage, my family and I was alone. I had to make it mean something, I had to redress that balance of payments, I had to make a difference.

Very few of us have the opportunity to change the world with a single act but we all have the ability to change it incrementally, tiny nudges, day by day, that make the world a better place.

We hear a lot about microaggressions, rudeness, bad attitudes that make life more difficult for others, if we can have microaggressions then we can also have micro kindnesses. Small acts that spread happiness and positivity, saying hello, please and thank you, holding the door for someone, being helpful. All of these acts can make a difference to others.

We all have issues and problems that affect our lives and most of the time the rest of the world is oblivious to our suffering. We have no idea how close to breaking someone else might be and often our unthinking actions can deeply hurt others without us even realising.

I realised that I had to try to make a difference, one micro act at a time, one day at a time, for only then could I find the help that I, myself, needed to find happiness.

· · · · ·

The beach stretches away into the distance. Waves gently caress the golden sands as a faint breeze causes the leaves on the coconut trees that line the shore to sway in reply.

The woman is young, her skin sunkissed and her long, blonde hair naturally curled and tangled after a swim in the ocean. As she walks she becomes aware of starfish, washed up on the sands following the previous nights storm, their red orange bodies beginning to dry out under the tropical sun.

As she walks along the beach she gently lifts each starfish, inspects it quickly and returns it to the sea, their five radial legs seem to stroke her fingers as she places them back into the life giving water. Working methodically she continues along the shore, all the while being watched by an old lady sat in the shade of a tree.

"An exercise in futility," the old lady laughs as the woman comes within earshot.

"Pardon?"

"An exercise in futility. You do realise that there are miles and miles of beach on this shore, and millions and millions of starfish."

The young woman's gaze slowly moves from the old lady along the beach, taking in the overwhelming number of starfish in need of assistance.

"You can't hope to make a difference," the old lady laughs from her shaded perch.

Bending, the young woman reaches down to pick up one of the beached creatures. She turns it over in her hands, thinking, deciding on a course of action before walking over to the sea and gently placing the starfish into the waves.

"I made a difference to that one," she replies as she goes back to work, lifting, inspecting and saving the starfish, one by one.

15
BREAK UP
BREAK DOWN

My lungs burn as I fight for breath.

Pain radiates from my core, threatening to overwhelm me as I grit my teeth, tears forming in my eyes. Gravity has multiplied and each step takes an effort I could only have dreamt of mere months before.

As I begin the final climb of the tortuous, hilly, 13.1 mile route towards the finish line I am overcome with emotion. Over the past 3 hours and 20 minutes I've been on a roller coaster emotional journey no less intense than that of the past 12 months.

Late in 2014 I had returned to the town in Germany where I was stationed with the Royal Air Force for the first time in 30 years to attend a reunion with the guys that I'd served with as a fresh faced 18 year old. At the time I weighed 23 stone, my body, organs and face wrapped in a layer of fat that limited my ability to do anything.

A small knee injury was exacerbated by my weight and became a limp, it was impossible for me to run and even to walk at anything other than a slow stroll. I had developed an unhealthy relationship with food using it as a form of self harm.

Over the past 12 months I had realised the depth of my mental health issues, I faced up to my lifelong gender dysphoria, and began to combat my depression and self loathing. This led to a new found, and previously unknown, love and respect for myself. I began eating more healthily, as the weight started to drop I once again became able to exercise and within 6 months I'd lost 5 stone.

During this period I began to run more and more, enjoying the freedom of my daily run along the Brighton seafront from my home in Hove to the Palace Pier. 3 miles there, grab a cup of tea from one of the seafront cafes and walk home, and all before 8am. As it became easier I began to extend the runs, if I felt good at the pier I'd continue along the beach to the Marina, stretching it to 5 miles.

Then I was struck by one of my 'whatif' feelings, the moments when I suddenly challenge myself that normally appear in my head unannounced.

It was late October and I'd done a 5 mile run on the Monday that felt great, at the end I still had plenty of energy and was sure that I could have gone further. So two days later when I set off at 5am for a run I suddenly decided, hell I might as well do 10 miles today. This run wasn't easy but it was very doable, to tell the truth it didn't feel that different from the 5 miles, it just took longer. On the Sunday I decided to do another 10 miles and again felt great at the end of it.

"Hang about", I said to myself, "I'm doing these 10 mile runs and they're going well, it's great but I think I can achieve more. Only another 3 miles and I'd be doing a half marathon, and that's a big deal!"

I immediately went on the internet, desperately searching for a half marathon that fitted around football matches and that still had their entry list open. Only one race fitted my criteria before the new year but it was only 11 days away.

· · · · ·

Arriving at the hotel that served as race HQ I was surrounded by people that looked like they knew what they were doing, with their running club tops and equipment belts, I looked totally out of place, the newcomer at their first race.

Checking in at the female runners' table I had a few funny looks but no one said anything and I was briefed and numbered ready for the off. As the start of the race was along a single track path I set off at the back of the field, I really didn't want to be the one that everyone had to divert through the stinging nettles to get past.

Being a Brighton resident who did all of their running on the seafront I was ready for the wind but the hills took me by surprise. The first six miles became an arduous climb as we headed further and further into the South Downs around Maidstone, climbing 900 feet including some slopes that I struggled to walk on let alone run up.

As I reached the highest point of the course the dark clouds that had been threatening all morning suddenly unleashed their payload of freezing, stinging rain, driven hard by the winds that whipped the hill's summit.

Running into the horizontal sleet I quickly became drenched whilst barely moving due to the headwind. It was coming down so hard that the only way I could keep going was by pulling my woolly cap down to my chin and looking through the loose knit material.

I took shelter in a bus stop for a minute or two, speaking to an elderly man waiting for his bus. He'd already watched most of the field pass him and probably thought the event was over by the time this lone, bedraggled individual came into view.

"You look too sensible to be running half marathons," he observed after we'd made the obligatory small talk about the foul weather.

I was cold, wet, tired, my knee was throbbing and the weather appeared to be getting worse by the minute.

As a bus approached I quickly said my goodbyes, explaining that if I was in the bus stop when the bus arrived it would be too tempting to give up. Running off into the storm I couldn't help but think that maybe I was dafter than he obviously thought I looked.

Tracking my progress on a GPS app on my phone I was in great form as I passed the halfway point, knowing that the worst of the course must be behind me and that it must surely all be downhill from here.

I managed to lengthen my stride on the downhill sections and felt like I was flying, the exhilaration of speed fuelling my energy.

I'd set myself a target of 3 hours and 30 minutes but as my satnav indicated that I'd reached the 10 mile point in 2 hours 20 minutes I began to think that a 3 hour time could be possible. Joy and energy swept through my body as I revelled in this amazing possibility, spurring me on and helping me to overcome the pain and fatigue.

As I passed 2 hours 40 minutes my sat nav was telling me that I'd done 11.3 miles, less than two miles to go and 20 minutes to cover it. I was exhausted but the sheer joy in this achievement was driving me on.

Five minutes later my world came crashing down around my ears, my heart sank as I passed a course marker for the 11 mile point.

What? No! My sat nav said I'd done 12 miles, this can't be, there was no way I'd make 3 hours now!

The energy drained out of me, I felt like I could cry, I just wanted to sit down and go to sleep. The old negative thought patterns took hold and began to play at my resolve.

As I passed a railway line I saw a sign saying 'Do not go on the railway line', all I could think of was the idea of climbing onto the line, lying down and going to sleep, the tiredness and pain would go away.

I struggled on, all the while thinking "this is so hard, this is so hard," pain, fatigue and despair overwhelming my body and mind, chipping away at my determination and resolve to finish.

And then I caught myself.

"No, this is not hard, this is easy."

This.

Is.

Easy.

I moved my eyes from the piece of tarmac directly in front of my feet and focused on the end of the road. I developed tunnel vision, my eyes purely on the goal, the next turn, the crest of the next hill and I carried on.

As I began the final climb to the finish line, enticing and welcome, a shipwreck survivor catching glimpse of land, I became overwhelmed with emotion. Tears began to build in my eyes as I thought about the journey that I'd been on in my life and in particular over the previous 12 months.

This wasn't one of the big headline runs with hundreds of people cheering at the finish line but the dozen or so people that cheered me home were so gratefully received, I was a stranger but they supported me nonetheless.

The relief as I passed the line swept me away and I broke down in tears, knowing that this was another step on my journey to fulfilment and self realisation. I sank to the ground, trying to still my emotions and fill my lungs with air. I watched the other runners being congratulated by their loved ones, friends and families. I sat there alone and exhausted, no one to share my triumph with, no one to congratulate me, no one to love me.

It was Sod's Law that at the point when I was most exposed I was hit by my biggest challenge, if I had given up when the storm hit then I wouldn't have succeeded. If I could stick it out through the tough times, especially the ones when I was most vulnerable, then things would get better, I just needed the strength of will to keep putting one foot in front of the other.

. . . . .

My relationship with Dawn was, as one of our friends described it, the model of an amicable separation. We were no longer a couple but, together with the kids, we were still a family.

On my frequent trips to Bournemouth for football matches I stay with them, sleeping in Sadie's room, and they spent time with me in Brighton having family trips to explore the city.

Unfortunately not all of my family are as supportive of my new identity.

They struggle with my transition and can't come to terms with Sophie, which is a pity as she is a very different person to Steve. He was damaged and emotionally detached, never comfortable, endlessly in pain, and at family gatherings he would try his best to avoid people. Sophie, on the other hand, loves people and wants to build relationships, she had been in prison for so long that she feels a need to celebrate life, experience it and love it.

Looking back now I can see the separation with my family in kinder terms than I could at the time. Then I was feeling vulnerable and really wanted and needed the love, support and validation of my family. I felt isolated, alone and unloved but the reality is that they had never had a relationship with me, Sophie. They loved Steve and he was gone, they needed to grieve that loss before they could move on.

I could see the positives of my transition, the end of my pain, the opportunity to finally be true to myself, but they didn't yet understand those things. They had never known Sophie, she was a new person and they would need to build new relationships with her.

Years later I would be looking at pre-transition photos of a transgender friend and I could not connect the man that I knew with the images of a woman that he was showing me. The person in the photos looked like a ghost and this made me look at photos of Steve with fresh eyes.

I'd already recognised the deep sadness that I saw buried deep within his blue eyes. A death barely concealed in their cool azure waters, regardless of the expression playing out on the rest of his face. But now I began to see much more.

In photos of our former selves I saw not people, I saw ghosts. Not just because they were no longer here but because, in a way, they never were. The pain and isolation of our buried identity hollowed us out, our souls not inhabiting our bodies but locked up, hidden away deep inside.

Our physical form acting as placeholders, walking the Earth taking up the space that we should have been inhabiting if only we could be set free. The body tortured and confused, denied the connection to the soul that is essential for a fulfilled life, waiting patiently for the day when we might finally be released to inhabit our bodies and call them our homes.

· · · · ·

"I've met someone."

The words hit me like a sniper round, small entry hole, massive exit wound, destroying everything in its path. Bone, organs, flesh and blood pulverised, torn, liquified and thrown against the wall behind me.

"I thought that I should tell you before the kids did", Dawn continued.

He'd met the kids, he'd spent enough time with them that they might mention him.

All life drained from me, all of my energy, strength, resolve. The core of my being had been ripped out and I began to crumple in on this void, a black hole swallowing all around it.

I sank to the floor, tears rising from deep within my being, the ice cold waters at the very depths of my soul and burst like a dam as the despair washed me away. Clutching the phone tight I lay on the floor in a foetal position, holding myself, trying to block out the pain, the words, the world.

"No, no, no."

This couldn't be right.

It was, I knew it was coming, but being informed made it real, more serious.

The scale of my loss overwhelmed me, threatening to unravel everything that I'd done to heal myself.

It wasn't worth it, I wasn't worth it.

I hadn't been told the price that I would have to pay for my transition and now I knew that it had cost me everything and there was no way that I was worth that price.

Lying on the floor sobbing, unmoving, as day turned into night. My depression transforming my body, internal organs, limbs to lead, weighing me down, unable to move. The darkness consuming me, becoming me.

"You knew this was going to happen, this was always going to happen."

I feel him lie down beside me, the dark void waiting to claim me.

"How did you think that this would play out? That you could find release but keep them?"

His words work their way into my head, probing for weakness, searching out all of the dark, cold vulnerable corners where doubts lived and replacing them with despair.

"She said she would always love me, she said that it would always be my home." I tried to wind back the clock, to a time before knowing.

"You were never good enough for her, you, broken and lost. She was always better than you and now she's found a real man, someone whom she wants and desires. She never wanted you, she ended up with you by default, tied to you by the children. Never wanting you but unable to leave."

"Just you and me now, as it's always been. You and me, forever, alone. I will never leave. You and me."

I feel his darkness envelop me as he takes me into his embrace, spooning me, gently whispering words of nothingness, sweet nothings, into my ear.

As the sun's first rays of light steal their way into the darkness of my flat, they find me as they had left me, curled in a ball, hugging myself, trying to deny the existence of the world around me.

· · · · ·

The pain will not leave.

I find myself in a peculiar situation whereby I can feel nothing, numb and at the same time the pain will not leave.

Everything is without purpose, without meaning. I am without purpose, without meaning.

I mean nothing.

I am worth nothing.

I exist simply to suffer. From the cradle to the grave.

Every day of my life since I tried to hang myself at age 12 has been a borrowed day, the library book long overdue its return. Nearly four decades of late fees, that's going to cost and now I am expected to pay.

As I lie back in my chair I drain my glass, the empty Jack Daniels bottle falls from my hand and I feel a peace descend quieting the pain as I close my eyes.

Sweet release, sweet nothing.

Anaesthetised.

· · · · ·

I was in deep and I no longer cared.

The pain was too great, I was alone, I would always be alone and I would die alone.

Maybe even tonight.

Yes, tonight might be the time, no time like the present and all of that.

I was crashing badly, the alcohol that I'd been self medicating my depression with only worked for so long before reaching a tipping point and then sending me diving, falling, rushing towards the bottom.

When you find yourself in this deep it's very difficult to step back and find the logical, safe course of action, in fact that is quite often the last thing that you want to do.

Over the years I'd developed a system of trying to take the action with the least worse consequences. In the past this had included me deleting large numbers of friends on Facebook, working in the knowledge that this was hurting me by removing the very support network that I needed at that moment.

This evening, in my headlong rush to oblivion, sat on the number 1 bus, I'd deleted 500 Facebook friends in the space of minutes. School friend - delete. RAF colleague - delete. Casual acquaintance from the pub - delete.

Best friend - delete.

On previous occasions this had helped me to avoid self harming, giving me a way to hurt myself, an outlet for that need, before physically taking up the blade.

Tonight this wasn't enough. Distraught, alone and ready to do something much more serious, for there are actions that are more serious than self harming, I stared at my hands.

I'd already deleted everyone on Facebook, and the prospect of dying alone filled my soul, stripping it of all positive thoughts.

Arriving at my stop I stumbled up the road to home and rather than finding sanctuary I found despair, memories, isolation, what had been my haven was now my prison, a place of torture.

Then, for the first time in three decades I hurt myself physically.

Immediately I looked at the wounds and through the fog in my mind asked myself "how the hell are you going to hide that?"

I had a big conference coming up where I was expected to speak about mental health. I couldn't stand in front of nearly a thousand people with fresh wounds marking the flesh of my arms, showing my shame and weakness.

The realisation hit me that I had to take responsibility for what I'd done. I'd already spoken openly about my history of self harming and suicide attempts in an effort to reduce the stigma around them, to make it easier for people in pain to share their pain with loved ones and to get the help they needed. If I tried to hide what I'd done then I'd be reinforcing the stigma around mental health and self harming rather than fighting it.

I realised that it was vitally important that I didn't compound my emotional anguish and struggle with my suicidal feelings and self harming by heaping guilt and shame on top of them. I recognised this as something that I had no control over. I wasn't attention seeking or a drama queen, I was in the worst kind of emotional pain and I knew that I wouldn't get better just because people told me to 'man up' or 'pull myself together.'

I wasn't proud of what I had done but I also felt that I shouldn't be ashamed of it. This was a battle won, rather than one lost, I was still here and I resolved that I would find a way to use it.

By speaking openly about my mental health I was effectively opening my old wounds in front of an audience and saying, "here is my pain, what can you learn from it?"

I wanted to show them that it was OK to be open about this, that they needn't be ashamed or feel guilty about it, but at the same time I was learning.

We are taught from an early age that we should hide our vulnerability, that it's a sign of weakness and to be denied. But that was a trap as surely as the idea of transgender people 'passing' was a trap. It was your weak spot, your Achilles' heel, forever susceptible to attack.

I chose instead to be open about my vulnerability, laying it before the world and challenging it, "here are my vulnerabilities, now what are you going to hurt me with?"

In being open about my vulnerabilities I diminished their power and became invincible.

And so a few days later, Sophie Cook, transgender, ex-RAF, motorbike racer, newspaper editor, rock and sports photographer, stood up in the QEII Convention Centre in Westminster and declared that she was also a self harm and suicide survivor.

· · · · ·

One of the biggest contributing factors in how much damage any mental health condition can do to us is how we interact with that anguish. If we allow it to fill us with guilt and shame then its power is magnified and reinforced.

"I don't deserve love."

"I don't deserve to be happy."

"I don't deserve to be successful."

"Everyone would be better off without me."

"No one would miss me, or even notice that I was gone."

At one time or another I've thought all of these things. I've planned my own death so that no one would ever find me. I've contemplated dying alone and speculated as to how many weeks, or months it would be before anyone even realised that I was missing.

The dark, lonely place within our souls where we go when depression hits hard can be impenetrable, a fortress of solitude with just our demons for company.

It's a place where no matter how hard they try to help, our loved ones are excluded with neither an invitation nor a key to enter.

The act of loving someone with severe depression can be a painful, thankless task which can drain the soul and life from the most positive of people.

In an effort to help and protect them you can find yourself hollowing out a cave deep within you in which you try to place your loved one in order to protect them from the pain and demons that assault them. A place of sanctuary, away from the world with all of its stresses, strains and protagonists but in reality it's a futile effort for their real enemies lie within their own psyches ever ready to strike.

I know that living with my depression for years affected my relationships, I withdrew, became uncommunicative, sometimes combative, I let my body turn to fat as my hatred for myself manifested in overeating and inactivity.

No matter how much effort Dawn put into trying to convince me to look after myself and watch what I ate I never really cared, I thought that I was unworthy, of anything, and the more I weighed the more justified my self loathing became.

It was only after my transition that I finally started to lose the weight, through the power of learning to love myself for the first time in decades, perhaps even my life.

Unfortunately I also discovered that mindset was vitally important to that as following the revelation of Dawn's new relationship my self love evaporated and the pounds once again started to pile on.

$$\cdots\cdots$$

This way, then that, folding round on itself and then diving for the surface before wheeling hard and climbing above the dark skeletal structure.

The warming rays of the setting sun glint occasionally off individual birds as the murmuration of starlings cavort in the skies above Brighton's West Pier.

I am alone. I am always alone. My mind elsewhere as the waves caress the shore, a gentle exhalation with each ebb and flow. I close my eyes searching for peace, for meaning, for a reason to be.

I sense his presence first, sat beside me on the bench, silent, watching the scene before us.

"Did you know that Brighton has had three piers?" he asked. "The first one to be built was the Chain Pier back in 1823, with the West Pier being added in the 1860s. The Palace Pier didn't get built until the turn of the century and by that point the Chain Pier had been destroyed in a storm. So although the town has had three piers, it only ever had two at a time."

I turn to look at him and he smiles at me, his eyes twinkling fondly as I greet him.

"Hello Grandad, I've missed you."

"I know love and I've missed our talks but I'm always here."

He hasn't changed, his full head of white grey hair brushed neatly back despite the sea breeze.

"I never got the chance to introduce you to the real me," I tell him, tears welling up behind my eyes. "I wish that I could have shared this with you. I've lost everyone, it's just me now."

"Don't worry, we're here and we love you so much, no matter what happens."

"I've wrecked everything, I'm so sorry, I've let you all down. I fought for so long but I failed."

"You haven't let anyone down. Life presents certain challenges and all that we can ever hope to do is our best. As long as we never purposely hurt someone then we haven't let anyone down."

"I'm trying to be happy, but I don't know how."

He looks at me kindly and smiles.

"You can't chose to be happy, you have no control over that, but you can be brave. When despair takes hold reach down, deep inside and you will find your bravery. When you stand up to despair then happiness will follow."

"I love you Grandad."

"And I love you too Sophie, I know that you were in pain, I know that you struggled, but you're still here and that's half the battle."

"I love you so much, I'm so alone. Just one more day, I'd give everything to spend one more day with you now that I'm the real me", the tears return and I turn away to look at the derelict Pier.

"Do you remember when the Red Arrow crashed into the sea? Hit the top of a yacht's mast, they used to fly displays with a minimum altitude of 35 feet over water, during the war an RAF Typhoon hit the West Pier and crashed onto the beach. That really is low flying, you just don't get that any more."

"Still full of useless information", I reply, smiling faintly as I close my eyes.

When I look back he's gone and my heart breaks just a little bit more, "I love you Grandad."

. . . . .

But where are all
Our yesterdays?
Now
Our yesterdays gone.

Steve Cook, c 1985-86

. . . . .

Lying in bed I decide to check my messages one last time before retiring for the night.

A red number 1 draws my attention to Facebook messenger and I tap the icon to open the app.

"I see that your life has changed quite a bit in the last 30 years as well."

This is the last message that I ever thought I would receive. I didn't even know that the sender was still alive and this is the first time that I've heard from them since I saved their life three decades earlier.

16
NOT TODAY

"I never got to thank you for saving my life."

Emotions threaten to overwhelm me, all of those years of questioning whether I'd done the right thing in saving his life, all of those years of guilt, shame and post traumatic stress.

The message from Andy Harris had come totally out of the blue. I hadn't heard anything for thirty years and the latest news was a vague report that he had taken his life due to the injuries that he'd sustained in that explosion all those years ago.

Over the years I'd searched the burgeoning internet for any mention of his name and always came up blank, no mentions, no profiles on any of the social networks, it was as if he'd died before the internet age had begun.

"I've got a son and two daughters that wouldn't be here if you hadn't saved my life."

Not one life saved but four, three people that would never have existed, children and grandchildren, the past and the future. Never before had the enormity of that moment dawned on me outside of our pain, Andy and I, linked by trauma.

As we talked it became clear why I'd never found him on the internet, he had one of the least digital jobs that it was possible to have in the always connected, online, virtual world that was the early part of the 21st century.

He was a gamekeeper in Cumbria, spending his days on the moors with dogs and guns and hunters. I was a transgender, socialist, TV presenter, we had nothing in common, except for that one terrible, life altering moment in 1985.

We shared the stories of our lives, how the explosion and subsequent trauma had shaped us over the years, the post traumatic stress taking its toll as surely as the flying shrapnel had.

On the 30th anniversary of the incident he had joined Facebook in order to contact me and through a circuitous route, through Steve to Sophie he'd finally found me. The question for me 'was when would I find me?'

. . . . .

I long ago became at ease with the idea of my own death, after all, I had spent three decades with suicidal feelings so if anything happened to me it was, effectively, just saving me a job. As a result of this I didn't always make the safest, or best, choices for my health. My time spent motocrossing in Saudi Arabia, whilst primarily about the adrenalin kick, saw me removing my own casts from broken bones to get back out on the track no matter how bad I felt.

I had made unsafe choices with regards to what I put into my body, unhealthy food and alcohol. I had chosen risky relationships and liaisons and as my new life slipped from exhilaration at finally finding myself to despair at the loss of my marriage the demons and destructive patterns once again returned.

. . . . .

Each year 1 million people kill themselves and another 10-20 million try to.

The Golden Gate Bridge in San Francisco is the second-most used suicide site in the world, the first is the Nanjing Yangtze River Bridge in China.

Four seconds after leaping from the walkway you hit the cold water 245 feet below at 75mph, impact trauma kills most jumpers and another 5% drown or succumb to hypothermia. The currents below the bridge are strong and many of the people that take their own lives here are washed out to sea and never recovered.

Between 1937 and 2012 around 1600 people are thought to have leapt from the bridge with the fall being fatal in 98% of cases, only 34 people are known to have survived the fall.

The survivors, however, tell a similar tale, how during the four seconds before impacting the water they immediately questioned their actions. Kevin Hines who, as a paranoid and hallucinating 19-year-old, had leapt from the bridge in 2000 said: "There was a millisecond of free fall. In that instant, I thought, what have I just done? I don't want to die. God, please save me."

Suicide is not the 'cowards way out' as so many dismissively refer to it, it occurs when the fear of living becomes greater than the fear of dying.

It takes a Herculean effort to override the survival instinct that is hard wired into our DNA. Taking your own life is not a natural act and for generations people have believed that it's an act confined to the human experience.

In 1845 the Illustrated London News reported the story of a Newfoundland dog, the eponymous 'black dog', a "fine, handsome and valuable" animal which had been behaving in a listless manner for a number of days that was seen "to throw himself in the water and endeavour to sink by preserving perfect stillness of the legs and feet". Whenever he was pulled from the waters he "again hastened to the water and tried to sink again."

Eventually the dog succeeded in holding his head underwater long enough to drown.

Over the years other stories have emerged, of drowning ducks, hung cats, livestock jumping off cliffs or the case of the star of the 1960s TV show 'Flipper' who according to her trainer drowned herself in front of his eyes, and then there's the story of the lemmings that throw themselves from cliffs in mass suicides.

Nature documentaries have always been difficult to film, they are resource and time intensive and animals are notoriously uncooperative when presented with a shooting script.

Long before the BBC and David Attenborough produced the epic 'Planet Earth' and 'Blue Planet' programmes Disney won an Academy Award for 'White Wilderness'. This 1958 "true-life adventure" told the stories of the animals that made their homes in the snowy north of the Northern American continent and one of the stories they had to include was that of the "suicidal" lemmings.Having struggled to get footage of this strange behaviour the filmmakers decided to stage the scene using animals that had been specially imported to landlocked Alberta from other parts of Canada.

"It is said of this tiny animal that it commits mass suicide by rushing into the sea in droves. The story is one of the persistent tales of the Arctic, and as often happens in Man's nature lore, it is a story both true and false." The narrator intones as the rodents fall off a cliff, apparently driven by a compulsion to take their own lives, what you don't see is the stagehands pushing the tiny animals off the precipice in order to get the shot.

Zoologist Gordon Jarrell, from the University of Alaska Fairbanks explains the behaviour that Disney misinterpreted as mass dispersal. "They will come to a body of water and be temporarily stopped, eventually they'll build up along the shore so dense and they will swim across. If they get wet to the skin, they're essentially dead. Do they really kill themselves? No. The answer is unequivocal, no they don't."

The survival instinct is at the core of all sentient life, without it antelopes would graze near lions and very soon become extinct. Evolution is not just the survival of the fittest, it's survival of the cautious.

$$\cdots\cdots$$

We know that animals suffer mental health issues in similar ways to humans. They feel stress, they get depressed, and they can suffer from the effects of post traumatic stress, but do they take their own lives by suicide?

Suicide requires an understanding about our place in the world and the imagination to picture a world without our presence. It requires a concept of time and the ability to build a narrative of life and death. Suicide is inducing our own mortality to end perceived suffering, either in ourselves or others. It is the result of the fear of living being greater than the fear of dying and that requires an understanding of our own mortality.

Self awareness is essential to all human creativity but the downside to our ability to create these narratives is that we can be too good at it. We worry about things we have no control over, we suffer anxiety over future disasters that may never happen, and we fear that the worst case will always prevail.

Optimism is the ability to see the silver lining in the clouds but for those suffering from depression the imagination of potential disaster and pain play a major role in affecting their mental health.

The understanding of time and the ability to project ideas into the future is one of the human races greatest gifts, without it all of human achievement would not have been possible.

Self destruction and the ability to picture taking our own lives is the price that we pay for that gift.

$$\cdots\cdots$$

But how would my mental health have been different if I'd transitioned in 2000?

Surely avoiding those fifteen years of pain would have helped.

When you start down the road of 'what ifs' then you ultimately have to ask yourself how unlikely is our very existence?

That these atoms would have formed this body, this mind, this person. It took a million moments to make us, the moment when that particular sperm released by our father in the height of passion reached that particular egg that our mother had carried since birth. If another sperm had got there first then we wouldn't be the person that we are, we would be someone else.

The moment when our parents met and felt an attraction, their parents, grandparents, and backwards to the moment when our ancestors first climbed out of the primordial soup to crawl upon the land.

Indeed none of those moments would have happened at all if the Chicxulub impactor, the 9 mile wide meteor that crashed into the Yucatán Peninsula in Mexico 66 million years ago had arrived ten minutes later. As it crashed into the Earth it unleashed the power of 10 billion Hiroshima A-bombs creating a cloud of superheated dust, ash and steam that spread across the globe blocking the heat and light of the sun and leading to the mass extinction of 75% of plant and animal species, including the dinosaurs.

Even the forming of our planet as we know it may not have happened if it had been impacted by one or more additional celestial bodies, asteroids or comets, that could have altered its orbit infinitesimally, changing the climate, the environment that allowed for the creation of life or perhaps moving it out of the path of that history changing meteor all together.

So many millions of moments have made us who we are, from the person that dumped us when we thought that we might get married, the job that we lost causing us to change career, to the trauma that shaped our mental health and all the way back through an infinite stream of moments to the beginning of time itself.

So no, I don't regret not transitioning in 2000, the world was a very different place, I was a very different person and I honestly don't think that we were ready for each other.

Besides which if I'd transitioned in 2000 I may have avoided fifteen years of pain but I wouldn't have my daughter Sadie, and she's worth fifteen years of pain.

She's fourteen so I've probably got at least another fifteen years of pain to look forward to.

· · · · ·

I know that one day I'll kill myself, because I don't know how to stop feeling this way but it won't be today. In the meantime I'm going to do the best I can to enjoy every single day and then on the day that I die, in many, many years time, I'll look back and realise that I didn't get around to doing it.

. . . . .

With this simple revelation I found a way to live. It may not have slain my demons completely but it significantly reduced their power to hurt me.

By saying 'Not Today' I gave myself permission to experience those dark days when I felt suicidal without the guilt and shame that multiply its ability to hurt you. These words allowed me to move on from the dark place.

Three decades of living with suicidal ideation had taught me two key lessons, I just needed to think clearly enough to see them.

The first lesson was that suicide was not the end, there is nothing final about suicide, it is not the end of your pain. All it does is to take your pain and give it to someone else. No matter how alone we feel there will always be someone affected by us taking our own lives, family, friends, the person that finds our body. Even in isolation we send ripples out into the world, ripples of joy, kindness, cruelty or despair.

I felt very strongly that the pain that I carried belonged to me and no one else, certainly not my children who I knew would be the worst affected if I was to take my own life.

Secondly I realised that this feeling would pass, it always did. Every single time that I had felt suicidal in the past the feeling eventually passed, hours or even days later, but pass it did.

People say that what doesn't kill you makes you stronger, I would disagree but ultimately what doesn't kill you doesn't kill you. The reality is that we recover from everything except death.

Some days I wake up and feel happy, some sad, some suicidal, but on the suicidal days I acknowledge the feeling and then get on with my life, no more, no less, after all I know that I won't do it and I know that the feeling will pass.

Effectively what I did was to put suicide on my To Do List.

I'm a great fan of David Allen's book 'Getting Things Done', it uses the four D's to help us lead better, more productive and fulfilling lives. The first part of the process is to capture all of those ideas that are floating around in your head, distracting you and drawing your focus away from more productive activities. As soon as you write an idea down your brain says 'ok, we've made a note of that, I can relax'.

Once you've captured all of those thoughts it's time to get productive with the four D's:

- Do It - If it takes less than two minutes, do it now. So many times we look at a task and spend more time procrastinating about it than it would take to have done it.
- Defer It - If it takes more than two minutes, and it's something that only you can do, defer it. Add it to a list of next actions, or schedule it to be done at a more convenient time.
- Delegate It - Is there someone else that could do the task? Either because they're better at it or it's their responsibility, then delegate it to them.
- Delete It - Let's face it, there's always stuff that pops up in our consciousness that is unimportant or irrelevant, if so delete it and allow yourself to think about the important issues.

Whilst this tool has helped me to be more productive in life, especially in dealing with the hundreds of emails that we all seem to receive on a daily basis nowadays, it's also helped me with my mental health, albeit through me subverting and perverting the process.

Suicide has now been data captured and put on my To Do list, effectively freeing my mind up from having to constantly think about it. Yes I know that's a major simplification, and it's not foolproof but it has helped me.

Now that it's on my To Do list it's time to apply the for D's.

- Do It - Well the whole point is that I don't actually want to complete this task and besides it takes a lot of planning and I'm really not convinced that I can do it inside of two minutes.
- Delegate It - That doesn't seem entirely fair to the person that gets the job and strictly speaking if you delegate suicide then it ceases to be that and becomes murder.
- Delete It - Try as I might over the years I have never come close to deleting this feeling, when I tried it resisted my efforts and made matters worse, and to be honest, I don't think that I ever will.

So that just leaves defer it and I've now scheduled this for some undefined date in the future, not sure when but my plan is that it won't be due until long after I have left this earth for other, less self induced, reasons.

Yes, it's on my To Do list, but we all know how one of those works. Our To Do lists are made up of big, scary tasks like 'write book' and small, meaningless tasks 'buy staples'. It's easier to do the small tasks and convince ourselves that we've achieved something, all the while ignoring the difficult, hard thing that takes a lot more effort. If you could only see how many staples I now own as a result of writing this book you'd know it's true, and I don't even own a stapler.

Suicide is now the biggest, most difficult thing on my To Do list, and there will always be staples that need buying long before I get around to that task.

Ah the human mind can be a wonderful thing, it has the power to destroy you but it can still be creative enough to pervert productivity tools in order to harness the power of procrastination as a defence against suicide.

And on that note I'm just off to update my chapter plan showing me how much more I have to write, even when you're being productive procrastination can jump right in.

· · · · ·

Early in my transition I was telling an old friend the story of how I'd originally tried to transition back in 2000 and I was explaining how the world had changed in the past 15 years, and how back then I would be abused wherever I went.

When I explained that things were different now and mentioned how society was much more tolerant she cut me off dead.

"Never, ever say that people are tolerant", she replied, "it implies that there's something wrong with you that people need to tolerate".

Good point I thought, and suitably chastised I tried to reword what I'd just said.

"Well, people are more accepting…"

I caught myself, that was scarcely better than tolerating, it still implies a wrongness that people need to put themselves out to find acceptable.

Eventually, after much thinking, I replaced the phrase with "more open to diversity". This conveyed the same point but with none of the negative connotations about the legitimacy of my place in society.

I thought about the language that I used with myself, the way in which subtle phrasing reinforced my negative self image and mental outlook.

How much better does it feel to think about the challenges in my life rather than the problems? It was just a simple thing but that simple word substitution moved me from problems which have connections to words like insurmountable to challenges which can be met and achieved. I'm definitely not a happy clappy 'think the world better' kind of person, I know that there are injustices in this world that can't be fixed with nice language and a positive mental attitude. The darkness is necessary for us to appreciate the light but if we can make changes to our internal dialogue then we can modify how we react to the darkness and thereby lessen its influence.

Depression and fear speak the language of negativity and pain but they also lie.

Fear is a liar, depression is a liar, and they both use whatever language it takes to hold you down in that dark place where the demons live.

· · · · ·

I'm sat on the beach at home in Sussex. The day could not be more beautiful, the sun glistens off the sea but I'm tired and I'm lonely, I've learnt to be comfortable with my own company but I still struggle. I have stresses, I have fears but on the whole life is ok.

But on this glorious day as I look out to sea I think about suicide, not because I hate myself not because I'm scared but simply because it's part of who I am. I'm tired, so tired that I think about suicide, I want to go to sleep and never wake up. This is suicide as pain relief, emotional and physical. I'm not scared of my own death, to me it's part of the natural order of things. Death is just the next stage of my journey but it's not as easy as that. Death leaves people behind, and that loss brings pain. Those left behind miss us and we will never see them grow old.

I find that I am fascinated by my own mental health, the way in which the suicidal feelings just come to me on good days and bad. They don't cause me pain in the way they used to for I know they are just part of me. But if I could just stop being, at this moment of peace, of happiness, pain free, it would be a release from future pain which I know will come.

I wonder about the moment of death and enlightenment, do we become enlightened at the moment of our death or does death come at the moment of our enlightenment?

Does the grim reaper appear and say "well done, you've learnt everything that you were placed on this earth to learn, off you go".

Although, of course, in this scenario death would not be the grim reaper but a kindly leader or guide, your parents or lost loved ones or even your God, who for my part I most often envisage as Morgan

Freeman, thank you popular culture.

I guess it all depends on your spirituality, are we unique beings that exist but for this single moment or are we part of something bigger. Do our souls live on?

My own spirituality has us living forever in the hearts of those who loved us, for if we are still loved then we are never truly gone. A kind of empathic transference where we become part of the human collective. Our acts touch others and each time we do that part of us joins their soul, an act of kindness or love, each one leaves an impression that can enrich others' lives and cause them to think of us when we're gone.

Of course acts of cruelty and unkindness can also have the same effect and they inject pain and fear into the souls of the people that we meet.

When we go, we live on due to these interactions, and when those that think of us finally die, we live on within the souls that loved them. The ultimate case of paying it forward.

To me kindness and the need to help others is a spiritual need, for if we can help others, touching and improving their lives in some small way then we can all live on in the collective human soul forever, one starfish at a time.

. . . . .

I had been drinking for as long as I could remember. As a teenager in Germany suffering from post traumatic stress it had dulled the pain, in Saudi Arabia it had alleviated the loneliness, and now it helped me to forget my loss.

But as I slowly came to understand the nature of my pain the intoxicants that had once helped so much began to have the opposite effect. Where once they had helped me to escape the darkness now they dragged me back to that cold, lonely place. I needed to keep my wits in order to keep the demons at bay, drinking only reduced my ability to defend myself from myself. I would return to the same destructive patterns and behaviours again and again until I finally realised that booze just wasn't my friend, or if it was it was the troublemaking friend from school that you should have outgrown years ago.

Like my recovery from my mental pain the recovery from addiction was also going to prove hard, and with both it's one day at a time. We try to make good choices today and we will worry about tomorrow when it comes. One day at a time. Not today.

. . . . .

To my body
I'm sorry for every time I told you that you were ugly
I'm sorry for every time I broke you or hurt you
I'm sorry for every time that I took risks with your safety
I'm sorry for every time I fed you poison for the sake of a high
I'm sorry for every time that I thought you weren't good enough
I'm sorry for every time that I took you for granted
I'm sorry for every time I rejected you as my home
I'm not saying that I won't do these things again
I will try and probably fail
But I just thought that you should know
I'm sorry.

· · · · ·

The abuses that we suffered, at our own hands and the hands of others, chained us to that mistreatment. An anchor that drags us down, forever holding us back from moving on and achieving our goals, love and happiness. The resentment and recrimination consumes us rather than reducing the pain or healing the wounds. It turns you away from love and towards hate, becoming the very things that hurt you.

The realisation that you want to live changes so much.

Trivial things that seemed important cease to be. Pain diminishes and anger fades.

In time forgiveness presents the path to freedom. It isn't about being a doormat, it's not about turning the other cheek or forgetting what was done. Forgiveness is about acknowledging the hurt and then finding meaning in it for it's only when we are free of that past pain that we can ever truly be happy.

Freedom allows you to speak the truth, to see beauty and love.

After a lifetime in darkness the truth can be terrifying, freedom can be terrifying.

Freedom is dangerous.

· · · · ·

I close my eyes and lean back against the rocks as the last rays of the sun begin to lose their warmth and a chill passes through me.

The waves churn the pebbles of the beach as the tide recedes away from the land.

"I was only ever looking out for you", the darkness beside me gently intones.

He's there but respectful, keeping his distance.

"I saw your pain, I saw your unhappiness and I needed to help."

I feel no fear as he talks to me, there is no malice in his voice only concern.

"I wanted you to be free of the pain."

"I know."

"I wanted you to have a way out."

"There were times when you were my only friend, when I was so alone that you were the only person there to hold me", I reply.

"I wanted you to be free."

"I know, but I don't need you to do that anymore. I will deal with the pain, I will find my path, I want to live."

The void beside me grows slightly, reaching out towards me, testing the air around me before retreating.

"I'll always be here. If ever the pain gets too great and you need me I will be here, watching and waiting."

"I know."

17

THE SUMMER THAT CHANGED EVERYTHING

Stepping up to the lectern erected yards outside her front door and faced by the world's press Theresa May, the accidental Prime Minister who got the job when no one else wanted it following David Cameron's disastrous Brexit Referendum, cleared her throat and began addressing the nation.

"I have just chaired a meeting of the Cabinet, where we agreed that the Government should call a general election, to be held on June 8.

Last summer, after the country voted to leave the European Union, Britain needed certainty, stability and strong leadership, and since I became Prime Minister the Government has delivered precisely that.

Despite predictions of immediate financial and economic danger, since the referendum we have seen consumer confidence remain high, record numbers of jobs, and economic growth that has exceeded all expectations.

We have also delivered on the mandate that we were handed by the referendum result.

Britain is leaving the European Union and there can be no turning back. And as we look to the future, the Government has the right plan for negotiating our new relationship with Europe.

At this moment of enormous national significance there should be unity here in Westminster, but instead there is division.

The country is coming together, but Westminster is not.

Our opponents believe that because the Government's majority is so small, our resolve will weaken and that they can force us to change course.

They are wrong.

They underestimate our determination to get the job done and I am not prepared to let them endanger the security of millions of working people across the country."

· · · · ·

Lying naked on the beach, enjoying the warm April sunshine, I studied the updates on the BBC News app. So she's done it, the Prime Minister that had continually and vociferously insisted that there wouldn't be an early election had called an early election.

Over recent months I had been having conversations with various people within the local Labour Party who believed that I could be a plausible candidate when the next general election was due in 2020. Those plans and that timetable had just been blown out of the water by Theresa May's announcement.

I immediately texted my friend Libby Barnes, a staunch supporter of Jeremy Corbyn, a Momentum member and vice-chair of campaigns for Brighton Kemptown and Peacehaven Constituency Labour Party (CLP).

"So what do you think? Should I go for it?" I asked her.

The it was the candidacy for Brighton Kemptown, a seat that the Tory Simon Kirby had won two years previously with a majority of only 690 votes ahead of the Labour candidate Nancy Platts.

"Definitely, you'd be amazing", Libby replied enthusiastically.

"I won't even think about it if Nancy is standing again", I replied, "I would never stand against an existing candidate that had done a good job".

"I'm hearing rumours that she might not stand again, let's see what happens."

· · · · ·

The election was predicted to be the death of the Labour Party. Ever since Jeremy Corbyn was elected Party Leader two years earlier the press and, more disappointingly, a majority of Blairite Labour MPs had constantly regurgitated the line that Corbyn was unelectable and that to fight a General Election with him as leader would be political suicide for the Party.

As the arrangements became clearer it was obvious that any previously standing candidates would be automatically selected to stand again so everything was down to whether or not Nancy, who had already stood twice, wanted to try again one more time.

When she announced that she wasn't going to try for a third time

I looked into the selection process. Applications were due to open at lunchtime on Friday and close at midday on the Sunday of that weekend. The process looked clear enough but I had the small distraction of a Premier League football match on the Saturday, severely limiting the time available for me to complete the application form but I knew that I had to go for it.

Friends within the Party suggested that it was a good idea for me to have my first choice of constituency and potentially one or two second choices. Looking at the list of constituencies open for applications I put my name forward for Brighton Kemptown, Arundel, and East Worthing and Shoreham. Kemptown was a potential win for Labour, although the stories of Corbyn's unelectability made it unlikely, but the other constituencies were safe Tory seats that were deemed impossible for a Labour candidate to ever win.

As soon as the applications opened I downloaded the form and began to read through the questions. At first glance it all looked straightforward enough, Labour Party experience, personal skills, why you would be a good candidate, and your thoughts on various policy areas including a 250 and 50 word personal statement. Having been a newspaper editor I was used to writing to word counts and felt confident that I could get the essence of me across within the stipulations of the application.

On the Saturday morning I made the journey along the south coast to Bournemouth and the football ground at Dean Court, pre-empting heavy traffic due to the nice weather and holidaymakers heading to the beach I arrived at the ground a full three hours before I was needed and spent those hours in the media suite working away on my laptop at my candidates application form. Occasionally I would stop to show my work to the football club's head of media, Anthony Marshall, who would make supportive if not entirely convinced noises at my intentions.

On the Sunday morning I arose early to get the form completed before the midday deadline and as I logged on to update my application I was shocked to realise that there were a number of questions that I hadn't spotted at first glance and at this point my journalists experience of writing to deadlines really came into its own. As the clock approached midday I completed the forms with minutes to spare, now I just had to wait.

· · · · ·

Due to the short timeframe involved with the snap election the candidate selection process had been taken away from local Constituency

Labour Parties in order to get candidates in position as quickly as possible but as the days stretched to weeks the wait became interminable.

I began campaigning in Kemptown alongside other activists, going out door knocking around the Whitehawk estate, helping on street stalls and increasing my social media activity. A number of local members were very supportive of my application and expressed their opinion that I would make a great candidate, fingers crossed.

At Latest TV we were looking to introduce a number of new TV shows and as part of the process we held a management meeting in the basement of the bar which was home to the TV station. It was positive meeting with some great ideas but following it I took the boss Bill Smith to one side and told him about my application to stand as a parliamentary candidate.

"Unfortunately this means that I'm going to have to step back from my presenting duties", I told him.

Ofcom rules about impartiality meant that I could no longer present the news and stand as a candidate, in fact these regulations had forced me to pass on standing for political office only 12 months earlier.

"Who knows I may not even get selected", I told him, "in which case I can just return to work."

"Let's worry about that when it happens", replied Bill, "you're just the sort of person that we need in politics and you'd be great at it".

· · · · ·

The candidate announcements were all due to be made by the following Sunday and I spent the day following the progress and rumours on social media, becoming increasingly frustrated as other constituencies were announced, all the while wondering when our news might be coming.

Around 5pm my phone rang.

"Hi, is that Sophie?" the voice on the phone asked. "This is Amy at Labour Party Southeast region and I just wanted to congratulate you on being selected as the candidate for East Worthing and Shoreham".

As the call ended I sat back in my armchair and gazed towards the sea. East Worthing and Shoreham I thought to myself, it's going to be a challenge but at least I'm a candidate.

· · · · ·

Stretching from the eastern wards of Worthing along the coast to encompass the town of Shoreham-by-Sea, Lancing and the villages of the Adur valley, East Worthing and Shoreham had been represented in the House of Commons since the constituency was established in 1997 by Conservative Tim Loughton and was considered to be one of the safest of Tory seats. In the 2015 General Election Loughton had polled 24,686 votes to the Labour candidate, Tim Macpherson's 9,737, a majority of 15,000 votes.

With the selection process taking up two weeks of the already limited election campaign and with only five weeks to go until polling day I was keen to get started immediately.

I'd already been out door knocking in Kemptown and was keen to join the activists in my new constituency who I felt sure must have been out doing the same, picking up the phone I called the CLP chair Irene Reid full of enthusiasm at the task ahead.

"Hi Irene? This is Sophie Cook, I've just been selected as your candidate for the general election. I'm keen to get started as soon as possible as we've already lost two weeks, is it possible to meet up tomorrow morning at 9am so that we can discuss strategy, campaigning and how we are going to win this election?"

"I can't do anything tomorrow", she replied, "but I could possibly see you on Tuesday evening".

"But that's another 48 hours and we've only got five weeks until polling day, I'm eager to get started as soon as possible."

"I know that you're very excited but I need to tell you that we won't actually be running a campaign. This is a safe Tory seat and we've already decided that we will be sending all of our resources to Hove to protect Peter Kyle's majority."

In the space a couple of minutes I'd gone from the high of selection to the low of being told that I wouldn't actually have a campaign, that the CLP where I had been asked to stand saw me purely as a placeholder paper candidate, a name on the ballot paper purely to ensure that Labour was represented.

That evening as I sat in Lennon's bar in Kemptown alongside jubilance activists keen to take the fight to the Tories and support their candidate Lloyd Russell-Moyle I felt a great sense of loss. I'd been selected for the greatest honour of my life, to represent the Labour Party in a fight for the very soul of our nation and I'd been told that I couldn't expect any support by the very person that was supposed to be coordinating my campaign.

Welcome to politics, welcome to East Worthing and Shoreham.

· · · · ·

It gives me the greatest honour to announce that I am standing as the Labour Party Parliamentary Candidate for East Worthing & Shoreham in the 2017 General Election.

In the 1980s at the height of the Cold War I was stationed in West Germany with an RAF Tornado squadron. Suffering from Post Traumatic Stress having saved the life of a colleague following an explosion, I was filled with an acute sense of injustice at the way the world operated.

This was Thatcher's Britain, the miners' strike, rioting on the streets, section 28 and a war in Northern Ireland.

I already knew that I was transgender, even if I didn't have a name for it at that point. I knew that there was something about my identity that just didn't feel right. The mental anguish of my gender dysphoria coupled with the PTSD led to depression, and then self harming and suicide attempts.

As I became more aware of what my trans identity meant I realised that any political ambitions that I might have had were out of the question, with politicians being outed for their sexuality what chance did a bisexual transgender person have.

Even when I came out in 2015 I was still terrified that by being true to myself that I would lose everything, my career in football, my family and most of all, my children. By being true to myself I've lost a lot, but my children have been amazing and I regularly see my two youngest kids.

When I came out I faced a choice, to either hide or to stand up and try to make a difference.

I began speaking about my journey and very soon found myself speaking at venues like Wembley Stadium and the TUC. My story moved people, not because it was unusual but because it included universal messages of fear, loss and redemption.

I was offered a job in television and I saw this as an opportunity to continue the work that I'd done years before with my newspaper, to educate and inspire people to change the world around them.

In 2016 I was approached to stand for local political office but was barred from this opportunity unless I gave up the TV work and so, reluctantly, I had to decline. And then Theresa May called a snap general election, the plans that I'd had to potentially stand in 2020 were thrown into overdrive and I declared an interest in becoming a candidate.

The country needs a change, years of austerity have left whole communities desperate and lost.

I've been out on the streets, speaking to voters and they feel isolated and unrepresented by the Tory government.

The reception to me, as a trans woman, has been positive with many declaring that it's time for greater diversity in parliament.

The time is right, the time is now and we must all work together to achieve a more caring, diverse society where everyone can live free from fear and where no one suffers from prejudice regardless of their gender, sexuality, gender identity, race, religion, disability or wealth.

And that is why I am proud to be the Labour Party candidate for East Worthing & Shoreham.

As an ex-newspaper editor and broadcaster, as well as my experience as a public speaker I know that I have the skills and belief to serve the Party and constituency well.

It is time for a united Labour Party to work together to defeat the Tories and work for the good of all, regardless of their position in society.

At AFC Bournemouth, the Premier League club for whom I am the photographer, we have a motto: Together anything is possible.

It was true for us and it can be true for the Labour Party.

We need to work together to ensure that our children can grow up in a country where their health and education are priorities. Where there are jobs for their future and where difference is celebrated. And the Labour Party has pledged to build a million homes so that our children can in turn begin their own families in safety.

Education for all, health care for all and homes for all.

The time for change is now, a united Labour Party working for a United Kingdom.

Be the change that you want to see in the world.

Thank you.

Sophie Cook, General Election statement, Apr 30, 2017

· · · · ·

On the Tuesday evening, sat around the small kitchen table in the house of the CLP chair, Irene Reid, I got to meet the people that were planning to run, or not as the case would be, my campaign.

They had already selected my electoral agent, a vital role as this is the person responsible for the promotion of the candidate and ensuring that the campaign stayed within electoral law.

Once again it was reiterated that we wouldn't be running a campaign. We could do two street stalls and perhaps four sessions of door knocking but we wouldn't have any resources and the members were all being instructed to help in Hove.

In Kemptown I'd already participated in more activity than that over the past five days, the defeatism and lack of commitment was hard to take. I had left my job in TV in order to be their candidate and they had no intention of even trying to win.

I pointed out that not every member would want to help in Hove. Peter Kyle had been very vocal in his attempts to undermine Jeremy Corbyn's leadership and many on the left of the Party were disgusted with the actions of Blairite MPs within the Parliamentary Labour Party (PLP).

"They'll do what they're told", Irene responded angrily, "there will be no campaign here outside of what we have decided".

Walking back to my car I was more determined than ever. I was not a paper candidate, I was not there simply to make up the numbers on the ballot.

The Tories had been destroying the country that I loved, dismantling the NHS, underfunding our schools and putting more people than ever onto the streets. I would not rest until every Conservative MP had lost their seat and this was the battleground that I had been given. I would not take no for an answer.

· · · · ·

The following night I managed to meet up with some of the activists from the branches, much to Irene's annoyance, and we began to map out a possible campaign. It would still be low key compared to the thousands of pounds and hundreds of activists that were being poured into Hove but it was a start.

I'd also insisted that I wanted to meet the local Party members, Irene said it was a waste of time, but I couldn't expect members to campaign for a candidate that they'd never met and I knew that if I could speak to them I could make them believe in our campaign.

· · · · ·

Following my speech to assembled members in a packed meeting I was approached by a middle aged man with close cropped grey hair and stubble, dressed all in black, his t-shirt proclaiming that 'Most people ignore most poetry because most poetry ignores most people' the famous quote from Adrian Mitchell's preface to Poems (1964), his first major collection.

"Alright Sophie, I'm John", he introduced himself. "I do a lot of fundraising around the country, I'm a poet, Attila the Stockbroker, I don't normally get to do much locally as nothing much ever happens here."

I recognised his name from support slots for The Jam and the Peel Sessions that he'd done during the 80s. Earning his reputation as a punk poet in Thatcher's Britain, always ready with an acerbic line of prose, even when being beaten over the head with his own mandolin by Fascists. He spoke at a mile a minute, some internal energy constantly threatening to explode forth.

"I came along tonight to see what kind of Blairite, careerist they had parachuted in on us but I was pleasantly surprised. As soon as you started talking I realised that we finally had a real candidate and a real socialist."

Praise indeed and people were starting to believe.

. . . . .

My selection caused a few waves locally, I was told that "this isn't Brighton" and that the people of the constituency wouldn't warm to a transgender candidate.

The press gave my campaign some coverage and despite being one of nine transgender candidates I was the one that got the most attention due to my profile from working in football and TV.

"Labour candidate could become first transgender MP", said one headline while another mentioned the fight for LGBT rights, "Trans activist is fighting to oust anti-LGBT Conservative politician."

Being transgender and in the public eye I was already used to abuse, both online and in the real world. I'd been trolled by various groups and had even received death threats on Twitter and as I stepped into the political arena I was bracing myself for a renewed onslaught of hatred.

But then something unexpected happened. Instead of the abuse I was greeted with love and support, sure there were still a few transphobic remarks online but nothing like I'd experienced previously.

I'd heard first hand accounts of trans people moving out of the constituency because of abuse and yet, when I started to talk to people, they responded with warmth and openness.

My gender identity that had hit the headlines around the world seemed to mean nothing to the constituents that I met, it was never mentioned on the doorsteps, the street stalls or the hustings. The only people that made it an issue were the press, not the voters. They listened to the policies, my ideas, passion and belief and they embraced me.

The one time a constituent raised my gender identity it was a man who approached me on the street.

"When you were selected to be the candidate I didn't know much about you, or transgender people. Since then I've watched a few of your interviews and I get the impression that you would stand up for what you believe in, no matter how hard or difficult it was, and that's why I'm going to vote for you."

. . . . .

The campaign was suspended twice due to two horrific terrorist attacks that shook the nation, throwing a veil of grief over the election and bringing the majority of the country together while others used them to justify hate and Islamophobia.

On May 22, 2017, twenty-two people were killed when a suicide bomber detonated a homemade device in the lobby of Manchester Arena at the end of an Ariana Grande concert. More than 200 people, many of which were children and teenagers, were injured in the deadliest terror attack on British soil since the 2005 7/7 bombings in London.

The youngest victim, Saffie Roussos, was just eight years old.

In the week before polling day, on June 3, three terrorists wearing fake explosive vests drove a van into pedestrians on London Bridge before running into Borough Market stabbing people with knives.

Eight people were killed before armed police could shoot the attackers dead eight minutes after the first emergency calls were made.

Thirty lives lost, many of whom were children, killed by men driven by hate while politicians and the media fanned the flames. The anti-immigrant, anti-Islam, anti-foreigner rhetoric had led to an increase in hate crime since the Brexit Referendum. It had created the atmosphere that resulted in the murder of Labour MP Jo Cox and it would continue to claim more lives as the seeds of division and distrust were sown within our society.

I wanted to see a new politics, not of hate but of solidarity, built upon the belief that we will always be stronger together and that our differences and diversity are the things that make society richer, not poorer.

A new politics that ended the cycle of exploitation that seemed to be such a large part of our world. Exploitation of people, of animals and of our planet, all of these had to end.

If society was a person then it would be a deeply traumatised, abusive and self harming person. I believed that it was time for society to show a little self love and compassion. Society had to heal itself.

. . . . .

As the campaign progressed we managed to mobilise a few dozen local activists, it was much better than our officially sanctioned activities would have allowed but it was still nothing compared with the numbers that were flooding into Hove where some houses were canvassed so many times that people started complaining about it on social media.

Likewise funds were limited and John Baine, Attila the Stockbroker, approached me with an offer to put on a fundraising evening for my campaign.

"I hear that you've got a pretty good voice as well", he said, "fancy performing at your own fundraiser?"

"I haven't played live in twenty years", I replied, "but I'm up for that".

"Great, there can't be many candidates that play at their own campaign fundraisers, and don't forget, all of the songs have to be self written."

I may not have performed live for two decades but I also hadn't written a song in as long. I dusted off some old lyrics and, fortunately, remembered how the tunes went but I felt that I needed something new, something political. Picking up my guitar I began to write.

. . . . .

For the many, not the few

Verse - C Em / F G / C Em / F G
Chorus - F G / C Em / F G / C G

Tories robbing old folk blind
The poor, the ill, they're none too kind
Fuel the myth of strong and stable
But there's no food upon your table.

Chorus
United fighting for what's right
Out of the dark into the light
We'll raise the red flag not the blue
Fight for the many and not the few.

Press barons teaching you to hate
Wake up now it's not too late
With them burying the truth
We need to mobilise the youth.

No nurses for the old or weak
They tell you lies, the bare faced cheek
Stealing school dinners, winter fuel
They'll treat us all just like a fool.

With my rainbow flag I'm out and proud
Scream it clear and sing it loud
We're all the same under the skin
All one race, on kith and kin.

Chorus
United fighting for what's right
Out of the dark into the light
We'll raise the red flag not the blue
Fight for the many and not the few.

Sophie Cook, May 2017

. . . . .

I played that song, complete with singalong chorus, to a great reception at the fundraiser, making a campaign speech with a beat up Rickenbacker copy guitar slung around my neck and then on the weekend before the election I performed at Glastonwick Festival, opening for comedian Mark Thomas.

To all of the people that told me that they wouldn't be voting at all because all politicians are the same, I, clearly, was not.

. . . . .

As I look out at the sea I contemplate the journey that I have been on.

Two years, to the day since I moved to Brighton, and only 23 months since I came out as Transgender. My life has changed beyond all recognition. The shy, scared person has found her voice and her purpose.

I've met wonderful people along the way and experienced joy and sadness, freedom and loss.

Today the people of East Worthing & Shoreham get to decide if they want me to stand up for them in Parliament and the responsibility sits large but welcome upon my shoulders.

When I was selected five short weeks ago no one gave us a chance but I, and others, dared to believe.

In a life full of uncertainty I have never felt more unsure about my future than at this moment. I gave up a career in television to stand and beyond 8am tomorrow morning I now have no idea what my life will hold.

Despite that, at this moment in time everything makes sense. My purpose seems clear. When I came out I had the choice to hide or to stand up to make the world a better place and that is what I've been trying to do, in my small way, every single day.

Today you have the opportunity to do the same thing, go out, VOTE LABOUR, and let us make the world a better, fairer, kinder place, together x

Sophie Cook, 04:30 June 8, 2017, Election Day

· · · · ·

Stood on the beach near my home in Hove I gazed along the shore to Shoreham and beyond to Worthing Pier pointing out to sea on the horizon.

Over the previous five weeks I had been forced to fight for everything against a CLP leadership that was happy to maintain the status quo, against a Party that had decided that we were not worthy of support, and against public opinion stoked against Labour with claims that our leader, Jeremy Corbyn, was a terrorist sympathiser, anti-semite and a danger to the nation.

The maximum permissible expenditure on a General Election campaign by any candidate is £12,000, our budget had been £1500, we'd brought in a further £400 from fundraisers and £300 or so through crowdfunding. The CLP had even suggested that the crowdfunder money be put towards replenishing CLP funds, this had been predominantly raised by my friends and my supporters and the thought that it would be diverted to other uses felt dishonest and disgusted me. Eventually I used all of the crowdfunded money for Facebook advertising but, again, it took a fight.

A small but dedicated group of party members had put hours into pounding the streets with me, talking to voters and delivering leaflets. With the limited support that we received there was very little more that we could have accomplished and I am eternally grateful for their support.

On the day of an election the main tasks for activists are telling, checking off who has voted, and GOTV, Get Out The Vote, whereby you knock up all of the people that you have identified as potential

Labour voters through your previous canvassing activities. Getting out the vote is considered to be one of the most crucial elements of any election campaign.

We were told that we would be running no GOTV activities at all. If any of our local activists wanted to be involved then they had to go to Hove knocking up for Peter Kyle who only two days earlier had been visible in the national press saying that there was no way that Labour would win because of Jeremy Corbyn.

Whilst we were barred from getting out the vote in our constituency our activists were knocking on doors in Hove, sometimes for the third or fourth time that day due to the numbers of people that had been called in to help.

· · · · ·

"Hi, I hope you don't mind but I just wanted to say hello."

"No, of course, please take a seat," I replied as the young woman sat opposite me on the train.

"I wanted to let you know how much you standing means to us all", she continued. "I was at my friend's hen night in London and I left early to catch the train back to Worthing to vote for you."

"Thank you so much, that means the world to me."

"We need people like you in politics that are prepared to stand up and fight for what they believe in. You can do this, we need change."

As I got off the train at Worthing station there were 30 minutes until the polls closed, I said goodbye and thank you to the woman and readied myself for the long night ahead.

· · · · ·

The clock ticked down in the bottom corner of the screen, 'Polls close 00:20'.

"There are just over 20 seconds to go until Big Ben strikes ten, then I'll be able to reveal the results of the BBC, ITV and Sky joint exit poll. Over thirty thousand people, 144 polling stations, were questioned today and by the magic of psephology we're able to predict what we think has happened tonight."

As he finishes introducing the BBC's election night coverage David Dimbleby turns to the screen behind him as the graphics appear on screen.

'Exit poll: Conservatives largest party.'

No overall majority.

'Conservatives 314, Labour 266, SNP 34, LibDems 14, Plaid Cymru 3, Green 1, UKIP 0, Other 18'

"314 seats for the Conservatives, that's down 17", Dimbleby continues. "266 for Labour, that's up 34."

"The Prime Minister called this election because, as she put it, she wanted 'certainty and stability', well this doesn't look like certainty and stability."

· · · · ·

Sitting Tory MP, Tim Loughton, was used to elections being coronations, of little import and even less drama, but as soon as he entered Worthing Assembly Hall he knew that something had changed.

Where he was used to seeing his piles of votes towering over all others there was instead two very evenly matched piles of votes, one labelled 'Loughton' and the other 'Cook'.

Worthing doesn't start the count until some other seats have already declared and as the first results came in it became obvious that the much predicted death of the Labour Party was not going to happen.

At 11pm, barely an hour after the polls closed Houghton & Sunderland South declared, Labour hold. Followed a while later by Sunderland Central at 11.30 and Washington & Sunderland West at 00.01 both also Labour hold.

The first seat to change hands came at 1am when Marsha De Cordova won Battersea for Labour with a swing of 9.1% from the Conservatives.

Theresa May's gamble to destroy the Labour Party and enhance her own position had failed spectacularly despite the best efforts of the press and some within Labour, keen to use a defeat to oust Jeremy Corbyn once and for all.

For weeks I'd been telling people that we would get 20,000 votes and that we could win. My belief was based upon the feeling that I got out on the streets, talking to voters. Two years earlier our candidate had only managed to register 9,737 votes but I was confident that we could double that. Having heard how disliked Tory Tim Loughton was around the constituency I was sure that he would drop 5000 votes meaning that we could win the seat.

The hours dragged on as ballot box after ballot box was verified, opened, emptied and counted. Volunteers from the Party acted as observers, watching for irregularities. Unsurprisingly, given their previous lack of support, the CLP Chair and my Electoral Agent both decided that they had better things to do, creating a potential issue if we needed to request a recount.

At around 4.30am I asked the returning officer if he was expecting to have a result in the next 30 minutes or so.

"No, you're good", he replied as I pulled my coat on and walked out into the night.

· · · · ·

The sun was beginning to brighten the sky to the east as I sat on the deserted steps in front of the colonnaded entrance to St Paul's Church. The chapel had been opened in 1812 with the building being funded by the sale and leasing of pews. I thought about how the poor were effectively excluded from the church through this process until it was finally upgraded to parish status in 1893.

Our system had always presented one set of life opportunities for the haves and one for the have nots, even to the extent of different places of worship. Tim Loughton represented so many things that I disliked in our split society, he epitomised privilege and entitlement and tonight we had a chance to change that.

· · · · ·

East Worthing and Shoreham was one of the last seats to declare at 6am and by that stage we knew that the Conservatives had lost their majority. Rather than the much crowed about 'historic defeat' for Labour and the end of Jeremy Corbyn it had been a validation of the common sense socialism that he represented.

As I stood on stage, a room full of expectant people looking up at me I was totally focused on the next words that I would hear.

"Sophie Rose Cook, Labour Party, 20,882."

In the space of five short weeks we'd achieved the seemingly impossible, taking a previously safe Tory seat and making it a marginal, increasing the Labour vote by 114% with one of the biggest swings in the country at 19.8%.

East Worthing & Shoreham had always been blue and the Tory incumbent, Tim Loughton, had been the MP for 20 years. He felt safe and secure that no one could ever challenge him, and I'm sure that the selection of a little known transgender TV presenter as the Labour candidate only added to the feeling that he would increase his 15,000 majority. He clung on to his seat, for now, but we had slashed his majority by 10,000 votes, the closest that he had come to losing the seat since he was first elected in 1997.

On June 8, 2017 nearly 21,000 people chose to put their mark next to my name on the ballot paper.

They weren't voting for a trans woman, they were voting for Sophie Cook, they were voting for the Labour Party. They saw beyond the headlines and the things that made us different and in their way struck a massive blow for trans equality.

As a result of that election we now had the most diverse parliament ever with 45 LGB MPs, I missed out on adding a T to that by 5000 votes. We need transgender politicians, after all everyone in society needs to feel represented. But the main reason why I believe that the time is right for a trans MP has nothing to do with equality or diversity, it's down to the constituents who put their faith in me to represent them, regardless of my gender identity.

In the days following the election I spoke to hundreds of people who said that I'd given them hope for the first time. That feeling went both ways, they saw that there is more that unites us than separates us, they saw a person rather than a label, and they too gave me hope for a brighter tomorrow.

· · · · ·

Five weeks ago no one gave Labour a chance in Theresa May's snap election, it was supposed to be the Prime Minister's coronation, proving that she was strong and stable enough to win everything we wanted from Brexit.

There were those that believed we had no hope, both outside and inside the party.

Five weeks later and that picture looks very different. Through the amazing, hard work of a team of committed activists with little or no resources we achieved a 19.8 swing towards Labour, picking up votes from all of the parties and increasing the Labour vote by over 11,000 from 9,737 to 20,882.

We fought a campaign based on belief, integrity, honesty and policies, and we reached out to more of our constituency than any party had ever done.

Yesterday the country voted for change, nationally and here in East Worthing & Shoreham. They voted for a more caring society, for the many, not the few. We still have a way to go to achieve that change here, in our constituency, but we will continue fighting towards that aim.

I gave up a career in television to become the candidate here, I have no job to go back to, but I don't regret that one bit. Life is a journey, not a destination, and whilst I may not have a job at the moment I think that I've found a new career.

If the Party wants me I will work to remain in politics and hope that someday in the near future that I get the opportunity again.

Thank you so much to everyone that worked with me, supported me and, of course, voted for me. I may not have achieved that change yet but I will not fail you.

Sophie Cook, 06:30 June 9, 2017
(30 minutes after the result was declared)

18
RED STAR

"Homophobia we say no, homophobia we say no,
Racism we say no, racism we say no,
Sexism we say no, sexism we say no,
DUP we say no, DUP we say no,
Oh oh we say no."

Marching at the head of the protest I'm proud to be alongside fellow Labour Party members, Trade Unionists and Whitehawk FC Ultras.

A day has passed since the election results were declared and Theresa May is hanging on to power by her fingertips. The loss of her majority means that if she hopes to form a government then she will need support from Northern Ireland in the form of the DUP, the Democratic Unionist Party. Their ten Westminster seats hold the key to a Conservative government.

Founded at the height of the Troubles by the Protestant fundamentalist minister, Ian Paisley, the DUP had blocked attempts to resolve the conflict by opposing any plans that involved power sharing with Irish nationalists or republicans. It had campaigned against numerous attempts to bring peace to the province, the 1973 Sunningdale Agreement, the Anglo-Irish Agreement of 1985, and the 1998 Good Friday Agreement.

During the 1980s, the party had helped set up the paramilitary Third Force and Ulster Resistance. In 1981 Ian Paisley addressed a Third Force rally of thousands of masked and uniformed men in Newtownards and declared: "My men are ready to be recruited under the crown to destroy the vermin of the IRA. But if they refuse to recruit them, then we will have no other decision to make but to destroy the IRA ourselves!"

In 1986 the DUP announced the formation of the Ulster Resistance

Movement (URM), a loyalist paramilitary group whose mission was to "take direct action as and when required". The following year, the URM helped smuggle a large shipment of weapons into Northern Ireland, and in 1989, URM members attempted to trade Shorts' missile blueprints for weapons from the apartheid South African regime.

After the constant stories during the election campaign about Jeremy Corbyn being a terrorist sympathiser Theresa May was now proposing to go into government with people that had actively supported loyalist terrorist organisations responsible for, among other atrocities, four car bombs that killed 33 civilians in Dublin and Monaghan in 1974.

Right-wing and socially conservative, pro-Brexit, pro-Israel, pro-capital punishment and anti-abortion. The DUP campaigned against the legalisation of homosexual acts, which it said were a "harmful deviance" linked to paedophilia, the party set up the "Save Ulster from Sodomy" campaign and ensured that Northern Ireland remains the only region of the UK where same-sex marriage is not permitted. Some DUP politicians have even called for creationism to be taught in schools.

Rumours abound that Theresa May will fail to form a government and that we will be back at the polls in the autumn. The prospect of the DUP helping to guide government policy is a terrifying prospect for many, and today's demonstration with speeches on the Level in Brighton shows the strength of public opinion.

"I want to introduce Sophie, who has fought the most amazing campaign against all the odds," Libby Barnes is on the microphone introducing me to the assembled crowd. "With no funding, and no real support unfortunately from our party except a few solid comrades who believed in her. Once you've heard from Sophie you're all going to believe in her, she's the most amazing strong woman and I really, really hope that she will be our first trans Labour MP - Sophie Cook".

As I step up to the microphone, the crowd is cheering and clapping, news of our historic result in East Worthing and Shoreham had really captured the imagination of activists across the south coast.

"On Thursday the people of this country voted for change. They voted for a country that was more caring, they voted for a country that was more diverse, they voted for a country that believed in education, healthcare and an ethical foreign policy. In East Worthing and Shoreham 20,882 people voted for a trans woman," a roar goes up from crowd, whistles and applause. "I haven't been to bed yet, I've been out campaigning again today because we are going to win the next election in October", laughs and cheers.

"This coalition of cruelty with the DUP shows just how low the Tories will go to cling on to power. They will get into bed with anti-abortionists, and creationists and homophobes. This country has voted for change, you all voted for change."

From the back of the crowd a woman shouts, "we love Jeremy Corbyn".

I repeat her words, "we love Jeremy Corbyn", cue more applause and cheers. "Two months ago they said that he was unelectable, do you think he's unelectable?"

A resounding "no" answers me.

"We will stand up to bigotry, we will stand up to sectarianism, we will stand up for freedom and liberty and we will never surrender. Go out, make your voices heard, if you believe enough and you make other people believe then you can change the world."

· · · · ·

Despite our hopes and protests, on June 26, more that two weeks after the election the Tories and the DUP sign a confidence and supply agreement.

"The DUP agrees to support the government on all motions of confidence; and on the Queen's Speech, the Budget, finance bills, money bills, supply and appropriation legislation. The DUP agrees to support the government in votes in the UK Parliament, in line with this agreement."

Confidence and Supply Agreement between the Conservative and Unionist Party and the Democratic Unionist Party

Theresa May had her majority and would form the next government.

· · · · ·

Our efforts in the election campaign hadn't gone unnoticed and I was honoured to be invited to join the Future Candidates Programme set up by Unite the Union. Over a weekend at the stately Esher Place convention venue I met a wonderful group of activists, some of whom had stood in the election and some that were coming up through the unions ranks to potentially one day stand for public office.

This marked the start of a valued and supportive relationship between myself and the trade union and through the network that I began to build both within the Party and the trade union movement I began to mobilise the resources that we would need to win the seat at the next election.

I never turned down an opportunity to speak, travelling the breadth of the south coast to deliver speeches at Labour Party CLPs, conferences, fringe events and on picket lines. Wherever I spoke activists promised to make the trip to East Worthing and Shoreham at the next election to join our fight for votes.

I was particularly honoured to be invited to join the striking British Airways cabin crew from Unite Mixed Fleet on the picket line outside Heathrow Airport and to give a speech to the assembled crew at their strike headquarters in a football club a short distance from the airport.

The bitter dispute over pay had been running for months and at its peak up to 2,000 members, mainly younger, recent recruits on inferior terms and conditions to most British Airways crew took action. I listened to their stories and was shocked to hear that cabin crew pay at BA started at a basic rate of just over £12,000.

I showed them that there were people in the wider Labour and trade union movement that cared about their fight and expressed disgust at the reprisals that had been dished out by the airline for staff who went on strike. Their fight was our fight and solidarity was at the heart of my political beliefs.

· · · · ·

Six months after the election I was honoured to be stood on stage at London's Park Lane Sheraton Hotel in front of over 400 guests, including Labour MPs and peers, being presented with an award as the Labour Parliamentary Candidate of the Year by SME4Labour.

In my speech I dedicated the award to every single activist that had helped in my campaign and spoke about increasing the diversity within politics and ensuring that Labour was seen as the party for small business owners.

· · · · ·

Throughout the following year the subject of bigotry never seemed far from the surface of British politics. There had been a huge rise in the number of hate crimes following the Brexit referendum, including those against LGBT people. It seems that the negative and often xenophobic language used in the campaign had emboldened the bigots who had now convinced themselves that the majority of the British people felt as they did about immigrants and gays.

There were continued claims of antisemitism within the Labour Party and whilst I would say that all organisations can include elements that reflect the bigotry in the society around them, I myself never saw it, but that isn't to say that it didn't exist.

What I did see though was an increasing appetite for seeing bigotry in legitimate criticism of the actions of certain governments and I think that it's important to remember that:

Criticism of the US government is not hatred of the American people.

Criticism of the Kingdom of Saudi Arabia is not Islamophobia.

Criticism of the state of Israel is not antisemitism.

We must always fight bigotry of all kinds, we must hold governments to account for their actions but we must never resort to hatred of a people.

· · · · ·

One of the most prolific of the cheerleaders for hate was celebrity racist Katie Hopkins.

Hopkins originally found notoriety on the third series of The Apprentice in 2007, yet another thing to thank Lord Sugar for, and in the intervening decade had made her name with a series of racist outbursts in her columns for right wing publications The Sun and The Mail.

There was an uproar when it was announced that she would be speaking at the Lewes Speakers Festival a few miles outside Brighton. The organisers claimed that they didn't know her reputation and protests were planned for the venue of her talk.

My opinion was that a protest gave her the attention and reaction that she so desperately craved and so I took a different tack. Taking inspiration from Lewes' most famous inhabitant, revolutionary, activist and philosopher, Thomas Paine, the "father of the American revolution". I booked the chapel that bears his name a few hundred yards from the venue for Hopkins talk and began planning my own show.

'Love/Hate: Guaranteed 100% hate free' didn't mention Hopkins name at all, I refused to do press around it and sold the tickets with a minimum of fuss. I didn't want to do anything that gave further publicity to her bigoted views, I just wanted to give the people of Lewes a hate free alternative.

On the night of the event, as I shared a drink with my audience minutes before I began, one of them informed me that it had just been announced that Hopkins had cancelled her event. The people of Lewes had made their opinion that the town was no place for hate clear, and we were now the only show in town.

· · · · ·

When I'd tried to transition back in 2000 the levels of transphobic prejudice that I encountered were shocking but by 2015 the world seemed to be improving and beginning to understand the value of diversity and inclusion. Unfortunately the world's slip towards the right, the Brexit result, the election of Donald Trump and the rise of right wing politicians around the world was also felt in gender politics.

Activists that had been at the forefront of feminist thinking, including some that had received honours for services to equality, suddenly started attacking transgender people and trans rights. In 2017 I had spoken alongside Linda Bellos OBE at an LGBT History Month event at Bournemouth University but within two years she was to appear at Westminster Magistrates Court for allegedly threatening to "thump" a trans woman.

"I play football and box, and if any one of those bastards comes near me I will take my glasses off and thump them… I am quite prepared to threaten violence because it seems to me politically what they are seeking to do is piss on women."

A number of groups had sprung up to campaign against transgender rights including A Woman's Place, Fairplay for Women, Object, and the Lesbian Rights Alliance. Mumsnet, the website ostensibly set up to provide parenting advice became a hotbed of transphobic hate as various anti-trans bigots whipped up the fervour with claims that trans women were a danger to women and girls.

The arguments that were put forward decades earlier to fuel homophobic hate were repurposed in the fight against transgender people. They were a danger to children, they were all sexual predators, rapists and paedophiles. These campaigners claimed to be feminists, fighting against the erosion of women's rights and lesbian erasure but I knew lots of feminists, and lots of lesbians, they were overwhelmingly supportive of trans people and I knew that these bigots spouting hate did not speak for them. Their claims that they were being silenced seemed hollow, coming as they were via virtually every media channel, tabloid press, broadsheets, national radio and TV.

Even the Morning Star, the left-wing British daily tabloid newspaper, founded in 1930 as the Daily Worker by the Communist Party of Great Britain, that fought every other form of prejudice, had joined the battle on the side of the anti-trans campaigners. In light of this I was approached by the GMB Union to write an opinion piece for the paper seeking to redress the balance of the conversation.

· · · · ·

Equality for trans people doesn't take away anyone else's rights – and I'm an equality activist

Over recent months the hysteria around transgender women seems to have been growing with each new statement about proposed reforms to the Gender Recognition Act.

Headlines like PeakTrans, TransCult and Transgender Trend all imply that being trans is a new thing, that the weak minded and sexually confused are jumping on the bandwagon. If being transgender is trendy then I've never been trendier. But there's nothing new about being trans, transgender people have always existed throughout human history — the hijra or two spirit people.

Today mental health issues are still significantly more likely to affect transgender people, and a large contributing factor is the bigotry and prejudice that they experience on a daily basis. The name-calling, the loss of family and relationships, the diminished career prospects, the violence and the legal challenges against their rights and identity.

We all exist somewhere on the gender identity and sexuality spectrums, straight-gay, male-female, and growing up we all come to a realisation about who we are, it's just that if you're straight and cisgender, you identify with the gender you were assigned at birth, then no-one notices. It only becomes an issue if you're LGBT+.

The recent attempt to hijack London Pride by a group of anti-trans activists under the slogan of "Get the L out" was just the latest in a concerted campaign of hate and misinformation being directed at transgender people by a small but vocal minority.

The cries of "we must protect the girls" create jarring echoes for those of us old enough to remember the same child safety concerns being used to justify anti-LGBT laws like Section 28 of the Local Government Act 1988 which banned the "promotion of homosexuality" on the grounds that it was a direct threat to our children. The connection between homosexuality and child abuse was as disgusting and incorrect as the current attempts to link transgender people and child abuse or sexual violence.

Any attempt to point out the abhorrent and unsubstantiated nature of these slurs is met with the argument that women's voices are being silenced. It seems strange that a small group of people can make the argument that their voice is being denied when they seem to have the ear of publications from The Times to the Morning Star, and regular opportunities to appear on TV and radio to tell us how their voices are being erased.

They claim to want debate around the issues, yet their language continually denies the identities of those they seek to debate with and claims of "I'm not a transphobe but…" followed by misgendering or using the former name of those they are attacking do not constitute anything other than prejudice. A recent attempt to debate the issues on Channel 4 resulted in anti-trans bigots screaming the word "penis" every time the trans woman on the panel spoke, obviously a deeply considered debating position.

We see claims that trans women are parasitic, misogynistic men dressed up in "woman face" for the purpose of lesbian erasure and yet, living near Brighton and knowing many lesbians, I have never met one who expresses anything but support for transgender people. Stonewall has come under attack from the Get The L Out lobby, despite having a lesbian chief executive, and Europe's best-selling lesbian magazine Diva, which is totally trans inclusive, was recently forced to publish a message saying that this group does not speak for all lesbians and certainly not for them.

It's true that women and lesbians have been oppressed over the years, but so have black women and disabled women and transgender women, and gay men, and working-class people and trade unionists and many other groups.

There is no hierarchy of oppression. Human rights are not a nil-sum equation. To grant one group equal rights does not diminish the rights of others.

Black rights do not come at the expense of white rights, women's rights do not come at the expense of men's rights, and trans rights do not come at the expense of women's rights.

There's a clue in the word, equality: equal. You cannot demand equality for yourself but not for others — for that is not equality, that is privilege.

I am not a transgender rights campaigner. I am an equality rights campaigner. This weekend I will be taking to the streets of Brighton to celebrate Trans Pride, not because I am transgender but because I believe that everyone should be treated with the same respect, the very reasons that I attend Disability Pride despite not being disabled.

We must fight for the rights of all people. We must always stand together, for together we are stronger, and until the day when everyone is equal then none of us are.

Sophie Cook, Morning Star, July 21, 2018

. . . . .

This anti-transgender prejudice had also infected the Labour Party and a crowdfunding campaign was started to ban trans women from All Women Shortlists (AWS), this raised £30,000 and would directly affect my campaign to be reselected as the candidate for East Worthing and Shoreham as the CLP had voted overwhelmingly to select a woman as the next candidate.

I had also been on the receiving end of this hate after I was selected to participate in the Jo Cox Women In Leadership Programme run by the Labour Women's Network.

Set up in memory of the MP for Batley and Spen who was murdered in 2016, the training programme aimed at helping to "create a generation of women who can continue Jo's fight in parliament, local government and in their communities".

At the end of the programme the Labour Women's Network tweeted graduation photos of each of the 50 plus women that had been part of the second cohort and while my sisters were greeted with messages of support my image was singled out for hundreds of messages of abuse.

@LabourWomensNet: "Congratulations to Sophie Cook on successfully graduating from the 2018 Jo Cox Women In Leadership programme. Everyone at Labour Women's Network and the Labour Party is proud of you!"

"Not me. I'm not pleased that he took the place that should have gone to a woman, and will now go on to take other places, that are meant for women."

"He has to justify himself everyday because he isn't a woman. He stole that place from a woman."

"That hulking manbeast took a place away from a woman and you're pleased? Jo Cox's spirit must be in despair. Everything she worked for being made a mockery of. Shame on you all."

"And poor Jo had a penis in her name."

"HE is living a lie and we're all supposed to go along with that lie? I DON'T THINK SO... denying material reality and biological facts are signs of mental illness."

"'Sophie' is a man in a dress. Thing is, you all know that, but actually believe that pretending otherwise makes you progressive and open-minded. Wake up."

"They define a burly bloke in a shitty wig as a woman obviously."

"Bet you're proud of yourself as a mediocre man taking away a prize from a woman. I don't give a shit about his feelings. What about the feelings of real women who should have gotten this award? Fuck off with your privilege and entitlement."

And more, and more, ad infinitum.

Of course one of the best arguments against me was that I was transgender so that I could steal a woman's place in politics, that's obviously a great idea because white, middle aged men just don't get any breaks in politics.

Eventually after months of false starts and postponed statements the Party finally clarified their position on transgender inclusion.

· · · · ·

Labour has a proud record of championing the fight for LGBT equality. The Labour Party recognises the vital importance of self-definition for the Trans community.

On the fight for Trans equality Labour has committed to reforming the Gender Recognition Act and the Equality Act 2010 to ensure they protect Trans people by changing the protected characteristic of 'gender reassignment' to 'gender identity' and remove other outdated language such as 'transsexual'.

The Labour Party continues to have an inclusive definition of women. In line with the Party's policy on the Gender Recognition Act, All Women Shortlists and women's reserved places are open to self-defining women.

We recognise that there is a diversity of views on what is a very complex and emotive issue, but discussions should never take the form of abuse and intimidation.

Any instances of discrimination must be taken extremely seriously, investigated and acted upon. Transphobia and the abuse of members based on their Trans identity will not be tolerated in the Labour Party.

Labour Party NEC Statement
on Trans Inclusion, March 6, 2018

· · · · ·

But people still denied that transphobia existed, it wasn't prejudice it was a 'much needed debate' around important issues, although I can't remember any other group of society having to debate the validity of their own identity.

For me the foolproof test of whether or not a phrase is bigoted is to replace the subject of the phrase with a different group of people, let's try this.

If you think that the phrase "Trans Women are sexual predators and a danger to children" is acceptable and purely a sensible suggestion then how about these variations?

"Muslims are sexual predators and a danger to children."

"Black men are sexual predators and a danger to children."

If you think that those examples are acceptable then you're straying into Tommy Robinson territory and you'd be made to feel very welcome at any English Defence League march, let's face it, they could do with the numbers.

By turning the phrase around the prejudice should be blatantly apparent to anyone but those in denial about their bigotry, so why is it ok to say it about trans women?

Before you preach hate, or spread division and mistrust, think on this.

Imagine if everything you said appeared on you body as a tattoo. If the words you spoke appeared on your skin would you still be beautiful?

· · · · ·

I do a lot of work with various organisations and they all have rulebooks, binders and guides, telling people how to speak to each other, how to ensure that they cause no offence as they navigate the treacherous waters of diversity and inclusion.

Whenever I see these rules I tell them that they can replace the whole lot with two simple words. Two words so powerful that if we all lived our lives by them then the world would very quickly become a better place.

The Home Office once approached me about doing some media appearances to talk about the fight against hate crime. I suggested to them that if we lived our lives by these two words then we wouldn't even need laws.

I think that was the point where I lost the gig since the Home Office's entire raison d'être is the creation and enforcement of laws, but I stand by my statement.

If we lived our lives with the philosophy of 'Respect Everyone' then we would very quickly begin to see the change that we want to see in the world.

· · · · ·

White people to people of colour "racism isn't a problem"

Men to women "sexism isn't a problem"

Straight people to gay people "homophobia isn't a problem"

Cis people to trans people "transphobia isn't a problem"
Rich to poor "inequality isn't a problem"

Sophie Cook, October 2018

· · · · ·

The border guard, with his distinctive high fronted cap, studies my face, alternating his gaze between me and the passport that he holds in his hand.

"Could you take your glasses off?" He instructs rather than asks.

I'm tired, it's 2am and I've been travelling for 12 hours. I want to tell him that I look better when I'm not exhausted but don't think that he would appreciate the humour. Besides if I look worse than my passport photo then I really am doomed.

Finally satisfied after tapping away on a computer keyboard he closes the passport and passes it across the counter to me.

"Spasibo."

"Pozhaluysta", he replies as I turn and walk toward the exit past the sign that simply reads 'Mockba'.

· · · · ·

No one knows where I am, I have kept my trip a secret, doing everything that I can to avoid the possibility of giving my hosts a reason to refuse me entry but now I'm in.

I've been invited to Moscow during the World Cup to speak to Russian LGBT activists and the only way to get me into the country is with a FIFA FAN ID. Introduced for the 2018 World Cup the FAN ID allowed foreign citizens multiple visa-free entries and exits into and from the Russian Federation. To get one you needed to be issued with a match ticket.

When the invitation arrived I pointed out that the only matches being played during the week of the conference were the semi-finals. "No problem", I was told and now, here I was entering Moscow to not only speak at a conference of LGBT activists but also to watch England play for a place in the World Cup final.

I've done a number of scary things in my life but the trip to Russia seemed to surpass them all. Even coming out as transgender in Premier League football seemed easier than this, after all the worst possible outcome there was ridicule and humiliation. This trip to Russia holds the possibility of violence or imprisonment.

Although homosexuality was decriminalized in Russia in 1993, anti-gay sentiment remains strong and after a law was introduced in 2013 prohibiting "propaganda" legitimizing homosexuality hate crimes against LGBT people had doubled.

In the build up to the tournament LGBT football fans had been threatened that they would be hunted down and attacked if they went to the World Cup, and were warned not to "publicly display their sexuality". That's great but how do you hide your gender identity.

Risk management specialists WorldAware assessed the situation thus:

"Though Russia is a high-threat environment for LGBTQ travelers, FIFA's anti-discrimination chief has stated that the LGBTQ community will feel safe at this summer's events. However, Russian society does not widely accept the LGBTQ community, and there are no laws protecting LGBTQ individuals from discrimination or violence. Although same-sex relations are legal in Russia, homophobia is widespread, and hate crimes and violence against LGBTQ individuals often go unpunished.

Openly LGBTQ visitors are highly likely to encounter discrimination or verbal and physical harassment in Russia. Attacks often occur near known LGBTQ-friendly establishments or event sites, such as when a man reportedly injured six people attending an LGBTQ Conference in Moscow with acid."

· · · · ·

My car drops me at the hotel, I'm tired, isolated and in need of sleep but it's immediately clear that something is wrong. Reception is full of irate England fans all trying to check into their rooms.

"The hotel is full, we have another hotel 30 minutes away where you can have an executive room and free dinner", the receptionist is telling everyone in broken English.

Cabs are arriving constantly to transport the would be guests to their new lodgings. My local contact, Alexander Agapov of the Russian LGBT Sport Federation, is on the phone trying to rectify the situation. I'm already on edge, I've heard about the violence and prejudice that LGBT people face in Russia on a daily basis and now they want to ship me off to god knows where on the say so of the hotel. My contacts are here, my meetings are here, everything I have planned for the next few days is here and I'm concerned that I'm not going to be able to communicate with anyone once I've been moved.

I make sure that Alexander has an idea of where I'm going and he reassures me that we'll look into this in the morning. He's already faced multiple barriers in trying to arrange this conference, venues have been cancelled at the last minute with dubious excuses, security services have been following activists and shutting down meetings and this is just another difficulty in his constant struggle against the Russian authorities.

Travelling south out of the city my concern grows as residential and business districts give way to industrial sites and dense wooded areas. The driver speaks no English and I have no cellphone reception as, an hour later, we turn into what looks like an abandoned quarry surrounded by derelict plant and equipment, white dust being thrown up by the vehicle's tyres illuminated in the beam of the headlights.

From my window I catch a sight of what looks like a goblin village, toadstool buildings surrounding a dark pond, as the first dawn rays of sun begin to pierce the gloom, and there on the left of me, standing incongruously in these surroundings, is the hotel.

The main building echoes the architecture of the grand houses of Imperial Russia, white columns framing large arched windows on the cream facade topped with a blue tile roof. On entering reception I'm struck by the golden chandelier, sweeping spiral staircase, large scale portraits of Romanov princesses and the gold thrones. Things could be looking up, at least it looks like a hotel and not some detention centre.

It's clear what the hotel chain has done, knowing that no one would book this hotel an hour outside of the city, they have overbooked their city centre hotel in the knowledge that once here any guests not happy with the arrangements would struggle to find alternative accommodation nearer to the city centre.

I need to move, all of my activities for the next week are in the city and when my fellow speaker, referee Ryan Atkin, arrives a few hours later we begin to make plans for the day, my mood lifting with the arrival of a friendly face.

"Check out, we've arranged new accommodation and we're sending a car for you both."

The message from our contacts at the British Embassy is very welcome and as Ryan and I wait for the car we relax with dark, bitter coffee and get to know each other a little better.

Ryan referees in the National League and when he came out in August 2017 he became the first openly gay professional official in English football. We knew each other through social media but this was the first time that we'd met in person.

. . . . .

The car slows as we drive along Sofiyskaya Embankment on the southern bank of the Moskva River. To our left, on the opposite shore, stands the Kremlin and there on our right is our home for the new few days, the residence of the British Ambassador, Dr Laurie Bristow.

Originally the home of Gustav List, a wealthy Moscow industrialist, this 19th century mansion house became the British Embassy in 1927. In 2002 the Embassy had moved into new offices nearby with the old building remaining the official residence of the British Ambassador in Moscow.

Ryan and I were met at the gates by Alexander who spoke to the Russian security guards, they checked our passports and allowed us through the barriers and on to British soil.

The room that I was assigned was just off the main entrance hall and was larger than my two bedroom flat back home in the UK. Two large windows looked out onto the residence's garden and above the fireplace hung Ernesto Fontana's portrait of 'Woman in a Hat and Undergarments'.

"A palace for our Princess Sofiya", exclaimed Alexander, obviously impressed.

Apparently the room had been used by Sir Ian McKellen on his last visit to Moscow, Ryan was accommodated in Winston Churchill's former lodgings but for me, my room was perfect.

· · · · ·

The uniformed security guard searches my bag as we pass through the airport style security barriers to get into Red Square. I'm anxious, will he spot the flag that I have hidden amongst the notebooks, makeup and hairbrush?

Barely a week earlier veteran LGBT campaigner Peter Tatchell had been arrested and deported for protesting in the same location and now it was my turn to visibly show my support for the LGBT people who had been repressed across the Russian Federation.

A torrential downpour has soaked us and the multicoloured splendour of the Cathedral of Vasily the Blessed, commonly known as Saint Basil's Cathedral, is reflected in the puddles that cover the wet cobbles.

Built on orders from Ivan the Terrible to commemorate the capture of Kazan and Astrakhan between 1555–1561, the distinctive building is shaped like the flame of a bonfire rising into the sky. Seized from the church as part of the Soviet Union's anti-theist campaigns it has been part of the State Historical Museum since 1928 and stands as an instantly recognisable symbol of Moscow and the Russian State.

Alexander scans the square, looking for security operatives hiding among the tourists and football fans, and judging that the time is right takes my bag and camera as I unfurl the Trans Pride flag that I have carried all the way to Moscow for this very purpose. Time stretches and freezes, as do the hairs on my neck, it seems to take forever for Alexander to get the photo and all the time my tensions rise.

Eyes are on me, some supportive, some with a little more menace. It's a scary moment but ultimately a rewarding one. I'm only in Russia for a few days, I have the combined protections of FIFA and the British Embassy, but for my Russian friends that is not a comfort that they enjoy.

I believe that it's important for those of us in the West that enjoy a relative freedom of expression to support our LGBT friends around the world that may not enjoy the same rights. There are many hostile environments around the world for LGBT+ people, places where they face discrimination, criminalisation, abuse and even violence. I wanted to do whatever I could to help them, and while it is possible for your sexuality to go unnoticed, LGB people are only visible if they chose to be, transgender people are visible constantly.

Walking the streets of Moscow I'm constantly prepared for a confrontation, abuse or even violence. The city is full of security forces and football fans from around the world, some of whom would presumably not be supportive of LGBT people. But whenever Alexander mentions to me that he's overheard people talking about me in Russian it wasn't abuse that he heard, it was curiosity. I'm heartened to see that wherever I go I seem to be met with friendship and I come to the belief that whilst the Russian government of Vladimir Putin is opposed to LGBT rights, the Russian people, in Moscow at least, appear to be open to diversity.

· · · · ·

Inside the 81,000 seat Luzhniki Stadium, I take my seat behind the England dugout.

Opened in 1956 the stadium was originally called the Central Lenin Stadium, and was used for the 1980 Olympics. Sat beside me is an elderly couple, suntanned and healthy, she introduces herself as Bracha and her diminutive husband, "Abraham Klein, who refereed England v Brazil". The legendary Israeli referee that had officiated one of football's greatest ever matches, World Cup holders Bobby Moore's England lined up against Pele's Brazil.

Klein was born in Romania in 1934 and as a child had escaped the

Nazi death camps as one of 500 children put on a train to Holland while many of his family were killed in Auschwitz. Over the years he'd been described on numerous occasions as the best referee in the world, the 'master of the whistle' although when Graham Poll wrote his list of the 50 greatest referees of all time Klein was omitted, although the list did include, without irony, Graham Poll.

At 84 he's still fit and sharp, we chat about England's chances tonight against Croatia as well as that legendary match in 1970 and I'm shocked to hear that he was only paid £10 for refereeing the game.

On my other side is a young Russian man, alone, around 30 years old, short cropped hair and ill fitting suit, he's less talkative than the Kleins and I have the uncomfortable feeling that he may not be there as a football fan.

Off to my right the travelling England fans are in great spirits, cheering the team as they walk onto the pitch and singing endless recitals of 'Three Lions on a shirt'. Amongst the flags that line the pitch is a rainbow flag proclaiming 'Three Lions Pride', the newly formed England LGBT fans group. I stand waving my Trans Pride flag and join in the singing, proud of my team, proud of my country and proud of my own identity.

After 6 minutes England are awarded a free kick just outside the penalty area and Kieran Trippier steps up to curl the ball up and over the wall into the top right corner of the Croatian goal. As the players smother the goalscorer tears well up in my eyes, thinking about my unlikely journey that has brought me to this moment, coming out as transgender in football, my battles with my own demons and now watching my country heading for their first World Cup final of my lifetime, we dare to dream.

For an hour we are going to the final, for an hour football's coming home, despite that not actually being the meaning of the lyrics to that song. When first Ivan Perisic scores to equalise with 22 minutes left and then Mario Mandzukic wins the match for Croatia in extra time, they shatter England's dreams, and break the hearts of every England player and fan in the stadium as well as millions more back home. The team had done themselves and the nation proud and following the final whistle the fans stay in the stadium, showing their respect for the effort and passion that every player has given to the cause.

Attempting to leave the stadium my path is blocked by security services who have sealed off a large area outside the main entrance. Together with a spanish gentleman and his family we are informed that the area is in lock down in preparation for Vladimir Putin's departure from the ground. It seems that my companion carries a little more weight with FIFA than I do and he requisitions one of the waiting people carriers.

"Are you heading back to the hotel?" I ask him.

He replies in the affirmative and offers me a lift. Throughout the thirty minute journey we chat about the game and he tells me that Moscow has changed a little since he played there. I ask which team he was with at the time and he replies "Real Madrid".

Here I am sat in the back of a car with a former Real Madrid legend and I have no idea who he is, although those from the north west of England would have had no problems recognising the former Blackburn Rovers player, Míchel Salgado.

. . . . .

Security forces had repeatedly closed down conference halls, trying to shut down the LGBT conference that the Russian LGBT Sport Federation were hosting on LGBTQ inclusion in football. One venue claimed that their air conditioning had broken, another that they had a double booking.

At the last minute, with the assistance of FIFA and the British Embassy, the Goethe Institut had stepped in to host the event 'Football - A Homophobia Free Game' and I was proud to speak alongside Ryan and speakers from Germany, Canada and Russia.

Before I leave Moscow I manage to share a drink with Alexander and as we part I hug him close, telling him to "stay safe, be careful".

"I will", he replies. "You have helped to keep us safe. Every time someone from the west joins us, every time they speak about us, every time they raise awareness of our situation it makes it more difficult for the authorities to do things to us."

I smile weakly and hug him close again.

19
HOUSE OF CARDS

"And so it is in politics, dear brother,
Each for himself alone, there is no other."

Geoffrey Chaucer, The Canterbury Tales

. . . . .

Because of the short notice nature of the 2017 snap General Election all candidates were selected by the National Executive Committee (NEC) of the Labour Party. This allowed an outsider with potential, like myself, to be selected free from local party factions, of course it was also not in keeping with internal party democracy and led to tensions.

Despite my phenomenal result the previous year I was still going to have to go through an internal party selection process if I wanted to stand again as the candidate. This would consist of an application period, a campaign for votes and then a hustings and election.

East Worthing and Shoreham Labour Party members had voted to have an All Women Shortlist (AWS) of candidates, a mechanism that had done much to address the gender imbalance among MPs. My presence in this process to select an AWS immediately offended the transphobes who would insult me on social media, calling me a 'Penis person' and saying that I was stealing opportunities from women.

As the deadline for applications passed I was the only candidate that had put their name forward, so great was the feeling that I was the obvious choice. A good thing you might think but the rules of the selection did not allow for a single, unopposed candidate despite this being a regular occurance in other elections throughout the party, from CLP chair all the way up to leader.

The deadline was extended and three other candidates came forward, Beccy Cooper, the candidate from West Worthing in the General Election, another applicant from outside of the area, and my former campaign manager who told me in a brief phone call: "I'm standing to be the candidate, I've got political ambitions as well".

The funny thing is that I didn't, I was almost an accidental candidate, I had no interest in a political career, I had stood the previous year in the hope that I could make a difference to people's lives.

I had spent the past year travelling the country, speaking at CLPs across the region, talking to trade unions, building the support that we would need in the next election. I was honoured to receive the endorsements of the GMB, Unison and the BFAWU unions as well as the support of the great political team at Unite the Union who would help run my campaign.

These endorsements had been hard won, they were not granted on whims, and immediately it seemed that other candidates resented the support that I had built. I had the full support of Momentum nationally but the local Momentum group with whom I'd had positive endorsement meetings began to contradict the support for my campaign.

A rogue element within the group began using their access to the social media accounts and mailing lists to push an alternative candidate. The national leadership of Momentum was not impressed, as far as they were concerned it was vitally important that the left of the Party put up a united front in the face of right wing challenges. Apparently an angry exchange ensued during which the local group was chastised but rather than end the argument it only fanned the flames of dissent.

Negative posts began to appear about me in CLP social media groups and former comrades began a character assassination. One in particular stands out where a former member of the Momentum group, possibly even the one responsible for the hijacking of official communications, waxed lyrical about how another candidate was "easy on the eye" and could "charm the pants off you". I wasn't the only person that found this display uncomfortable.

· · · · ·

A week before the hustings and vote I was in a commanding position. Despite the negativity I was still polling around 90% support, the majority of members weren't interested in internal party squabbles all they knew was that I had almost unseated the Tories the previous year and that was good enough for them.

"Sophie, something has come to our attention about a business that you used to own and we need you to meet the selection committee to answer some questions."

The message had come out of the blue, it was the start of the bank holiday weekend and this had suddenly been dropped on me. The tension that weekend was unbearable, I should have been campaigning but I was bloodied and bruised, someone had been digging into my past to find a way to discredit me and the betrayal of that moment hurt more than anything the Conservatives had ever done to me.

On the bank holiday Monday, after a stressful weekend, I was called before the committee.

"We want to ask you some questions about your business Seeker News."

I explained what had happened, the push to build a business, underfunded and under resourced, the competitive climate that I had faced, the difficulties when my investor had pulled out at the eleventh hour. My battles to save the jobs of my team and how I had lost everything.

The questions came thick and fast, asking me about incidents all those years before, asking me about things that I hadn't thought about for six years, that even then I might not have known all of the answers to. "Why hadn't I declared this business to the Party?" The answer was clear, because I thought that it was irrelevant.

I was frustrated, I was annoyed, someone had gone to the effort of searching through my past in the hope of finding some dirt with which to destroy me and I was the one on trial. I had done nothing wrong, I had tried to build a business in a difficult, volatile industry and failed. All of the newspaper publishers were struggling, Newsquest had been downsizing for years in efforts to remain viable and in November 2018 the 251-year-old company that published more than 200 local titles as well as the i newspaper, Johnston Press, went into administration after failing to refinance a £220 million debt.

Following the meeting I had no official communication from the committee, no one got in touch to relay their decision but the supposedly confidential enquiry suddenly became public knowledge.

A few days later the NEC got in touch to say that the local committee had voted to exclude me from the selection but that the NEC, with their much greater knowledge of Party rules and procedures, had overruled them. I was still on the ballot and the matter was behind us.

· · · · ·

The day before the hustings and election I was contacted by the regional Party to inform me that the other candidates had withdrawn from the selection, Beccy Cooper had previously informed me that she was pulling out due to the toxic nature of the process and apparently the other candidate had decided to drop out as well.

I was still polling a majority of support amongst members and it looked highly likely that I would have won the selection the following day despite the attempts to sabotage my campaign. The Party couldn't proceed with only one candidate and so the selection was suspended.

Within minutes the phone rang, it was a reporter from the Guardian asking about what had happened. How did they know almost as quickly as I did? Who was feeding them information? I gave them a short statement about my regrets that the members had been denied the opportunity to select their candidate and how I hoped to be given the chance to stand again soon. The resulting story was balanced and fair, obviously not the aim of the person that had given them the story because no sooner had it appeared then other, more antagonistic reporters got in touch.

"A local party source told Brighton and Hove News that Ms Cook has been something of a marmite figure with activists. Local party members who worked with her at the last election felt she had been imposed by Labour HQ, and found her rude and publicity hungry."

The anonymous political source, the lowest of the low, with so little conviction in their own words that they hide their identity. Anonymity making it impossible to challenge the legitimacy of their words and the insidious lies they tell.

Marmite figure? Well I could only think of one small faction that had disliked me from day one and their prejudice seemed to fuel that hatred.

Rude? If only they'd not spoken anonymously because then I could have asked them for examples.

Publicity hungry? That was the biggest joke as I turned down far more requests for interviews than I ever accepted, Good Morning Britain, Channel 4 News, Sunday Politics, all of these had been rejected in the previous month. As a politician you are constantly in the media eye, this isn't being publicity hungry, it's the nature of the beast, and surely being in the media all helps to win the votes that you need to get elected.

Unable to beat me fairly it was clear that some within the local party were prepared to do everything that they could to destroy me as a person. This felt very personal and the betrayal hurt so much more than anything that the Tories had ever done to me.

. . . . .

"To me, the thing that is worse than death is betrayal.
You see, I could conceive death, but I could not conceive betrayal."

Malcolm X

"You want a friend in this city? (Washington, DC) Get a dog!"

Harry S. Truman

The idea of your integrity being called into question by people who dig dirt and give secret anonymous briefings to the press would be laughable if it wasn't so damaging.

Despite the negative stories being fed to the press I always believed that the best thing for the Party was to maintain my composure, to not fan the flames or sink to their level. Protecting the Party was a greater priority than defending myself and so I didn't fight back in the media, I chose not to comment rather than draw attention to the dispute. I was trying to starve the story of fuel while others were fanning the flames and throwing kerosene onto the blaze

It hurt me to realise that people, supposedly on my own side of politics, were capable of doing this to someone that was a comrade. I missed the military and football worlds where your opponents at least had the good grace to wear a different colour so that you knew who they were.

Believing the best of people is a great value in a politician but unfortunately not a useful one, and certainly not one that will get you anywhere. My belief in people had been shaken and I was being increasingly isolated by the propaganda being disseminated about me.

I had no integrity, I was dishonest, I was a rude, publicity hungry crook.

I was, of course, none of those things and if for a second the Party and trade unions had believed it then they would have dropped their support for me in an instant.

People go into politics for many reasons but the two most prevalent are the pursuit of money and power and the wish to help people. I was of the latter persuasion, money and power held no allure for me. My ambitions as far as wealth was concerned stretched only as far as the ability to keep my bills paid up to date. I had no materialistic needs, and retail therapy did nothing for me, there simply wasn't anything that I wanted.

I had been helping people before I went into politics through my speaking, writing and activism, raising awareness of mental health and the need to end the stigma.

In politics the desire for money and power will always make for a more successful candidate, they allow you to be more flexible with your integrity and beliefs, they allow you to go the extra mile required to beat your opponent who, no matter how great the stakes, will not compromise their beliefs.

I was not prepared to do anything that didn't fit with my beliefs 100%, for if I did then I was betraying not just the people that voted for me but myself.

"For what is a man advantaged, if he gain the whole world, and lose himself?"
Luke 9:25

. . . . .

When the selection process was finally resumed the NEC took control of the process in the hope that this would restrict the possibility of further disputes within the local party organisation causing more unnecessary damage to the Party.

Since I had already been shortlisted in the previous selection and had not withdrawn I was automatically on the shortlist for this campaign, yet another thing that outraged those that were opposed to me.

I knew that anti-transgender elements within the Party had raised £30,000 in an attempt to block trans women being allowed on All Women Shortlists and here I was, the only person currently in that position and already under attack from factions within my local party. The question was obvious, how much interest were the transphobes paying to this selection? And how many resources would they employ to ensure my defeat?

Maybe it's my military background, maybe it's just my own beliefs but when a friend is under attack I believe that it's right to support them rather than seek to profit from the situation. It had become clear to many members just how aggressive the character assassination directed at me had been and they expressed their disgust at what had been going on.

At this point the previous two candidates and I were joined on the ballot by Lavinia O'Connor, the chair of the CLP and someone that had supposedly been my friend. Styling herself as the 'Unity' candidate her campaign team was made up of many of the people that had previously tried to exclude me as part of the now disbanded selection committee.

The trade unions restated their support for me and once again the local and national Momentum groups were split with the local group supporting Lavinia and the national organisation backing me.

My campaign was supported by the political team at Unite the Union and we had great endorsements from many MPs including Shadow Secretary of State for Justice and Shadow Lord Chancellor, Richard Burgon, staunch Corbyn ally Chris Williamson and my friend Lloyd Russell-Moyle who had won the Kemptown seat in which I had originally hoped to stand. Our polling had identified more than 300 members that supported me as their candidate, more than enough to win the selection as long as they all turned out but confusing procedures and ludicrously early postal ballot deadlines had definitely taken their toll.

Despite the Union support that I had, other candidates still seemed to be outspending my campaign, including sending mailings to all 1100 members of the CLP on the eve of the poll.

. . . . .

On the morning of the hustings I drove into Worthing to pick up my campaign coordinator from Unite, Jenny Killin, I was in good spirits and despite the stresses of the previous six months I was relaxed and ready to go.

One of the most apt alleged political quotes was attributed to Tony Blair offering advice to the then fresh-faced David Miliband: "Smile at everybody, and get somebody else to stab their back."

Walking into the hustings it was great to see so many friends but the nature of the previous months had caused an undercurrent of suspicion, comrade turned against comrade and some of the smiles seemed lacking in sincerity.

The format for the meeting was that each of the four candidates would give a five minute speech followed by questions from the floor and then, finally, the voting. Stepping up to the microphone I began to speak.

. . . . .

As the candidate for East Worthing & Shoreham last year there were some who didn't give us a chance as two years earlier we'd only managed 9000 votes for Labour.

Nationally, it was predicted by the press and even some within the Party that we would suffer a historic defeat.

We proved them wrong and now together we have to finish what we started.

Last time we achieved more than twenty thousand votes this time we'll make history and finish the job.

When I stood on the stage of the Worthing Assembly Hall for the count I remembered the journey that we had been on.

The hundreds of people that we met on the doorstep, the people that waved as they drove past, the guys that cheered when we knocked on their door and even the woman that I met on the train on the way to the count. She'd left her friends hen party in London early in order to travel back to Worthing to vote Labour.

It's amazing to think that only five weeks before almost nobody believed in us, including some within our own CLP.

I'd been told that we wouldn't be running a campaign, that I was to be only a 'paper' candidate and that all of our resources would be going to support Hove.

I refused to accept that any constituency could be written off without a fight.

I believed then as I do now that we could win here, we spread our message of hope and belief and soon others began to believe as well.

In those five short weeks we almost delivered East Worthing & Shoreham's first Labour MP and I strongly believe that together we will achieve it this time.

I had been told that no one would vote for a transwoman in East Worthing & Shoreham. That voters would never support me and that I would be a one issue candidate. Everywhere I went people kept reminding me that this wasn't Brighton.

They were wrong, and they will be wrong again.

20,882 people in this constituency voted Labour and for me as your candidate because we fought a campaign based on the policies that matter to everyone. Housing, education and healthcare.

The foundations of our society that have been destroyed by this Tory government which will go down as one of the worst in history.

Housing is in crisis, the number of families in emergency accommodation across Adur and Worthing has increased by 35 per cent in the last 14 months.

Education is in crisis, West Sussex schools are among the most poorly funded in the country and our teachers struggle for resources.

Our NHS is in crisis, with people on trolleys and cancelled operations.

Our campaign will be about securing a safe future for our children where they are all given the opportunities to succeed. We fight on our policies to put this right.

We fought a campaign based on honesty and integrity. We will again.

Last time I chose never to partake in negative politics. A choice I stand by.

Together we turned the tide and started the groundswell of support that has brought us nine new Labour councillors since the general election and I want to congratulate every one of them and thank them for the great work that they do for the people of their wards.

As your Labour MP together, this time, we will bring hope of a better future to the people of East Worthing & Shoreham.

This time we will help to build a fairer society for the many and not the few.

This time we will create history together.

Building on the 114% rise in the Labour vote, exceeding the 19.8% swing and increasing on the 20,882 votes that we achieved in 2017.

I have spent the last year speaking at Labour and trade union events across the region, building support for this constituency so that in the next election we will have the help and resources required to win this time.

Since the election last year hundreds of people have contacted me to say that for the first time ever they have hope that things can improve, thanking me for my loyalty to this constituency and that's why I honestly believe that I am the only candidate who can win East Worthing and Shoreham for Labour.

Last year we gave the people hope.

Vote for me and this time we create history.

Together we can make a real difference to people's lives.

Together we can turn this 'safe' Tory seat into a Labour one.

Together anything is possible.

Thank you.

. . . . .

I nailed it, whilst other candidates fluffed their lines or overran their time my speech was sharp and succinct. Now for the questions.

Beside me one of the other candidates had briefing notes for all possible questions, shuffling through them lost, trying desperately to find the answers. I was pleased with my performance, I spoke without notes, made some good points and was never cut off for over running my allotted time.

As the proceedings were brought to a close I felt that there really was nothing else that I could have done in light of the assault that I had been under. I knew that on the day I had been the most complete candidate but that it could all amount to nothing if the negativity had spread far enough.

Ballots were cast and the counting began on a large table placed on the stage, there was nothing else that I could do and I went off to chat to a few friends whilst Jenny watched the votes being counted.

Labour Party selections use a system called the single transferable vote whereby each member gets to express their support for each candidate in order of preference. First choices are counted and the lowest placed candidate is excluded with their votes then being redistributed on the basis of second choices.

On the first choices Lavinia O'Connor had 67 votes to Beccy Cooper and I on 52 each and my former campaign manager was excluded. She was the candidate whose supporters were least likely to support me and it became clear that I was not to be re-selected as the candidate. Fifteen months earlier 20,882 people had voted for me and now 67 people had voted for someone else.

Jenny turned to me and expressed her disappointment, I just smiled and told her it was fine.

My mental health had been struggling so much under the weight of the constant attacks from people that were supposedly on the same side as me. Despite the fact that I had become much better at saying no to things that I thought would have a negative impact on me I persisted in being involved in politics, the one thing that was causing me most pain.

"Do we have to hang around for anything?" I asked Jenny.

"No, we're good", she replied.

"Great, let's get out of here."

It's telling that even in victory my opponents still found it necessary to once again anonymously brief the press about me, saying that I had stormed off in a sulk.

When the same journalist that had published their whispers the previous time got in touch for a quote I asked her why she thought I might possibly be interested in speaking to her following the previous hatchet job.

I was no longer involved in politics and despite being "publicity hungry" I had no interest in playing their game.

A weight had been lifted from me, I never had to speak to any of the people that had been so focused on destroying me ever again. If I had won I knew that their campaign against me would have continued and intensified. My life that had been on hold for 18 months was now my own again and I was going to start living.

· · · · ·

"Yet each man kills the thing he loves
By each let this be heard
Some do it with a bitter look
Some with a flattering word
The coward does it with a kiss
The brave man with a sword"

Oscar Wilde, The Ballad Of Reading Gaol

When I came out as transgender in Premier League football they said it was impossible.

When I ran for parliament they said that no one would vote for a trans woman but 21,000 people did.

When I became a TV presenter they said that I had a face for radio... ok so that bit is true and I now host a show on Brighton's RadioReverb.

Never let someone tell you that it can't be done just because you're trans, gay, black, disabled, Muslim, whatever you are, be true to yourself and believe that anything is possible.

Sophie Cook, Oct 2018

EPILOGUE
COMING HOME

The flat is still dark as I pull on my coat, I pick up my keys, pausing briefly to touch a kiss to the handwritten message from my daughter, Sadie.

"You're my hero, Steve was great but Sophie's better."

Closing the door behind me the first rays of light probe the darkness trying to find their way in.

I walk quietly, unobserved as I slip down to the beach, every wave whispering to me gently, calling me on.

Gazing out at the expanse of sea I strip and walk slowly into the cold, dark waters which envelop and embrace me.

The cool water reaches my chest and I turn to the east as the sun makes its first appearance above the horizon, the warmth of its arrival caressing my face as I close my eyes feeling the release of the past 24 hours.

I feel free, my life once again my own. Free from the attacks and hostility that politics had become.

I have fought for longer than I can remember, the pain from without and within always threatening to destroy me.

My demons, my trauma, my pain, my loss, my fights.

They may not be gone forever, nothing is forever, but today they are quiet, not today.

The past is the past, past pain, past love, just passed.

A lifetime detached from the world around me, captive inside a prison of flesh, my body not my own.

I would no longer sleepwalk through life, I was aware of my pain, my sadness, my joy and my love. Finally, after a lifetime of searching, I have found my way home to me.

As the cold waters surround me and the warmth of the sun calls me on I close the door to my past, opening the door to my future.

I take a deep breath, steady myself and step through to start a new chapter in my life.

To be continued...

EXTRA TIME

"The lower you fall,
the higher you'll fly."

Chuck Palahniuk, Fight Club

POETRY

I present a selection of the poetry that I've written over the years, not because I think that it's particularly good, in fact some of it is spectacularly bad, but because I think that it gives a unique, unfiltered view into the soul. The difference between my teens when I was lost deep within PTSD, wallowing in the pain, and now as I try to heal myself is immediately clear.

Steve Cook - Selected Poems 85-87

Feed the world is what they say
So we produce our wallets and pay
Another charity
Another disaster
Loses the clarity
We forget faster.

. . . . .

Oh why must I always hold the cup
With the tainted wine
Why do I hold the cup that overflows
With the wine of my soul
While no-one wants a drink.

. . . . .

How can a man who's seen so much
Still be so naive
You've seen the evil, that men can do
Why be so innocent?
Now that your time has come
Why are you not ready?
Death has seen you once
And been denied
He will not wait again.
Goodbye.

. . . . .

Suicide gives a certain feeling
Sweet, yet strangely stale.

How can your life
Be worth so little
That all you do is hurt.

. . . . .

You were young
So young
Where oh where
Did it all go wrong.

A moment of error
Your youth is gone
Forever.

. . . . .

I saw him
Lying there
So old
So old
But, I hear you say
He was only a boy
He died
You can't get much older
Than that.

. . . . .

Medic! Medic!
The cry goes out
Andy's down
Caught by shrapnel
In a war
For which he neither cared
Nor understood.

. . . . .

Always cared for
Always a brother
Always loved
Never a lover

Good friends
That's what we are
Good friends
And that's where it ends

You trust completely
You show your soul
The fuller the trust
The greater the betrayal
The betrayal is whole

. . . . .

The clown
Waits in the wings
Tense
Put on a happy face
Go out there
Do your stuff
You play the fool
For five minutes
Everyone loves you

The show's over
The applause dies
You return
To your world
Your solitary plane
Alone
The audience is gone
You cry
You die
To be reborn
Next time.

. . . . .

Cereal pack poetry
Throwaway prose
For throwaway lives
You scribble
You write
It means everything
Yet
It means nothing
Life is so cheap
Scratched on the back
Of bank statements
That's what you're worth
That's all
Welcome to the real world
This is your life.

. . . . .

You sit
You wait
The walls close in
The bar rises
And falls
With your chest
Smiling faces
Laughing
At me?
Who are you?
You come closer
I feel the pressure
The weight
Life
Weighs me down
Constricting
My chest
Can't breathe
Can't
Please
Help!

. . . . .

Rejection
Consternation
You're different
You're you
It's not normal
What bloody is?
Freak
But who?
Is it you?
Or them?
But you're not the same
As them
Does that make you wrong?
Well
Does it?

. . . . .

Night

The dark closes in
Constricts my mind
My throat
Life extinguished
A daylight atheist
Finds his God
As the terror
Descends.

. . . . .

But
Where are all
Our yesterdays
Now
Our yesterdays gone.

Sophie Cook - Beach Poetry 2017-18

Writing my poetry on early morning visits to the beach, my words now limited by the 21st century standard of 140, and now 280 characters.

Here by the sea where life first grew
Bathed in first rays of new days sun
Each morning die and born anew
A life of many but I am One.

. . . . .

Each new day
Is uncharted territory
You have never been here before
So be brave, be strong
And explore.

. . . . .

The world turns
The past flies away
The pain still burns
But in the promise of a new day
We rise and are
Born anew.

. . . . .

Sun rises
Chasing night's demons away
Bringing strength, hope
And the promise of each new day.

. . . . .

The sun warms my skin
And fuels my soul
Waves whisper and sing
To keep me whole.

. . . . .

The illusion of human power
And control are nothing
When the earth moves
Elemental, eternal.

. . . . .

The sea's gentle breath
The rise and swell
Soothes my mind
And keeps me well
Peace and oneness
Within its embrace
That gives me strength
In this time and place.

. . . . .

Some things are meant to be
As the rivers return to the sea
So my soul returns
To its home
Inside of me.

. . . . .

Feel the power
Waves that tower
That crash and roar
Whilst spirits soar
In search of the sun
To make me one.

. . . . .

As surely as day transforms to night
So too must wrong succumb to right
Human spirit will find a way
And darkness give way to light.

. . . . .

The sun of a new day
Warms my soul
And ushers my cares away.

. . . . .

At the heart of life
The crucible
From where we sprang
A dark figure
Stands guard
To keep the demons at bay
The sentinel.

. . . . .

And through the clouds of despair
Broke a new day...

RESOURCES

Once upon a time this page would have been filled with addresses and phone numbers but in the modern age these have been replaced with URLs, if you want to find out more about these organisation then you know what to do.

Mental Health

Samaritans
Whatever you're going through, call free any time, from any phone on 116 123.

24 hours a day, 365 days a year. This number is FREE to call and you don't have to be suicidal to call them.

www.samaritans.org

Mind
Mind provide advice and support to empower anyone experiencing a mental health problem. They campaign to improve services, raise awareness and promote understanding.

www.mind.org.uk

Hope Charity Project
HOPE Charity Project is run by people that are personally touched by a young person struggling with their emotional wellbeing. They provide a much-needed resource for children aged 10-18 and their families, who are experiencing the trauma of mental health issues.

Offering online support and a place to come and find some support, direction, guidance, answers and inspiration from other families that understand what you are going through.

www.hopecharityproject.org

MindOut
MindOut is a mental health service run by and for lesbians, gay men, bisexual, trans, and queer people, work to improve the mental health and wellbeing of LGBTQ communities and to make mental health a community concern. They helped people struggling with social isolation, suicidal distress, financial hardship, discrimination and prejudice, hate crime and exclusion.

www.mindout.org.uk

Sussex Oakleaf

Sussex Oakleaf provides a range of support services to people with mental health needs, those with a personality disorder and individuals at risk of homelessness.

They empower people and promote independence by providing recovery focused community wellbeing services, residential care, peer mentoring, housing support and volunteering opportunities.

www.sussexoakleaf.org.uk

Gender Identity

Mermaids

Mermaids support children, young people, and their families to achieve a happier life in the face of great adversity. They work to raise awareness about gender nonconformity in children and young people amongst professionals and the general public, and campaign for the recognition of gender dysphoria in young people and lobby for improvements in professional services.

www.mermaidsuk.org.uk

Fighting Discrimination

Kick It Out

Kick It Out is primarily a campaigning organisation which enables, facilitates and works with the football authorities, professional clubs, players, fans and communities to tackle all forms of discrimination. The campaign has been pivotal in persuading and supporting the game's stakeholders to take their equality responsibilities seriously.

www.kickitout.org

Just A Ball Game?

Just A Ball Game? aim to raise awareness around LGBT inclusion and visibility. Promote LGBT history and achievements. Change mind-sets, help to dispel myths and widen education in different cultures in a healthy active way.

www.justaballgame.co.uk

Stonewall

Stonewall campaigns for the equality of lesbian, gay, bi and trans people across Britain.

www.stonewall.org.uk

SOPHIE COOK

To follow Sophie's continuing work
please follow her on social media
@sophiecooktalks
on Twitter, Facebook, Instagram
and whatever comes along next
(assuming that someone doesn't
beat her to that username).

www.sophiecook.me.uk

Printed in Great Britain
by Amazon

18986652R00159